The
Adoptive
Parents'
Handbook

The
Adoptive
Parents'
Handbook

A Guide to Healing Trauma and Thriving with Your Foster or Adopted Child

Barbara Cummins Tantrum
MA, LMHC

North Atlantic Books
Berkeley, California

Published by
North Atlantic Books
Berkeley, California

Cover illustration © gettyimages.com/butenkow
Cover design by Jess Morphew
Book design by Happenstance Type-O-Rama

Printed in Canada

The Adoptive Parents' Handbook: A Guide to Healing Trauma and Thriving with Your Foster or Adopted Child is sponsored and published by the Society for the Study of Native Arts and Sciences (dba North Atlantic Books), an educational nonprofit based in Berkeley, California, that collaborates with partners to develop cross-cultural perspectives, nurture holistic views of art, science, the humanities, and healing, and seed personal and global transformation by publishing work on the relationship of body, spirit, and nature.

North Atlantic Books' publications are available through most bookstores. For further information, visit our website at www.northatlanticbooks.com or call 800-733-3000.

Library of Congress Cataloging-in-Publication Data
Names: Tantrum, Barbara Cummins, 1973- author. | Tantrum, Barbara Cummins, 1973-
Title: The adoptive parents' handbook : a guide to healing trauma and thriving with your foster or adopted child / Barbara Cummins Tantrum, MA, LMHC.
Description: Berkeley : North Atlantic Books, 2020. | Includes bibliographical references and index. | Summary: "The essential guide to parenting adopted and foster kids—
learn to create felt safety, heal attachment trauma, and navigate challenging behaviors and triggers"—Provided by publisher.
Identifiers: LCCN 2020005390 (print) | LCCN 2020005391 (ebook) | ISBN 9781623175153 (trade paperback) | ISBN 9781623175160 (ebook)
Subjects: LCSH: Parenting. | Adopted children—Psychology. | Foster children—Psychology.
Classification: LCC HQ755.8 .T358 2020 (print) | LCC HQ755.8 (ebook) | DDC 306.874—dc23
LC record available at https://lccn.loc.gov/2020005390
LC ebook record available at https://lccn.loc.gov/2020005391

1 2 3 4 5 6 7 8 9 MARQUIS 25 24 23 22 21 20

This book includes recycled material and material from well-managed forests. North Atlantic Books is committed to the protection of our environment. We print on recycled paper whenever possible and partner with printers who strive to use environmentally responsible practices.

What is broken in relationship
must be healed in relationship.

—DAN ALLENDER

Acknowledgments

A SPECIAL THANKS to my husband: my partner in crime and the one that actually suggested that I should write this book while we were on a date night.

And to my children: my pride, my joy, and my source of continued laughter and amazement.

My friends and family and their continued support even when you often think that we're crazy.

And my colleagues, as we have done our work together, sharpening each other and supporting each other in the hard work that we do.

Yeah, it's a little nuts, but that's the sort of thing you do.

My friend Jamie Henning, on finding we were taking in three refugee children while I was pregnant and finishing my master's, when I asked her if she thought I could do it. It's the encouragement I needed at the right moment.

Contents

Part 3. Identity

Part 4. Living and Thriving with PTSD

Foreword

MAKE A PLACE on your bookshelf for this book! Barbara Cummins Tantrum's *The Adoptive Parents' Handbook* covers the range of topics that are significant to raising children and teens after adoption or guardianship. Barbara's expertise is based on her successes as both a parent of adopted children and as a therapist who treats children and families.

The book is a pleasure to read. The author has a fresh, interesting writing voice. My favorite parts of the book, and there were many, included recounted conversations between Barbara, her husband, and her children. This was an enjoyable way to "see" into Barbara's home, absorbing the daily, practical use of the topics that she writes about.

This book is well-organized, which allows readers to find what they need without plowing through previous chapters. Her treatment of topics like trauma, regulation, attachment styles, sensory issues, racism, and identity are parent friendly. Most importantly, she provides scripts and straightforward advice for parental intervention. Her advice is written clearly, and is often numbered.

I have worked with children and families for over thirty years, but I still found many new suggestions within this book that will enrich my work. Barbara includes fresh insights on multiracial family identity, food, and sleep. She lays out processes for families that are reasonable to follow. I was pleased to find she discusses the topic of gender identity. Barbara provides helpful research and guidance on this essential issue.

Throughout the book, as she writes on topics that stem from children's early life adversity, She gives examples that deepen the reader's insight and sensitivity. Barbara's material will enable the success of families. She provides the stepping stones for a parenting path of compassion and competence.

—DEBORAH D. GRAY, MPA, LICSW
Author of Promoting Healthy Attachments: Hands-on Techniques to Use with your Clients;
Attaching Through Love, Hugs, and Play; Attaching in Adoption; and
Nurturing Adoptions: Creating Resilience after Trauma and Neglect

Preface

I WROTE THIS BOOK intending it to be the book I would have wanted to read when I was at the beginning of my foster-adoptive-guardianship journey. I have read so many dry and clinical books, or books written by people that seemed not to have a clue of what it was really like to be a parent, so I wanted to write something that was a little different. And so I wrote a book that was personal and informative, and I also tried to be a little funny—because we all know that there are times that you have a choice between laughing and crying. But no book is a substitute for therapy—if your family is having trouble, please get help. If you are feeling overwhelmed, get help for you too. Parenting a traumatized child is hard enough if your brain is fully functioning, but if your trauma is getting triggered too, it will be nearly impossible. Take care of yourself; secondary trauma is no laughing matter.

I wrote this book to be able to be read cover to cover if you so choose, but also you can pick and choose chapters as you wish as well. This book is also meant to be partially triage—identifying where there might be bigger problems to tackle and where you might need to do more research; or maybe it's an area where a chapter's worth of info is enough. To be honest, I could easily write an entire book about most of these chapters (and for some of them, someone has). So look around and explore as you need to do it. No issues with food and sleep? Count your lucky stars and skip that chapter. Food and sleep are your daily struggle and major issue? Skip ahead! However, they might revoke my good-therapist badge if I didn't say that it is mandatory that everyone read the self-care chapter. I know you're tired of hearing about it, but trust me that foster and adoptive parents are so good at taking care of others wa-a-ay before they take care of themselves. Please promise me you'll at least take a look at it.

Let's dive in!

PART 1

Creating Felt Safety

ORIGINS

I CLEARLY REMEMBER the moment that I realized I was in over my head. I have always been an expert at projecting confidence, and when I announced that we were taking in a sibling group of three refugee children from the Democratic Republic of Congo on top of our three-year-old bio-child and the thirteen-year-old daughter from Ethiopia we already had, people thought we were strange, but it wasn't completely out of character for our family. Even though I was finishing up my graduate degree in counseling and soon afterward realized I was unexpectedly pregnant, my unsquashable optimism shut down any naysayer that came our way. The girls came, I somehow finished my degree and my internship through the dizzying nausea and an almost comical level of unpreparedness, and then my son came, bringing our total family number up to eight. We have crazy stories from that time; stories of hijinks about raising kids that got off an airplane not speaking a word of English, and more serious stories of difficult behavior and tears and so much misinformation. But through it all, I was going to survive and we were going to make it.

But then there was the night that I was crying while washing dishes. It was my birthday, and I had just started a new, very part-time job working as a therapist for an adoption agency—the first step in the direction I had been dreaming about. Instead of coming home to flowers or a card, I came home to a serious conflict that had arisen while I was at class that involved physical aggression (no serious harm, but it had scared people) and a call to the social worker. We had celebrated my birthday with friends the previous weekend, but it just felt so wrong to have my actual birthday spent trying to negotiate this conflict. For the first time I let my mind wander a bit and wonder if I were actually cut out for this. I knew what I needed to do—my mantra had been calm, predicable parenting—but suddenly I wondered if I was in way over my head. Could I parent six kids, four with trauma? Would this all just descend into chaos that I could no longer control?

My husband heard me crying and came down to the kitchen. I think he instinctively knew that no words would be helpful at that point, or maybe he simply had no idea what to say. He held me, let my tears wet his shirt, and didn't offer any shallow platitudes of "it will get better" or "don't worry." Anybody who has been in the trenches of trauma knows those sayings for how worthless they are. The only thing that speaks the language of trauma is connection, and that's what I needed at that time.

I wrote this book with wanting that in mind. Connection is the key to trauma, and what is broken in relationship has to be healed in relationship, according to one of my professors from graduate school.[1] And I write this book as an expert, yes, but as an expert that has been through the fire of parenting traumatized kids as well, and I am still learning. Let's take this journey together.

First off, I want to say that no book is a substitute for therapy. Personalized therapy, where your therapist knows you and your child, helps everyone communicate better, and working with someone who can make personalized recommendations is always the best situation. But I know that when I was waiting for a placement, when I was in the trenches waiting for an appointment, and even in working with a therapist, I read everything I could get my hands on, hoping that something would help. This hopefully will be that book—something to help. I wrote this book as the book I wish I could have read back when I was naive and thought that love could overcome everything. And part of what I wanted from experts wasn't just dry, cold theory; rather, I wanted comradery and a knowledge that I wasn't alone in my worries and my fears. And so I'm writing this book as an adoption and trauma therapist, a foster-adoptive mom, the sister to a sibling that was adopted, and a bio-half-sister to a child placed for adoption.

But before I can write about brain structures and cortisol, I should tell you that I never intended to be a child therapist. When I went to grad school, I thought it would be fun to be a marriage therapist, or maybe work with college students, as I was doing at my current job. But then one of my professors said something that shook me to my core and completely changed the course of my professional life. She said that the best therapists worked in the areas of their trauma—and if your trauma was in your childhood, you should work with children. This statement floored me. I had never seriously considered working with children. I liked children—I had a two-year-old and our eleven-year-old Ethiopian daughter at the time. But I'm not one of those women who dream about being a second-grade teacher or who have opinions on the best method of teaching a child to read. I had never even put together a decorated bulletin board, something I thought was a prerequisite for someone wanting to work with children.

But, when I heard my professor talk, I knew she was right. I had done very little work in my marriage; it was comfortable and safe. But childhood trauma—that was something I understood at a deep level. I understood sitting with my younger sister and her sobbing about her birth parents not wanting her; I had grown up as the middle child and "counselor" that had helped her work through that early trauma. I also understood being the object of abuse in my own desperate flight from my older sister's abuse, which caused me to create an elaborate fantasy world into which I frequently escaped. And, at my core, what may have been casual career advice to many of my colleagues shaped my life's calling—I knew that I was going to be working with kids with trauma, because that was something that I understood deeply; something in my very bones.

Why did you choose this path? This is a question I always ask foster and adoptive parents that I work with. The reason that brings people to raising a child that they did not give birth to informs much of what they bring to the table. Was it the grief of infertility? Was it wanting to do something good for the world? Was it the lack of a partner? Was it seeing and hearing the statistics of kids in foster care and wanting to do something to help? Was it already having two boys and wanting a girl? All of these reasons are good reasons, and all of these reasons have drawbacks. But I would invite you to think about your origin story, and what brought you here. We need to know where we come from before we can adequately know where we are going.

My Professional Origins

I think it's also fair that you know my origins as a therapist. In treating trauma as a therapist, I come from a lot of different backgrounds. I was trained as an interpersonal therapist; I also have training in cognitive behavioral therapy, trauma-focused cognitive behavioral therapy, play therapy, as well as the attachment, regulation, and competency (ARC) model. I believe strongly that what is broken in relationship needs to be healed in relationship, but the tools available through cognitive behavioral therapy (CBT) and dialectical behavior therapy (DBT) can be very helpful for calming our brains down enough to get us to that place.

The largest influence on how I treat trauma in children is the ARC model. To explain the ARC model, I also have to reference Maslow's Hierarchy of Needs,[2] which I remember calling Maslow's triangle as a college student in Psych 101. It's basically a triangle where the bottom layers are needs like food and shelter, and as you move up the triangle, you get to things like relationships, purpose, and finally what Maslow calls self-actualization.[3] Maslow's theory was that people needed to have the lower needs on the triangle met before they could fulfill the needs on the upper parts of the triangle. For instance, recognition and respect are much less important to you if you are starving or if you're living in a situation that is radically unsafe. And being able to pursue inner creativity and talent means that you have met relational needs as well as basic needs.

The ARC model is built on some of the same ideas, with a triangle as well.[4] At the bottom of the ARC triangle is Attachments—what the parents do to create attachments with kids. The next level is Regulation—emotional identification, regulation, and expression. Then the *C* is Competence—which is executive functioning and self-development and identity. Then there can be the integration of the trauma experience.

Just like Maslow's triangle, the ARC triangle is built so that the bottom blocks need to be in place before the top blocks can be worked on. Kids need to have the basic safety blocks of Caregiver Affect Management (their caregivers being able to stay calm and attune to them), Attachments (and attunement), Consistent Response (have a predictable, consistent environment with all their caregivers), and consistent Routines and Rituals before they can work effectively on their own Affect Identification, Modulation, and Expression.[5] This makes a lot of sense—how can we expect a child to be able to modulate their emotions if their caregiver isn't able to do it first? How can a child identify and express emotions if they are too preoccupied with whether or not their living situation is stable and consistent? And children need to be able to identify, modulate, and express affect and emotion before it is really developmentally appropriate to think about addressing executive functioning with them. Just like it would be difficult for a starving person to talk about their favorite historical period, it is very difficult for a child that doesn't feel safe with their caregivers to work on their table manners or write out their trauma narrative to help integrate it into their lives. My colleagues and I developed a program that we call PATCH (Parenting Adopted and Traumatized Children) that works with families affected by adoption, foster care, and early trauma to help parents understand trauma, have the tools to parent more effectively, and help children process and regulate memories and emotions associated with trauma.

So as I write about how to survive parenting a child with early childhood trauma and attachment breaks, I wanted you to know some of where I come from, my origins. I come from being an earnest mom that would do anything to get the raging kid in front of me just to trust me. I come as the grown-up sister of an adopted sister who grew up feeling less-than because of her adoption, and never feeling as if her questions got answered. I also come as a therapist who has worked with incredible, brave, and enduring kids and families that have fought the good fight to love, to attach, and to beat the odds when it seemed as if the world was stacked against them. And I wanted to bring to you the best of what I've learned and continue to learn about the brain, about attachment, trauma, and healing.

I also want to say as we embark on this journey of healing together that healing and attachment are a gradual process—a slow upward journey in the same direction. One client I have had likened it to the movement of the stock market. If you are a short-term investor, you are likely to lose your shirt, and if you look from day to day, you might panic. However, if you are a long-term investor even when the market is down for a while, you will notice that the overall movement will be up and to the right. That is how this process is for kids. Using the principles outlined in this book—creating a safe place, connecting with your child, helping them regulate and form identity—your child's brain will begin to heal. Most of the clients I work with will notice a gradual lessening of behaviors and a gradual growth in tenderness. Sometimes they will try to drive themselves crazy by figuring out the magic formula—was it what they ate? Or how much they slept? Or sometimes they won't trust it, thinking that if they let their guard down that the child will hurt them more. Healing looks like longer periods of regulation, more capacity to talk about emotions, turning to parents for comfort, and the ability to regulate more easily when they do dysregulate. Children with a traumatic early childhood will most likely always have periods of dysregulation, but their ability to care for themselves in the dysregulation is what's important. And if parents can keep in mind the idea of the long investment, it can make it much easier to see and trust the progress when it happens.

TRAUMA

How a Gastroenterologist Changed How the World Thinks about Trauma

IMAGINE YOU ARE on a gravel road after a rain, and your tires find comfortable ruts you are driving in. These ruts work well—until you spot a large puddle ahead. Not wanting to splash through that puddle, you try to swerve—but find it difficult to get out of those ruts. Your car seems unable to hop onto the higher bank, and it seems inevitable that you will splash through the large puddle ahead.

This is a crude picture of how the brain works as well. Certain pathways in the brain can be the ruts that are easier to go down—and these ruts are formed by either repetition or by something very traumatic happening. You probably barely had to think about how you got dressed this morning, made your breakfast, or drove somewhere familiar. These are ruts of familiarity—and everyone has them. If you think you don't have them, then drive a different way to a familiar place or change your usual order for your morning and see how odd it feels. Children who grow up in dysfunctional homes also have these ruts, and these are the ruts that you see when they expect every negative emotion they see in an adult to end in violence, or that every time a foster parent gets angry, they have to move.

What Is Trauma?

Trauma is any event or situation that causes a person to feel terror and horror to the point of feeling like your life and safety are in serious jeopardy. Trauma is inflicted when a person either experiences or witnesses such an event; in fact there is little difference between experiencing or witnessing to the amount of trauma. This type of incidence of trauma may temporarily or permanently alter a person's ability to cope, their self-concept, and their ability to identify what is a threat. Types of trauma include abuse (sexual, physical, and emotional), hospital trauma (life-threatening injury or illness), violence within the family or in the community, war, natural disasters, parental loss (by death, neglect, divorce, mental illness, or substance abuse), rape, assault, being suddenly removed from your home, changing foster homes, and so on. Different traumas have different effects on children—the death of a parent is worse than the death of a neighbor for most children. One researcher writes, "Intentional acts by other human beings that threaten the life or bodily integrity of children or their primary support systems and caregivers—interpersonal or complex trauma—have particularly severe and wide-ranging adverse effects on children's psychosocial functioning and neurodevelopment."[1]

Kids that are adopted are often exposed to many different kinds of trauma, including separation from original caregivers, neglect, physical abuse, and sexual abuse. For children born into an unsafe house, this abuse is perpetrated by the very people that are supposed to be caring for the child. Then, if this takes place over a span of months or years, this can compound and create complex trauma. The more severe the trauma and the greater the duration, the more difficult it is on the child. This trauma increases the risk for the child to have debilitating behavioral, psychological, and physical problems. Dr. Bruce Perry writes,

> *A brief sampling of recent studies gives some feel for the incidence of [post-traumatic stress disorder] (PTSD) following a traumatic event. Thirty-five percent of a sample of adolescents diagnosed with cancer met criteria for lifetime PTSD . . . Seventy-three percent of adolescent male rape victims*

develop PTSD; 34 percent of a sample of children experiencing sexual or physical abuse and 58 percent of children experiencing both physical and sexual abuse met criteria for PTSD. In all of these studies, clinically significant symptoms, though not full PTSD, were observed in essentially all of the children or adolescents following the traumatic experiences.[2]

Perry goes on to explain that trauma is worsened if there is physical injury to the child, if there is death or physical injury of a loved one (especially the mother), the perpetrator is a family member, the victim is of a younger age, they have absent or unengaged caregivers, or the caregivers are affected by the trauma. And, obviously, ongoing trauma is much worse on children than a one-time event. Children with loving caregivers and community support are much less affected by trauma.[3]

The children who have been adopted or are in foster care have generally undergone a great deal of trauma with a breach in their family support, which intensifies and makes this trauma more difficult for them to cope with. A Harvard Medical School study found children in foster care to have PTSD at twice the rate of U.S. war veterans.[4] Spinazzola found that, "in addition, although interpersonal trauma and attachment adversity were each separately associated with affective-somatic and attentional-behavioral dysregulation, their combination was particularly strongly associated with self-relational dysregulation, independent of the effect of PTSD."[5] What these studies have found is that children in foster care and with attachment disruption have a much higher chance of having clinically significant PTSD symptoms. What this boils down to is that if you want to adopt or foster children, you're going to have to become an expert in trauma.

How a Gastroenterologist and an Insurance Company Redefine Trauma

Several years ago a gastroenterologist named Vincent Felitti, who was working for an insurance company called Kaiser Permanente, was puzzled by some results he happened upon in his data collection. The patients he worked with that had the worst outcomes at his obesity clinic were the ones that had suffered from childhood sexual abuse. Could there be a link between the trauma they experienced as a child to the outcomes for the obesity treatment he was offering? Together with a researcher named Dr. Robert Anda, he decided to study this trauma as well as nine other areas of childhood trauma, naming these adverse childhood experiences (ACEs). These are the ten areas that make up the ACE score:[6]

physical abuse

sexual abuse

emotional abuse

physical neglect

emotional neglect

exposure to domestic violence

household substance abuse

household mental illness

parental separation or divorce

incarcerated household member

His study was deceptively simple. Working with a large group of people with Kaiser Permanente insurance, he would assign someone a number based on the number of ACEs they had personally experienced growing up, calling that their ACE score. Then, he followed them for several years and looked at their health outcomes not only for obesity treatment but many other areas of their health. And what this gastroenterologist found startled and shocked the psychological world. Not only did the people's ACE score affect obesity and mental health outcomes, which Dr. Felitti expected, but he found that their ACE score affected just about every health measure he measured. He writes,

> We found a strong dose response relationship between the breadth of exposure to abuse or household dysfunction during childhood and multiple risk factors for several of the leading causes of death in adults. Disease conditions, including ischemic heart disease, cancer, chronic lung disease, skeletal fractures, and liver disease, as well as poor self-rated health, also showed a graded relationship to the breadth of childhood exposures. The findings suggest that the impact of these adverse childhood experiences on adult health status is strong and cumulative.[7]

This is shocking. What Dr. Felitti is saying is that *childhood trauma is the leading cause of death in adults.* He's saying that trauma affects almost every area of health; from cancer to skeletal fractures to heart disease. And this is changing how we are viewing health, mental health, addiction, and violence. We have always expected that trauma and abuse can create emotional and behavioral problems, but it is "less well known that adverse experiences like violence exposure can lead to hidden physical alterations inside a child's body, alterations which may have adverse effects on lifelong health."[8]

What Is the Impact of Trauma on the Child?

Humans respond to trauma by their neural pathways and brain structures changing. Adults can create new pathways in the brain and change existing ones. When trauma happens for a young child, this can become the organizing framework for their brain. For instance, if an adult is bitten by a dog, she can take that trauma and use her thinking brain. She might feel more nervous about meeting a new dog, but she has a lifetime of good dog experiences to help regulate her response to dogs. She can get to the place of saying, "Hey, that one dog was pretty bad, but that doesn't mean they all are. I just have to be a bit cautious with new ones." For a child, this can be a defining event and make it very difficult ever to feel safe around a dog as an adult. For the adult, the neural pathways are somewhat changed; for the child, it is an organizing framework. One researcher writes,

> We have learned that trauma is not just an event that took place sometime in the past; it is also the imprint left by that experience on mind, brain, and body. This imprint has ongoing consequences for how the human organism manages to survive in the present. Trauma results in a fundamental reorganization of the way mind and brain manage perceptions. It changes not only how we think and what we think about, but also our very capacity to think.[9]

It is much easier for us as a society to make accommodations for a child with a physical handicap than with a mental health one. But trauma in a young child quite literally causes a specific type of brain damage that makes it impossible to function normally.

The brain can be compared to hikers going through a forest. On paths that are used frequently, the paths are worn and easy moving. On paths that are less frequent, they can become overgrown or hard to see. You can create new paths in this forest, and old and unused paths can become overgrown. If you had trauma as a young child, then these well-worn paths are about safety and hypervigilance. It takes time to build new pathways of trust and safety in the brain. Jamieson writes,

> *When an individual experiences trauma, the limbic system sounds the alarm and lets the prefrontal cortex and body know that danger is impending. This brain structure tells us when to run and when to stay and fight, providing the necessary chemicals to ensure survival. Because the limbic system is mostly unconscious, a traumatized person often does not know why they feel what they feel. Sometimes they are unable to identify what they are feeling. This is the main reason why some children respond to kindness from adult helpers with anger, fear, and aggression. They are literally fighting for their life, whether there is an actual threat or not.[10]*

Thinking versus Doing Brain

Most of the time, most of us operate in our thinking brain—or prefrontal cortex. This is the reasoning part of the brain, and the last one to develop (and it is actually not fully mature until your mid-twenties).[11] Teenagers are able to do risky and brave things, whether it's skateboarding or striking off for horizons unknown, because their prefrontal cortex is not fully developed yet. With our prefrontal cortex comes cause-and-effect thinking, decision-making, and recognition of errors.

The amygdala is a structure in the middle of the brain that is responsible for regulating memory, emotions, and fear. This is part of the limbic system. When the amygdala is activated, it creates the fight, flight, or freeze response by triggering the hypothalamus to secrete adrenaline.

> *All of these changes happen so quickly that people aren't aware of them. In fact, the wiring is so efficient that the amygdala and hypothalamus start this cascade even before the brain's visual centers have had a chance to fully process what is happening. That's why people are able to jump out*

of the path of an oncoming car even before they think about what they are doing.[12]

How Does Trauma Impact a Child's Development?

When children believe that the world around them is dangerous and it is up to them to keep themselves safe, then they become hypervigilant, or always watching. This level of arousal and alertness makes other developmental tasks take a backseat, and it also impacts relationships for the child. This can also contribute to otherwise bright kids struggling in school, because so much of their mental energy is being used to keep alert and vigilant. This alertness will often cause a child to misread another person or situation as dangerous, and then act to protect themselves (often in not very socially acceptable ways). This leads to behavior problems, peer problems, and home problems.

Neurobiology

Scientists have found that childhood trauma actually physically alters the structures of the brain. Having childhood trauma not only increases your risk of mental illness, but research shows that 40 to 50 percent of those that have experienced childhood neglect and abuse will develop a substance abuse problem.[13] Many scientists believe that this is due to an actual change in the structure of the brain, namely in the hippocampus, the amygdala, and more recently, they've found it might even affect the volume of gray matter.[14]

So what does it mean to have an altered hippocampus and amygdala? For a nontraumatized person, their body will most likely only react to things that are actually dangerous, with only the occasional false start. For a person with trauma, this means that they live in a state of constant hypervigilance and overarousal, which means that small things trigger big reactions, and they are always on the lookout for those small things. A sudden loud noise like an unexpected door slamming might make everyone in a room jump a bit, but someone with an overactive amygdala might actually be triggered by something like that into fight, flight, or freeze. Living in that state of hyper-arousal is exhausting.

Top Symptoms of Children with Early Childhood Trauma

Though every child is, of course, their own unique person, the symptoms of early childhood trauma are pretty consistent throughout the kids and adults that I work with. It can actually be relieving to a lot of parents to realize that their child, who feels like a control freak that dysregulates all the time and hoards food, is actually very consistent with a lot of kids that I work with. So here is a list of the most common things that we see with kids with trauma:

Control Issues. One of my professors in graduate school said, "If you are sitting with an adult with control issues, look for where they've been orphaned. Control is an orphan wound."[15] This statement has had a profound impact on how I view and treat children and adults with early childhood trauma. It's absolutely correct; a child that has grown up with love, attention, and all their needs met doesn't feel the need to control the world around them because the world is safe. Babies decide in the first year of life whether or not the world is safe, and for the ones that the world isn't safe, they do their best to try and make it safe by seeking a high level of control on the environment around them. Kids don't seek control to drive their caregivers crazy; they do it to try and make what seems like a crazy and unstable world safer for them. Control-seeking is a subconscious and very hard pattern to change, and it will get worse when a child (or adult) feels less safe.

Hypervigilance. This is the subconscious need for traumatized people to always be aware and alert to everything around them, constantly scanning for danger and assessing what's going on. With this hypervigilance comes a great deal of anxiety, however, because it takes up a lot of bandwidth in a child's brain and can often lead children to jump to the wrong conclusions. After trauma has been properly processed, however, this increased sensitivity does have its benefits—people who have done their trauma work are excellent at reading emotions and responding quickly, and make excellent counselors, nurses, teachers, etc. I once worked with a police officer that had come in for trauma work, and when I talked with him about hypervigilance, he smirked and named the three cars in my parking lot as well as full descriptions of the two people he passed coming into my office. When I work with children, I call it their superpower: this increased sensitivity can be used for good once it no longer controls them.

Delayed social and emotional development. When I first start working with a family, I usually give the child an assessment that is aimed at assessing the child's development in five different areas. In nearly every child that I work with that has had early childhood trauma, the child will score below average or delayed in the social and emotional development. This is due to several factors—including the fact that if you're existing in a family where you are just trying to survive neglect and abuse, it can be really difficult for your brain to learn and develop in this way. The brain needs safety to learn and grow effectively in this area, and kids that haven't had this felt safety aren't able to grow.

Difficulty connecting with caregivers, especially the mom. It is heartbreaking to me that often frustrated and heartbroken moms come into my office feeling like there must be something wrong with them that their new foster child seems completely at ease with their new foster dad but wanting nothing to do with the foster mom. I always assure them that this is what it's like with probably 90 percent of the families that I work with. This is because the original attachment break is usually with mom, and so kids come into the foster family feeling like Mom isn't safe and feeling a lot of angst toward the mother figure in the family. And for kids that have been in multiple foster placements—well, they've been there, done that. They know that at some point you're going to tire of them and they'll be packing up again. With every move, their shell gets harder, and the next caregiver has a harder job cut out for them for trying to make a connection.

Difficulty connecting with peers. Kids with trauma usually have a lot of difficulty with same-age peers. Because of their social and emotional delays, many of them feel attracted to playing with younger peers, as they are actually developmentally more appropriate for them. Kids that have come from a dysfunctional family system might also have not ever learned good people skills and may lack the ability to make and keep friends. Also, the emotional volatility that sometimes comes with early trauma can also make keeping friends hard as well.

Sensory processing disorder. This is so common for kids with trauma that I do a screening for it with kids that I work with. It's because one of the strategies that babies can use to survive early trauma is dissociation, which causes difficulty then for how the brain interprets sensory information. And typical experiences that babies should have to help them process sensory information and regulate emotions aren't available to a dysfunctional family. For instance, holding a baby and gently talking to him as you feed him is a typical, soothing parenting technique. But what if the baby is left to cry for a long time, hungry and scared? And then when she's fed, she's left in a crib and handed a bottle hastily, not rocked and talked to? Being held while fed is critical for eye development, being sung to and talked to is critical for auditory development, and being held and rocked is important for regulation and touch. We'll talk more about this in chapter 13, on sensory processing.

Emotional dysregulation. This is the ups and downs of emotions, and the difficulty that the person with PTSD has controlling the highs and the lows. People without PTSD are usually able to "regulate" their emotions—to keep them within a functional range most of the time. For people with PTSD, this is a much more difficult thing. They experience more extreme emotions— higher highs and lower lows. This is most likely tied to some of the neurobiology that goes along with early exposure to trauma.

Impulsivity and a lack of cause-effect thinking. Kids with trauma are unable to look ahead and think, "If I do this, then this will happen," very well. This is why traditional disciplinary tactics don't work very well on them, because it's so hard for them to think ahead. It can be very hard for them to think, "If I don't bring my jacket, I will get cold," or even, "If I don't do my homework, I will get this consequence." This is one of the areas where a kid with trauma can look a lot like a child with attention deficit hyperactivity disorder (ADHD).

Bad dreams, sleep, and bathing issues. Not all kids experience bad dreams and nightmares, but it is common enough to mention. It is very common for kids with trauma to have issues going to sleep; and this could have several reasons. One reason could be that the abuse happened at bedtime or in a bath (common for sexual abuse), it could be that it feels vulnerable to try to turn their brain off to sleep, and it could be that Mom and Dad feel far away.

Avoiding triggers. A trigger is anything that reminds the child, even sub-consciously, of their trauma enough to cause a PTSD (fight, flight, or freeze) reaction. For instance, a child removed from their first parents in October could be triggered by things associated with Halloween. Anything that triggers a kid will feel so bad to them that they will usually go to great lengths to avoid it, even resulting in strange rituals or magical thinking. For instance, a child triggered by riding in a shopping cart might begin to try to avoid the grocery store in order to avoid riding in the shopping cart.

Food issues. It is very common for kids who spent some time in a dysfunc-tional home before removal to have food issues. If there were any issues around there not being enough food in the house, then the child will have issues around being fed and getting enough food and other resources.

After looking at a study about attachment and PTSD, one researcher writes:

> *Finally, results from this field trial show in bold relief the potentially most vulnerable high-risk subpopulation of polyvictims: children and adolescents who endure disruption or impairment in their primary caregiving rela-tionships while attempting to grow up in the midst of chronic familial and community violence. For such youth, love often is in short supply, danger abounds, and attempts to survive can take the form of clinical problems that may be best understood and treated as resilient adaptations to trauma during childhood and adolescence.[16]*

To Learn More about How Trauma Affects People

Bessel van der Kolk, *The Body Keeps the Score: Brain, Mind, and Body in the Healing of Trauma* (New York: Penguin, 2015).

3

INFANT TRAUMA

"HOW MUCH TRAUMA can he have had?" one parent asks me skeptically when I label her child as having early childhood trauma. "He was three months old when we got him. He doesn't remember anything before he came to us."

That is a great question, and one that for many years most people would have agreed with. How could a tiny baby remember? Science is finding more and more not only how early infancy profoundly affects a child but also pregnancy. Maternal stress levels during pregnancy affect the child's IQ and future mental health,[1] regardless if the mother takes drugs or anything to do with genetics. Studies have found that children adopted at birth, even when controlling for other factors, are roughly twice as likely to have diagnosed mental health conditions than nonadopted peers.[2] Adopted children succeed less at school, have more conflicts with classmates, and have more diagnosed behavioral problems despite having advantages such as typically wealthier, more educated, and more involved parents.[3]

But why would adoption, which seems like such a fairy-tale solution to the problem of kids without stable homes and parents who want more kids, cause so many problems? It would be a gross misinterpretation of the data to say that adoption was bad, but rather the problem lies in the brain, and in attachment. Babies aren't blank slates when they're born, ready to be imprinted upon; they have spent the time in utero becoming attached to the woman carrying them, growing used to her voice, her scent, and her surroundings. Studies have shown that infants grieve when separated from their birth mothers,[4] and they are not developmentally capable of soothing themselves. Adoption is the way we as a society care for children in this particular situation, but children in the situation of having an early attachment break are a particularly vulnerable population. One researcher writes:

> The most important stage for brain development is the beginning of life, starting in the womb and then the first year of life. By the age of three, a child's brain has reached almost 90 percent of its adult size. This rapid brain growth and circuitry have been estimated at an astounding rate of 700–1,000 synapse connections per second in this period. The experiences a baby has with her caregivers are crucial to this early wiring and pruning and enable millions and millions of new connections in the brain to be made. Repeated interactions and communication lead to pathways being laid down that help memories and relationships form and learning and logic to develop. This means a human baby's brain is both complicated and vulnerable.[5]

This is absolutely critical to understand early trauma in an infant—their brain is developing at an astounding rate, and the patterns that they are laying down in their first year of life are going to affect them for the rest of their life. Infants decide in their first year of life whether or not the world is safe, and then that belief and felt safety becomes the basis on which they pattern future relationships.

All adopted children have an attachment break, and all adopted children have grief and loss. Some children are able to recover from that grief and loss easier and attach to their caregivers, and for some children this causes more problems. Not all adopted children struggle in school—they are just far more likely to do so.

So how can an adoptive parent help their child grieve, adapt, and soothe themselves? Here are some ideas.

First, recognize that the child is grieving and cannot soothe themselves. Throw away any book that tells you that you need to train your child to sleep or that your child is manipulating you (for more on manipulation, there's a chapter for that—look at chapter 11). Your child needs you to connect with them and soothe them, not to train them right now. Later we can work on sensible sleep for everyone; right now, you need connection. And if your child doesn't seem to be soothed easily, just tell yourself that if they're that upset, at least they have a sympathetic buddy holding them while they're upset. Responding to them and soothing them are building attachment.

Second, recognize that their grief is not your fault. Guilt and a lack of confidence in the face of your child's grief can actually be a barrier to attachment and relationship building. One researcher writes, "The mother may be called upon to contain and bear witness to the child's profound distress, which can undermine her confidence as a mother."[6] Part of becoming a foster or an adoptive parent is bearing witness to a child's profound grief and loss, and to do that in a way that they feel seen, heard, soothed, and their story honored. While a baby doesn't necessarily need to have a lifebook (a book with pictures and their foster or adoption story in it) made right that moment, they do need an engaged and loving parent to be with them in their distress.

Third, a parent should be as prepared as they can be and try to give the baby the calmest start in life that they are able to do. Consistent, calm, and predictable parenting from the very beginning is going to be key.

The Three Hot Topics

There are three main "hot topic" issues with newborns, and this is how they play out for adoptive parents:

Breast-feeding versus bottle-feeding: Breast-feeding usually isn't an option for adoptive parents, so this isn't as much an issue. However, I have known adoptive parents who have gotten disparaging remarks about not breast-feeding from people when they bottle-feed their children in public. Just remember you owe strangers no explanations, and people should mind their own business on how people choose to feed their babies.

Diapering issues: Cloth versus disposable doesn't have anything to do with trauma or attachment; one of the few things that doesn't.

Sleep issues: The mother lode of parenting issues. You will probably hear so much conflicting advice that it will make your head spin and will make you feel like a bad parent no matter what you choose. In *Brain Rules for Baby*, John Medina writes about sleep for typical babies:

> *A predictable schedule may not make itself visible for half a year, maybe longer. Between 25 percent and 40 percent of infants experience sleep problems in that time frame. . . . Babies eventually acquire a sleep schedule; we think it is actually burned into their DNA. . . . Even after a year, 50 percent still require some form of nighttime parental intervention.*[7]

So please, if you hear nothing else, realize that it is very normal for kids to have disrupted sleep. If half of one-year-olds need some nighttime intervention from their parents, it can't really be called a sleep problem, can it? Here are some truths in dealing with the sleep issue with babies with early trauma:

1. All children are intrinsically different in their sleep patterns. Yep, your best friend's baby that slept through the night at six weeks and your sister's baby that didn't sleep well until two were not the results of superlative or lax parenting; they were more likely just how those babies were. There are things you can do to make sleep issues better or worse, but babies are going to do their baby thing—whatever that is.

2. Adopted babies are grieving, often recovering from erratic cortisol levels if the mother was experiencing stress, and sometimes recovering from exposure to substances in utero.

3. Adopted babies have had an attachment break and need a bit of help to feel more secure.

In popular culture there are two polar opposite opinions on sleep strategies with babies. One is the "cry-it-out method" made popular by Dr. Richard Ferber, also called "Ferberizing" your child, and the other is co-sleeping. There are costs and benefits to each extreme, as well as a more moderate middle ground. Let's look at the different options and how they work with children with attachment trauma:

Cry-it-out method: This is a method of "sleep training" your child where the child is left to cry for gradually longer and longer periods of time, with the parent going in to reassure the child at gradually lengthening intervals. So, you put the child to bed, and wait for them to cry for five minutes, then go in and reassure them, then wait ten minutes, and so on. There can be many variations of this method, but this is the basic method. The idea is that eventually the child will be able to self-soothe and will put themselves to sleep with little protest if just the parents stay strong and are able to endure the cries and protests.

Pros: For some kids, this works.

Cons: For babies that can't soothe themselves, they will simply escalate until they are sick or exhausted. This doesn't work well for children with attachment issues.

Co-sleeping: This is the lovely, earthy, and back-to-our-roots sort of idea of the family bed where the baby sleeps in bed with the parents. Given the recent worry about the baby being smothered, there have been recent innovations such as the "co-sleeper," which is like a crib that clips onto the side of your bed, or a bassinet-like contraption that lies in your bed to protect the baby.

Pros: Cuddly and nice, baby sleeps better

Cons: Risk of smothering, limits parental intimacy, makes it difficult with multiple kids, interferes with parental sleep

Sensible sleep for all: I would like to propose a sensible sleep solution for everyone, and it's not a new concept. It's how my mother raised me and how her mother raised her before the psychologists started getting so involved in how children should be sleep-trained. It also works really well for attachment, because it is responsive to a baby's needs. Think of the baby's sleep in phases, and follow their lead on when they're ready for the next phase. And if they're sick or teething, just realize that they're going to have a few rough nights, and that's okay. Any change you make to their sleeping arrangements needs to be made slowly and carefully, with nothing drastic or sudden.

Phase 1 (zero to three months or so): This is the newborn stage, and usually when the mother is recovering from birth. Even though you didn't give birth to the child, you should mimic this natural rhythm as much as possible and "cocoon" with your baby, spending as much time cuddling and being together as possible. During this stage the baby should sleep in a bassinet in your bedroom, beside your bed if possible to make nighttime feedings easier. During this time you should establish a basic routine with your baby, doing things always in the same order. When they awake, you should feed them, and then when they finish eating, it's play time. When they're really little, this looks like cuddles and them looking around, but as they get a bit older, they'll get more interactive. Then, when they get fussy, rock them or soothe them to sleep. It's best not to make them dependent on always eating before they sleep. However, as they start getting ready to sleep more at night, you will notice them "tanking up" in the evening by eating more and more before bedtime.

To sleep, the child will need a dark and quiet place, maybe some soft music, to be swaddled, and often a pacifier. Rocking can also be really helpful as well, just to help them calm and then put them down to sleep. Babies in the womb find when the mama is awake and walking soothing, so they tend to sleep more during the mother's waking time and wake more during the mother's sleeping time, so this sets them up for being diametrically opposed to the mother's schedule upon birth. Yikes! Gently transition them into being more awake during the day by making the day more interesting and the night more boring. For your sanity, try as much as possible to sleep as much as you can. My husband and I tried to institute a six-hour rule for our first baby—while on parental leave we didn't leave the bedroom until we'd had at least that much sleep. It didn't always work, and even though it was broken up, we tried our best.

Phase 2 (three months to one year): When they start being able to sleep for longer stretches at night, maybe getting up twice or so, or they simply outgrow the bassinet, it's time for phase 2. This is when they can either graduate to a crib in your room, if you like them being in your room, or a crib in their own room if you're ready for some privacy. If they are in their own room, though, a monitor so you can hear them is a really good idea. In this phase you want to do the same routines as before, but try putting them down just before they fall asleep, and patting their back and being with them as they fall asleep in their crib. The goal here is to make their crib a pleasant, happy place. If they cry or are unhappy, soothe them and comfort them.

Phase 3 (one to two years): This is the age they transfer to a toddler bed and will often start having nightmares. Once they're mobile and in a toddler bed, a good trick to have is some sort of mat under your bed that they can sleep on if they have nightmares, are sick, or have other problems. That way they aren't climbing into your bed but are comforted by you being nearby if they need you, and they are at least starting the night in their own bed.

Maternity and paternity leave: If both parents are working and are both planning on returning to work, hopefully you have some family leave coming. Please take it! Many workplaces don't differentiate between adoption and giving birth, and if that's the case, use it to its fullest. If you don't have good family leave options, do your best to get at least some time off. Having some time at the beginning to bond with your child is very important.

My Favorite Baby Care Books

Tracy Hogg, *Secrets of the Baby Whisperer: How to Calm, Connect, and Communicate with Your Baby* (New York: Ballantine, 2001).

Harvey Karp, *The Happiest Baby on the Block: Fully Revised and Updated Second Edition: The New Way to Calm Crying and Help Your Newborn Baby Sleep Longer* (New York: Bantam, 2002).

BOOKS TO AVOID FOR ADOPTED CHILDREN:

Gary Ezzo and Robert Bucknam, *On Becoming Babywise: Giving Your Infant the Gift of Nighttime Sleep* (Mount Pleasant, SC: Hawksflight, 1990).

Richard Ferber, *Solve Your Child's Sleep Problems* (New York: Touchstone, 1985).

IF YOU WANT TO READ MORE ABOUT INFANT ATTACHMENT TRAUMA:

Nancy Newton Verrier, *The Primal Wound: Understanding the Adopted Child* (London: BAAF, 2009).

PTSD AND FIGHT,
FLIGHT, AND FREEZE

It's so funny how I think of myself as an expert, and I am usually prepared for reactions from my children, and even travel with an emergency kit of scented lotion, lollipops, and spicy gum in my purse at all times. Once, during a thunderstorm, I was caught in a hotel with nothing sensory but slightly scented hotel lotion and Tic Tacs, and so vowed to always be better prepared after that. And the first few years with our trauma-tized kids were a matter of sorting out the triggers—getting in trouble, check. Loud noises, check. Mom gets an angry look on her face because she gets angry at something she sees on her computer, check. And as I learned to identify the triggers, I learned to soothe them as well—backrubs, things that smell good, lollipops, and so on. But then I found myself utterly confused when I was riding on the Tube in London, and as soon as the train went underground, one of my children with a traumatic background suddenly curled into a ball on my lap and became nonverbal. I'm not sure why I didn't recognize it; perhaps because it wasn't in one of my predetermined categories? I turned to my husband and said, "What's wrong with her?"

"PTSD reaction," he answered, with cool confidence, as if he were the therapist and I was the statistician. "You have a lollipop in your purse?"

Nearly laughing at myself at my own incompetence, I quickly found a lollipop, popped it in her mouth, started rubbing her back, and then we made plans to do the rest of the London trip by cab. Now that I knew what was happening, I knew how to handle it—and I also knew that as soon as we were in the early spring sunshine again, she would unfreeze and be fine as well. Patting her back rhythmically while singing one of her favorite songs, I reflected on how different one of these reactions was for us eight years ago when I didn't know what was happening and it was much scarier for us both.

I KNOW THAT when people hear the term *post-traumatic stress disorder* they often think of returning war veterans. But did you know that kids in the foster system actually have PTSD at a much higher rate than soldiers returning from active combat?[1] Part of this is the difference between a child's brain and an adult's brain. When an adult has a traumatic experience, say they are a seasoned surfer and they have a little trouble in a rough wave and get slammed into the sand, they will most likely shrug it off as bad luck. But if a young child on their first trip to the beach gets slammed into the sand on their first time venturing into a wave, it will likely create a fear of the big waves that will be hard to overcome.

This isn't exactly worthy of the *Diagnostic and Statistical Manual of Mental Disorders (DSM)*, but here is my working definition of PTSD: When you have an outsized fear reaction to something not inherently dangerous (trigger) based on something that has happened in your past (trauma), this is a PTSD reaction. If we were in my office and a growling bear or a man with a gun came into my office, we would all have a reaction—probably something within the fight-flight-freeze realm. This is typical and appropriate—those are certainly things that are inherently dangerous. But what if a small dog came into my office? Well, I like dogs, so as long as it looked friendly, I would probably greet the dog and pat it on the head. But if you'd been bitten by a dog as a small child (trauma), you could have the same reaction to that small dog (trigger), no matter how friendly it looked, as I would have to a grizzly bear.

So for my daughter in the Tube, the trigger was the darkness and the noise, which triggered a trauma from her past that is probably mostly forgotten, except in her subconscious mind. We were all perfectly safe; thousands of people travel by the Tube every day and it is exceedingly rare that someone is injured by it. But her brain equated something about that experience with something from her early trauma and signaled that she wasn't safe, and she went into fight-flight-freeze mode, which for her is freeze mode. This was her mind trying to keep her safe. And you don't have to recognize and identify the source or the trauma to identify the PTSD reaction.

All of us have a fight, flight, or freeze reaction to stressors or being startled. This is actually a very good and developmentally appropriate way for us to be built! Imagine being one of our hunting and gathering ancestors out gathering food in a small group and suddenly being set upon by a large angry bear. If your brain had to think, "Well, what is the logical thing to do here?" and run scenarios in your head, you would be a bear snack. The part of your brain responsible for logical thought is the prefrontal cortex, which is a very complex part of the brain, and it also is slower at processing. The part of the brain responsible for the fight, flight, or freeze part of your brain is the cerebellum, which is also responsible for automatic parts of your body like your heartbeat and breathing. It is also sometimes called the "reptile brain" because it is an old brain structure, and it also processes information incredibly quickly. People will often talk about a fight-flight-freeze reaction as being so automatic their body does it almost without their permission or knowledge, and that can be a good way to think about it. Van der Kolk writes,

> *Psychologists usually try to help people use insight and understanding to manage their behavior. However, neuroscience research shows that very few psychological problems are the result of defects in understanding; most originate in pressures from deeper regions in the brain that drive our perception and attention. When the alarm bell of the emotional brain keeps signaling that you are in danger, no amount of insight will silence it.*[2]

People tend to have one main mode of either fight, flight, or freeze when they are startled. This chapter is designed to help you figure out what you are and what your kids are, and this will be enormously helpful in figuring out the dynamic that happens between the two of you. For example, a fight parent and a fight child have a much different dynamic than a flight parent and a freeze kid.

Caveat: There are a few things that can change your fight-flight-freeze reaction, and the main one is military training. When I work with parents that have a background in the military or law enforcement, I always ask what they were before they served, because military training actually trains people to overcome their initial reaction. The other branch of professionals that train against this reaction are any sort of emergency workers such as paramedics or ER nurses or doctors. The other thing that can change your reaction is certain circumstances— for example, I'm flight most of the time unless one of my children is threatened, and then I'm a fight person. So when we talk about these categories, we're trying to talk about what people are in general, so think in broader terms.

Fight

People for whom fight is their primary mode are people who tend to react very defensively when threatened, who seem to "have their fists up." Fight kids tend to be highly oppositional, difficult, argumentative, and both yell and cry easily. When triggered or startled, their body will often react into a defensive stance, with their fists clenched. If you touch the shoulder of a fight kid to comfort them when they're triggered, you could easily get punched, to the horror of both the kid and yourself.

Fight kids usually end up in my office faster than other kids because they tend to drive parents crazy and get into trouble at school, but in a lot of ways they are easier to work with in therapy because they have better access to their emotions. Oftentimes, with some tools and some work with communication, fight kids can do really well.

Flight

Flight people want to get away when startled. These are people that have restless, jumpy legs, that scan every situation looking for how to leave the room, and really hate feeling trapped. A flight kid, when feeling triggered, just won't want to stay in the room, and when they feel forced to stay in the room, they will leave in their minds, either through fantasy or disassociation.

Freeze

Freeze people are the literal "deer in the headlights" people. When startled they often have a heart-pounding sense of dread; they often hold their breath and try hard not to breathe. Children will often seem much younger than they are and will sometimes become nonverbal and unresponsive. Most people who are freeze will have difficulty feeling any emotion when they are triggered, beyond fear and dread.

Freeze kids can also be overly compliant when they are triggered, so often it can be very difficult to tell when they are triggered. Freeze kids also tend to be better behaved overall, so they don't tend to get into an office with a therapist until something happens with them that often feels out of the blue to the parent—like cutting or a sudden outbreak of panic attacks. Some people identify another category, called "fawn," where a person placates and pleases as a triggered response, but this could also be seen as a freeze response of being overly compliant.

I've had a similar experience with fight, though it is much rarer for me. I live in a house near Seattle with a green area behind the back fence, and sometimes we get large raccoons in our yard. About ten years ago a large raccoon attacked one of my dogs in our backyard, leaving her with emergency surgery and scars. Recently when I let my small dogs outside, I heard them yipping, and when I realized there was a raccoon out there engaged in combat with the more foolhardy of my dogs, I charged out, in full fight mode. I didn't pause long enough even to grab a broom for a weapon, and went out screaming at the raccoon at the top of my lungs and charging it, with every intention of doing whatever it took to protect my little dog. I had no thought to my own safety; raccoons can be quite nasty creatures when threatened, being naturally armed with sharp teeth and long claws. But the raccoon took one look at me, and my little dog that was putting up a valiant fight against an opponent twice her size, and decided it wasn't worth it, and took off over the bank and up a tree. (Side note: the dog was fine; the vet just had to clean up a few nasty lacerations and give her a round of antibiotics.)

Do you know what you are? If you are fight or flight, you probably identified yourself pretty easily. If you are freeze, it was probably harder. I usually tell people if they don't know what they are, then they're probably freeze, because when you freeze your brain turns off, so it makes it harder to realize what's happening and to remember what it feels like when you are triggered. Once, when I was about eleven or so, my parents took me to a haunted house section of a wax museum. I remember being very scared seeing the creepy scenarios set up, but then when something jumped out at me, it startled me so much that I knocked my mom, my dad, and my older sister onto the ground in my efforts to run out of the door to get out of the room. Clearly, I'm a person whose main mode is flight. I didn't think about what I was doing; my body took over in order to keep me safe.

Once you've figured out what you are and what your child is, then think about how they interact. Fight-fight is the most volatile, especially if the parent has had trauma in their childhood. This is because when the child gets triggered, their outbursts and aggression will trigger the parent, and then their attempts at control will continue to trigger the child, and it becomes a vicious cycle. But whatever the parent is, it is important for them to recognize what they are so that they are able to care for their reaction when they are starting to get triggered. Identifying for yourself when you are getting triggered is the first half of the equation; caring for yourself is the second half. The next chapter talks more about how to care for yourself when you are triggered, in order to keep yourself regulated.

Do you know what your child is for fight-flight-freeze? If you don't know, think about what the child does if someone in authority yells at them, or if someone startles or scares them. If someone the child is a little intimidated by yells at your child and they yell back, this is good evidence for a fight child. If the child is overly compliant or doesn't answer, this is probably a freeze kid. If the kid just tries to get out of the room, then this is probably a flight kid. If your child yells back at a playmate but freezes with a caregiver or teacher, this is a freeze kid. If your teenager is sassy with you unless you use a really stern tone and then they flee, then this is a well-adjusted teen that is probably flight and doesn't get triggered as easily. You have to think about how the child is when they are actually frightened or triggered and how they react.

Our brains are amazing things! Do you know that it is easier to induce the fear of snakes and spiders in mammals than it is to induce a fear of bunnies and mushrooms?[3] Our brains are hard-wired to find some things threatening and other things not as threatening. Kids with trauma often have similar things that trigger them, and I think it's very similar to how our brains are hard-wired to become afraid of snakes. So I've made a list of common triggers that I've seen many times with kids and some ways to address them. Every kid is unique, however, and every kid will have their own unique triggers. Often you can identify a good idea of what triggers a child, but often you can still get surprises (as I did that day in London). Sometimes you can also figure out why a certain thing is a trigger, such as an easy one like the child you adopted from a war zone being triggered by fireworks. But sometimes it is not very clear at all; you figure it out years later, or maybe never at all. It's okay to understand that loud noises trigger your child and not understand why; knowing why is very much less of the point than what you can do to help your child with how to help the trigger.

Common Triggers for Children

Being told no: This is one of the ones that can be very hard to understand for new parents, as they see it as a normal part of parenting (which indeed it is). This triggers children in two ways—one is that it triggers the control button for them (look at chapter 2 for how trauma affects the brain for why control is such an issue) and the second is that it can feel as if a need isn't getting met (felt needs often don't feel any different than real needs to children with attachment challenges). Parents can often avoid this trigger by trying to answer the question in a way that can avoid the no if they can. So a question of "Can I run around outside in my swimming suit?" when it's snowing can be answered with "I really wish it were summer too. That sounds lovely when the weather is warmer."

Getting in trouble: A child is at their most vulnerable when they are being corrected for doing something wrong. Any correction or discipline you do with a child that has had trauma must be done through the lens of realizing that just doing something wrong and being in trouble are probably going to be very triggering for the child. More on this in chapter 8, dealing with discipline strategies.

Being hungry, thirsty, hot, or cold: Physical discomfort puts all of us on edge, but these are especially hard for kids that have experienced trauma around these issues at preverbal ages. Kids that experienced hunger in their first year of life will probably not be able to vocalize why being hungry is so triggering for them, but you can often see the trigger happen. If this is a trigger for your child, make sure you always have snacks available. I work with kids that were cold as very young children, and they are very comforted by their caregivers making sure they have warm, safe beds and coats.

Holidays or significant events: Kids in dysfunctional homes often can't read a calendar, but they can read the weather and they can read holidays. And families with domestic violence often get worse around the holidays because people are home, there is often more drinking, and there is less oversight by school authorities. Because of this, many kids coming from dysfunctional backgrounds are very triggered by holidays, even if they were removed from their homes at relatively young ages. I recommend that families keep holiday celebrations simple and trauma-informed, with good sensory input and lots of space for children to regulate. Taking a traumatized child to three different houses to visit relatives, giving them treats all day to eat, opening stimulating presents, and then expecting them to stay regulated in unrealistic. Even kids adopted at birth or shortly after can be triggered by holidays or significant events as well, as those events might bring up mixed feels about where their bio-family is and if they're safe, and how they would feel about where the child is now.

Trauma anniversaries: This is similar to holidays, except you don't necessarily know when these anniversaries are. Kids have a biological clock that often can tell the time of year when traumatic things happen. I once worked with a teen who had disrupted from his foster family every October for the past four years. I asked the social worker, "So, what happened in October before he went into foster care?" She didn't know, but after some research she found out that he was removed from his parents pretty traumatically at five years old in October (his parents were taken away in handcuffs) and then he was placed with his grandma, who then died in front of him four years later, also in October. Of course this kid had trouble navigating October! His blood pressure started rising as soon as he saw pumpkins put out. It might not always be as clear as that, but if your child has a time of year that she struggles, then listen to that.

Transitions: Any type of transition is going to be hard for a traumatized child. School ending or starting, getting a new teacher, going from play to work, dinner to bed, or anything like that. Transitions feel out of control for traumatized kids, and they most want to feel in control in order to feel safe. Helping with this trigger usually helps children feel as if they have more control in the transition—doing things like giving warnings, giving them choices, and setting up expectations ahead of time.

Seeing someone hurt: Some kids get really triggered seeing another person hurt. One of my kids was like this, so if something happened like a kid scraped their knee or got their fingers slammed in a door, taking care of the triggered child was just as much a part of the first aid as Band-Aids and ice packs for the injured kid.

Professionals such as social workers, police, and therapists: This one is really tricky because obviously we want kids to be able to trust the professionals to help them, but if they saw police arrest their bio-parents or had a social worker remove them from their home, then they might not be as friendly toward them. I've worked with kids that have had a bad experience with a therapist before as well, and it can be doubly hard to do any work with them because of the mistrust. If your child has this issue with police officers, try and see if you can meet a police officer at your local station, a fund-raising pancake breakfast, or when they might visit your child's school. Fire fighters can sometimes be a happy medium for scared kids as they are like police officers but a little less scary.

Sights, sounds, or smells associated with previous life: This trigger can be things like cigarettes and alcohol, a certain perfume, or people yelling at each other. Sensory triggers, especially scent, can be very strong and overwhelming for kids.

Visits with bio-relatives: If you are fostering and have regular visits or have visits as part of an open adoption agreement, then you might already know this as part of your child being triggered. There are so many options in the whole arrangement that are fraught with triggers for kids—what if the relative doesn't show up? What if they do and are mean? What if they are nice and the child is sad they aren't living with them? What if they are using? What if the relative expects the child to do something the child doesn't want to do? What if this means reunification and the child leaves a beloved foster family? What if the child wants nothing more than to return home and is worried that their behavior at the visit is the deciding factor? It's enough to make a poor child's head spin.

My best advice for visits is to have expectations set up ahead of time as well as possible and try to make it as good an experience as possible for the child. For instance, a park is a good place for a child to have a visit, so they can be playing rather than fretting if someone is going to show up. Also, have a good transition plan for the end of the visit with time warnings, and have a good aftercare plan with sensory input. For instance, at the child's weekly visit with bio-dad, a plan could look like: they go to the park and play on the swings; then afterward the child cuddles with their special blanket and sucks on a lollipop in the car on the way home. At home, the child gets to jump on the trampoline while foster mom makes his favorite dinner, and then afterward he gets to watch a show with his foster parents. Having that plan written down, or drawn if it's easier for the child, can show how he's going to take care of himself to help him stay regulated.

Going to bed and bathing: These are very vulnerable times, especially for a child who was sexually abused, being groomed for sexual abuse, or has bad dreams associated with PTSD. First, make sure you have a gentle, loving routine and set very good boundaries for the child around these times to respect her privacy as much as possible. Try good sensory input during the bath and at bed through smells, touch, and sounds. Think soft music, scented lotion, and so on. If your child has a lot of issues around going to bed and bathing that you haven't been able to address with a gentle loving routine, this is definitely a place to get a therapist involved.

Praise: This might seem like an odd one, but for kids that have some of the more difficult attachment difficulties, praise can actually be a trigger for them. Most kids with trauma have a deep-seated belief that they are bad or broken, and when you praise them, they will sometimes feel that as a conflict with this deep desire and react negatively to that. Their self-image of being broken and wrong is so entrenched that any evidence to the contrary can feel threatening. If your kid is doing this, then instead try to focus on your enjoyment of them instead, so instead of saying, "That's a good drawing," instead say, "I am enjoying looking at this drawing so much," because it shifts the pressure to you rather than on them.

Vacation: I know this seems like a strange one to be on the list, but vacationing with traumatized kids can often be pretty challenging. Whether you go to a theme park and they get overwhelmed with all of the sensory input, or you go camping and the child gets dysregulated by the change in schedule, vacation is fraught with pitfalls. My best advice for vacation is to plan it as restful as possible and as predictable as possible. Do not go for surprises here, and do not try to cram as much as possible into your time off. Going on a road trip? Draw up a schedule, with the child involved if possible, so they know where you are going on what day, and a basic routine and expectations. Are you going to Disneyland? If you can, give yourselves a few extra days so you aren't rushing through the park in case people get triggered, read some blogs or watch some YouTube videos so kids know what to expect, and pack lots of good sensory regulating tools. In our family we break into team roller coaster (the sensory-seeking faction) and team not roller coaster (sensory sensitivities) and then go on different rides and meet back together. Respect kids' needs—Splash Mountain might be a lot of fun for some kids, but could be triggering for others.

Attachment: This is a hard one, because technically a child that reacts to attachment sounds like the diagnosis of reactive attachment disorder (RAD). Please do not Google this diagnosis, it will scare the socks off you, and it is not helpful for most parents. RAD is seen as mostly untreatable, and kids with it are seen as unadoptable and unable to be part of a family. Full-blown RAD indeed is very difficult to treat and very frightening, but what I want to address here is children who react to attachment, or to overtures of attachment from their caregivers. For children with a history of severe abuse and neglect, friendly overtures from caregivers always came with a price tag. They have learned to be suspicious, and this has kept them alive. So of course when this new "foster family" says they are safe, this child is not going to believe them. But the reaction to attachment comes when the child does start to believe, and that triggers them because it feels incredibly vulnerable.

This happened with one of my kids, and it nearly killed me before I recognized the pattern that was going on. In my defense I was not a trauma therapist at the time, and was just beginning to read the books about the theories.

It started when she had been with us for about nine months, and we started having moments of genuine emotional connection—where we had mutual enjoyment for a short conversation. Then, afterward, it would seem that she would hate me for a week. It was a hard week, where I felt betrayed and like a failure as a mom. I looked at a RAD checklist and could have checked nearly every box for her—and I worried that I was never going to make a connection with her. How could I when every connection ended in her hating me? But then I realized that it wasn't about me—I wasn't the one she really hated. I was the convenient and safe punching bag; I wasn't the cause.

And so I persisted stubbornly; I was going to love this child whether she liked it or not. And when she was over her reaction, I tried to connect again—tentatively, gently, but always trying again. I noticed as time passed that her reaction time went from a week, to five days, to three days, and so on. We didn't get to the point where she had no reaction time at all until she was an adult and no longer living with me. But now, many rocky years later, I can now have a real, intimate conversation with her and even hug and kiss her, telling her that I love her, and she says it back. She has formed real connections and friendships with others too, and is a gloriously amazing and imperfect human being that I respect and admire. I am truly grateful I am still allowed to be in her life to see who she has become.

OLYMPIC-LEVEL SELF-CARE

"HOW DO I KEEP from feeling like I'm twelve years old?" I asked my therapist for what felt like the tenth time. I felt hopelessly locked in the pattern with one of my daughters—she triggered one of my trauma buttons so hard that I was sometimes finding it very difficult to even stay in the same room with her when she really got going. Growing up, I had often been the victim of my mentally ill, capricious, and often cruel older sister, so learning to read the temperature of the room and escaping at the right time were survival skills that I had learned from a very young age. And when my adolescent daughter would rage, yell, and threaten violence, it was very difficult for me sometimes to keep calm about that and provide what I knew she needed—me as a calm, steady, and unreactive presence in her life.

But it was so hard to keep ahold of my flight response, and I would often want to flee anytime I could feel her ramping up. The other children didn't seem to trigger that same response in me, although to be fair my husband was triggered more by another one of the children. But with this one particular child I was deep in the realm of secondary trauma, where her trauma was beginning to make me feel victimized as well. The random thoughts I would have sometimes of feeling like I was a battered wife startled me in their intensity, and I felt shame that I wasn't able to handle her dysregulation in a better way. My husband would say, "Let her yell; it's okay. When she gets it out of her system, she'll be more reasonable." But I felt that I couldn't help but internalize fear, guilt, and shame when she raged, and it was so hard not to take it personally when she raged at me. I feel like I could write a whole book on this subject alone and there would still be more to say and more topics to explore, but I decided on settling on what has really helped me in this area.

I once read a book that said that the deepest shame that most mothers held was about how much they weighed and how messy their houses were.[1] Reading this book together with other women gave me a sense of freedom from that shame, and it made me laugh to think that other women had the same shame that I did. And for adoptive parents parenting traumatized kids, I would add that their own emotional regulation in response to their children's outbursts is as high in their shame list as anything else.

Caring for any children can really take a toll on caregivers, and the caregivers that give the most are parents of traumatized children. And tied up in that care can also be a self-evaluation too, wondering if we're doing a good enough job and if there is something that we could be doing better or differently. It's incredibly hard not to take it personally when a child rages, when they say they hate you, when they seem frightened of you, or when they just can't seem to make eye contact. But if I could tell parents one thing that is absolutely critical for their mental health, it would be to not take the things your child does and says personally. The fact that your child feels safe enough to act up with you means something; they would not be yelling at someone they thought was going to beat them or kick them out of their house. If you parent in a loving, kind, and consistent manner that gives a place for a child to work out their grief and trauma, often that can be very ugly. But in order to give them room to do that, you need to not take it personally if they are triggered or angry or sad. You are not graded in parenting based on how well your child behaves. There will be no mid-term exams, and they do not submit parent evaluations.

I found that in some ways self-care could be a lot like asthma. I didn't grow up with asthma; it was something that I developed later in life. Part of the learning curve that I figured out is that there are two medications that really help with asthma—one is the long-term medication and one is the rescue inhaler. The long-term medication contains a low dose of steroids that has to work over weeks in your lungs to reduce inflammation, and it is useless in an asthmatic crisis. For a crisis situation, you need albuterol, which is a rescue inhaler. If you try to manage asthma without both of these medications, it won't work. I tried for a while not to take the long-term daily medication, but then when a crisis arose (like when I got a cold), my lungs freaked out and it was too late to take the daily medication, because it took weeks to work. So I had to rely heavily on the rescue inhaler, which really isn't meant for that type of use. Likewise, if you only take the daily medication and have no rescue inhaler, you might be better prepared for a crisis, but if a crisis overwhelms you, you don't have a rescue option. An asthmatic needs both, and so does a parent to a traumatized child.

I hope I didn't overwhelm nonasthmatics out there with this analogy, but it was a revelation to me to realize that I needed long-term self-care as well as the instant rescue sort of self-care. Too heavy a reliance on either one won't work well in the long run. You need the disciplines of long-term care like exercise, therapy, date nights, good social connections, and community. You also need rescue self-care strategies that you can employ in the minute if you're feeling overwhelmed in order to stay calm and regulated yourself. Shortchange yourself on either one of those and you will not operate as well.

People avoid the topic of self-care, and they feel that it is unnecessary, or they feel depressed because they feel that they have neither the time nor the resources to do it properly. I am under no delusion that everyone reading this book will read this chapter—I know that many people will skip it and get onto "more important and useful things." But the core of self-care is actually the core of what we're trying to teach our kids as well—if we can model how we care for ourselves and our emotions, then that teaches them.

Please take this self-assessment to see how you're doing in these areas. Rate yourself a 1 (I don't do well at this at all) or a 5 (I excel at this) to each of the statements below.

1. I find time to exercise regularly.

2. I always get a good night's sleep.

3. I eat healthy food that makes me feel good.

4. I am completely caught up on all of my health-care appointments (doctor, dentist, optometrist).

5. I get an adequate level of mental health care.

6. I feel that I can identify and express my emotions.

7. I feel my emotions stay within good limits, neither overwhelming nor numb.

8. I feel and can cope with my emotions without unhealthy coping skills such as alcohol.

9. I have been able to engage with a like-minded community that I enjoy. For example: church, yoga class, book club.

10. I have space in my life to pursue something creative that I enjoy.

11. I have regular time with my friends.

12. I feel like my friends understand my struggles with my kids. They listen to me more than give me unwanted advice.

13. I am part of a support group for parents with traumatized kids.

14. I find time to have dates with my spouse or enjoyable time with any partnerships in my life. For example, if you are single, do you have enjoyable time with your parents or friends that are partners to you?

15. I feel that my relationships are mutually respectful and gratifying, and I have pursued therapy where appropriate.

This isn't a scored quiz that will give you a number that will tell you if you're doing it right or not, but rather these are questions to try to get you thinking about how you are caring for yourself and where there might be some holes.

Long-Term Self-Care

Long-term self-care is the type of self-care that deals with the core of ourselves. For raising typical kids, self-care can look like good date nights and bubble baths and maybe an art class, but for raising traumatized kids you need to up your game. I think of raising typical kids like playing intramural sports in college—you break a sweat, work hard, and go have a beer at the pub afterward. For raising traumatized kids, this is like the Olympics—pretty much as hard as it gets. So you need Olympic-level self-care as well. An Olympic swimmer doesn't say, "Well, that was a good mile in the pool today, think I'll call it a day, have a bit of time in the hot tub, and then head off." She analyzes everything about her life and workout to make sure she's maximizing how she can care for her body so she can succeed. We need to do the same as parents to traumatized children as well, to look at our lives to make sure we're getting all of our needs met so that we have the stamina for the race ahead. This breaks up into categories: physical, emotional-psychological, spiritual-creative, social, and partnership.

Physical: This is probably one of the easiest to quantify, and probably one of the things that came to mind when you think of self-care. Studies have shown that for psychological benefits, exercise just needs to be consistent and enjoyable. Even as little as five minutes of light to moderate exercise will boost your mood![2] Caring for your physical self also means healthy food that you know makes you feel good, getting enough sleep at night, regular health-care appointments, and wearing clothes that you like and that fit you.

Emotional-psychological: This category can be a little harder to quantify than the physical one, but it is no less important. Often parents of traumatized children feel overwhelmed emotionally, or numb. People often feel that they have to do this in order to survive the stress of raising children with the effects of trauma. Sometimes what's hard is hearing the traumatic stories the kids tell; sometimes it's dealing with the physical effects of the abuse (such as children affected by in utero exposure to drugs and alcohol); and sometimes it's the behavior challenges that come from a brain raised on heightened levels of cortisol. Raising kids with these challenges is really hard emotionally for parents with typical backgrounds, and if you come with a childhood with trauma in it yourself, then you have an even harder challenge ahead of you. Most parents that I work with that have childhood trauma can really benefit from therapy as they parent traumatized children in order to keep themselves regulated and help process the emotions that arise for them. Most therapists that I know that work in trauma make room in their lives for their own personal counseling, and it is seen as a good practice of self-care to continue the work they do.

Spiritual-creative: This is a fun one! Everybody has a need to connect with themselves in a spiritual and creative way. Whether this is attending services as part of your faith community, doing yoga, painting, writing poetry, mountain climbing, or walking on the beach, our human hearts crave engagement with something greater than ourselves. What is it for you that makes you feel connected to something outside of yourself that inspires awe? A visit to the forest on a sunny afternoon? Travel to a house of worship that has housed believers for centuries? Seeing a painting that inspires you? This category is incredibly personal but also has so many possibilities.

Social: This area does differ from person to person, but everyone has a need to connect socially with others. Parents under stress often separate from their relationships for many reasons; fear of judgment, well-meaning advice that falls flat, lack of child care, and sheer exhaustion can all play a role. But the resulting isolation makes parents feel worse, not better. Olympic-level parenting requires a lot of creativity with your social life, which can include creativity about making coffee dates after the kids go to bed, setting good boundaries about unwanted advice, or perhaps making a few friends with similar struggles.

Partnership: For many parents, their marital partner is their main partner in raising their child. But for many parents, they get partnership elsewhere, either because they are single or because another person provides that partnership for them as well. That person could be a mother, sister, nanny, grandpa, or friend. But I firmly believe that parenting is always done better in partnership, and maintaining those partnerships is very important for the mental health of the parents. With a marriage, maintaining that partnership can definitely look like having date nights, overnight trips, mutual encouragement, and friendship. Maintaining other partnerships can have a lot of the same ingredients—that it's important to enjoy the people in your life, and to have time with them that's not just about child care.

Instant Self-Care

Long-term self-care is absolutely critical, and without it the instant self-care will just be putting out fires and not helping you regulate over the long term. However, instant self-care is another very important piece of the puzzle as well, and without some good instant strategies when your child dysregulates, you could be not far behind. There are three steps for good self-care, and these steps can happen very quickly in the heat of the moment.

1. Recognize that you are being triggered. Become acquainted with how your body feels when you are at the beginning stages of feeling dysregulated—do your fists clench? Legs twitch? Stomach churn? Self-care works best at the beginning stages, so the earlier you can recognize the moment of needing some self-care, the better.

2. Remind yourself of a truth in the situation that helps you. Common mantras could be something like, "My child dysregulating isn't my fault; I shouldn't take it personally," or "My child isn't trying to attack me; they just have big emotions that they can't handle right now."

3. Employ some form of instant self-care. I'm going to give you a list of things that I use on a regular basis that are helpful to me, but there are lots of things that can be helpful in this category. The main idea is to do something that interrupts the escalation of emotion; caring for your emotions usually through something sensory or through giving you some time to calm down.

These are good instant self-care strategies:

* Count to ten out loud. Breathe deeply. I know this seems like something someone would do on a cheesy sitcom, but it actually works. My kids know I do it to regulate and to not yell at them, and I've actually begun to see them employ it when frustrated with each other. Success!

* Take a time-out, as they are actually supposed to be used! Say out loud that you are having trouble regulating and are going to take a time-out so that you can calm down and feel better. In the car I do this by announcing that I need a time-out and will not be talking to anybody for the next five minutes. During your time-out, do something calming, like deep breathing, yoga, or reading.

* Make a cup of tea. This smells good, tastes good, and feels warm and comforting.

* Light candles. Hmm, I love the smell and the light. I have a funny story about candles and one of my daughters, and I would always light

them when she started getting dysregulated to help me stay regulated. One evening I went to her apartment as an adult and after a particularly difficult time with some of her bio-family, she lit candles as a comfort measure for herself.

- Gum, chocolate, mints, scented lotion, putty, glitter jars, essential oils, or anything that can get your mind to focus on some other sensory process rather than the stress pathway currently operating in your brain.

I was once speaking to a group of foster parents about techniques to help calm foster kids when they were triggered. I went over my usual recommendations of sensory interventions and breathing techniques, and then afterward, we all adjourned and I left, expecting to head back home with little other thought. This was not to be, however, because just prior to the talk, one of the parents had gone grocery shopping, and her trunk had been full of groceries. Unbeknownst to her, a pack of toilet paper had nestled up against a loose brake wire, which had then smoldered during the evening while we were inside. Her car had really started smoking by the time we arrived in the parking lot. Someone had called the fire department, which had come quickly—blocking off the parking lot and pulling the burning material from the trunk of her car.

The woman who owned the car was, understandably, somewhat stressed by this progression of events. Imagine standing in the parking lot watching firefighters pull smoldering groceries out of the trunk of your car as lights and sirens flash all around.

I walked up beside the woman, who seemed on the edge of panic, and said, "Do you want some gum? I have some in my purse."

"Okay," she replied, hardly thinking.

I handed her some from my supply that I usually carry for my kids, then waiting another few moments. "I have some lovely scented lotion as well," I tell her. "It smells like lemons. Want to try some?"

"I know what you're doing," she tells me with a brittle laugh, accepting some of the lotion. "I heard your talk you just gave."

"I know," I answered. "I was hoping it might help."

"It does help," she answered in surprise, smoothing the lotion over her hands and smelling it. "Who would think something as simple as gum and lotion could help when your car is on fire."

6

ATTACHMENT

WHEN YOU THINK of attachment, it's easy to think of hipster parenting and baby wraps. However, when a therapist talks about attachment, they're talking about it in the context of how a child attaches to their primary caregiver in their first year of life. This attachment to the caregiver provides a blueprint for the child's relationships for the rest of their lives. For a child that comes from a relationship with a fraught attachment in their early childhood, this is bad news. One researcher found that participants in their study that experienced child abuse were found to be six times more likely to be experiencing difficulties in adult love relationships than those who had not experienced child abuse. They found that when investigating attachment style, self-esteem, and relationship attributions upon this phenomenon, only avoidant and ambivalent attachment styles explained this amount of relational turmoil. The researcher writes, "These findings indicate that avoidant-ambivalent attachment style, but not self-esteem and relationship attributions, is a mediating factor in the route from child abuse to adult relationship abilities."[1]

Attachment is the trust and bond that builds between a child and caregiver over time. When a child is born, they come into the world looking to attach.

They are built for it—everything in their brain and body is built for it. The mother's body is built for it as well; from the oxytocin (also called the bonding hormone) released when she nurses to the biological hormonal interactions that happen in the first few weeks of a baby's life, it is bound to happen. When a caregiver holds and rocks a baby, the distance between their faces is the perfect distance for the baby to focus and attach.

For a healthy baby and a healthy caregiver, this is how the attachment cycle works:

Baby has need → need expressed → need met → attachment

Rinse and repeat about a million times. Seriously, though, it may feel daunting when you think about the infant attachment cycle and think that if you don't respond perfectly every time, your child won't be properly attached. It's not true at all! You can respond well about half the time and still have a good, healthy attachment with your children. The key to the healthy attachment cycle is that the child has the expectation that most of the time their needs will be met, that they can express their needs, and that they will be listened to.

For babies in some sort of situation where they don't have responsive caregivers, this is what the infant trauma cycle[2] looks like:

Baby has need → need expressed → need not met → mistrust develops

The important thing to remember with the infant trauma cycle is that not only does attachment not form, but mistrust actually develops. If a child in this cycle has a parent that sometimes meets their needs, then their trying to get their needs met will look desperate. If they have had very little success in getting their needs met, they will give up completely.

Attachment Styles

In order to classify attachment styles, researchers decided to see how very young children reacted when their mothers left the room and when they returned. They set up what they called a "strange situation," which was the mother and child entered a room with toys in it with a researcher, stayed there for a short while, and then the mother left for a short time, leaving the child with the researcher. The mother would then return a short time later, and the child's reaction to her return would be measured. The researchers then classified the reactions of the children, and categorized them into four distinct attachment categories:

Secure attachment: Child was distressed when the mother left and then comforted when the mother returned.

Ambivalent attachment: Child was very distressed when the mother left, but wasn't comforted when the mother returned, pushing the mother away.

Avoidant attachment: Child didn't seem to notice when the mother left and didn't seem to notice when the mother returned.

Disorganized attachment: Child acted aggressively, erratically, and unpredictably.

These categories were then developed into what they termed attachment styles, and they theorized that people could be roughly divided into these four different styles. These are what those styles look like.

Secure Attachment

This attachment style is the style that is by far the most common in general, and makes up 65–70 percent of the general population. One of the hallmarks of a securely attached child is that when the parent is there, they use the parent as a "safe base" and explore the world around them while checking in with the parent periodically. A securely attached child also seeks out the caregiver when distressed and is easily comforted by them.[3] John Bowlby, one of the pioneers of attachment theory, writes that a person who has a secure attachment is "likely to possess a representational model of attachment figures as being available, responsive, and helpful."[4]

Children who have a secure attachment grow up to be adults who are able to attach to partners and friends well, as well as children that they raise. Secure attachment instills in children that they are safe, that they can trust others, and that others are responsive to their needs.

The good news for parents raising children is that you do not need to be responsive to your children's needs 100 percent of the time to have a securely attached child. For a typical child, a parent being sensitive to the child's needs most of the time is really all that's needed. Children with a secure attachment feel free to express negative emotion to their caregivers, and seek them out to feel soothed.[5]

Ambivalent Attachment: I Need You, Now Go Away

This is the most common type of attachment that I see in kids in foster care and that have been adopted out of foster care. It is also called the insecure resistant or the push-pull attachment style, because you see it played out by a child that seems to seek out attachment with their caregiver but then pushes them away.[6] This attachment style happens when a child has an inconsistently responsive caregiver. One researcher writes that parents of children with this attachment style have "[i]nfants whose caregivers respond in inconsistent, unpredictable, or 'involving' ways, such as expecting the infant to worry about the caregiver's own needs or by amplifying the infant's distress and being overwhelmed. . . . They display extreme negative emotion to draw the attention of their inconsistently responsive caregiver."[7]

Children with this attachment style, therefore, have learned that their caregivers are inconsistent, unpredictable, and are trying to get their own needs met through the child. So the child tries to get their needs met through displaying negative emotion and trying to draw the attention of the caregiver. Children with this attachment style are likely to seem like they are seeking attachment with their foster or adoptive parents, but then can often push away when the parents can seem like they are coming too close. They are confused by calm, consistent parenting and often try to get an emotional reaction out of parents because they think that will not get their needs met. This is caused by less maternal availability; they see parents as nondependable and capricious.

It can be confusing to try to attach to a child with this attachment style—they seem so desperate for you one minute and then push you away the next. They go to desperate lengths to get your attention, and then seem uninterested in it the next day. They are clingy and desperately want attention, but nothing you can do ever seems to satisfy their never-ending need for attention.

Avoidant Attachment: Don't Let Them See You Cry

Do you have a child that doesn't seem to notice if you leave or when you come back? Does your child not seem to care who is taking care of him or prefer you to other caregivers? Your child might have what's called an avoidant attachment style, also sometimes called an indifferent attachment style. This attachment style is developed in infancy when "caregivers consistently respond to distress in insensitive or 'rejecting' ways, such as ignoring, ridiculing, or becoming annoyed," and the infant responds by developing a coping strategy "in that they avoid their caregiver when distressed and minimize displays of negative emotion in the presence of the caregiver."[8] Children with an avoidant attachment style were most likely abused and neglected—they were punished and rejected for relying on a caregiver, and so they have learned to avoid this reliance. They avoid using bids for attachment because these have gone unanswered, and they avoid showing distress because these aren't met with soothing—they have been met with punishment or rejection.

But the key to understanding children with this attachment style is that even though they don't appear to be in the same amount of distress as their ambivalent counterparts, psychophysiological studies show that they are. When they measure the child's heart rate and levels of cortisol (a stress hormone) upon separation from the attachment figure, the levels were the same as for the ambivalent child that is freaking out when the parent leaves the room.[9] So even though they look cool and uninterested, their bodies are in distress.

This suppression of their physiological responses to the caregiver leaving is present in other areas as they grow as well. One researcher writes,

> *Over time, avoidant individuals learn to suppress physiological responses related to distress. It does not mean that they do not feel distress, but it appears that they cannot generate a solution when they feel overwhelmed. As a result, they overregulate their affect to appear as if they are unaffected and are in essence emotionally paralyzed. Hallmarks of the personality of an individual with an avoidant attachment pattern are aversion to physical contact; a brusque, halting, and impersonal relational style; and flat affect, which can appear as depression or apathy.[10]*

Children with this attachment style grow into adults that appear unaffected by emotion, but are in fact deeply affected and do not know how to deal with how overwhelmed they are feeling.

It can be harder to connect with a child with an avoidant attachment style because they aren't making bids for attachment or are engaging in attachment-seeking behavior, but they need attachment just the same as the ambivalent child.

Disorganized Attachment

A disorganized attachment is the rarest of the attachment styles in the general population, but it can be up to 82 percent of infants that were maltreated by their parents. Rates were higher in samples of families experiencing poverty, psychiatric illness, substance abuse, and similar stresses.[11] It usually comes from situations where the parents are mentally ill and erratic, or just have unresolved trauma of their own. Caregivers in this situation are "frightening, frightened, dissociated, sexualized, or otherwise atypical,"[12] and these parenting behaviors are displayed by the parents whether the child is in distress or not—and usually really no matter what the child does.[13]

This is a very difficult environment for a child to endure, and it usually severely delays them in major milestones of child development. The child has a very difficult time making social relationships as they grow up, and by preschool the child has developed strategies for survival in school. One strategy for kids with a disorganized attachment is to focus on the needs of others and be impatient or hostile to their own needs.[14] Another strategy that kids can use is to "adopt controlling (caregiving or punitive) strategies to help manage dysregulated, unpredictable, or frightening caregiving environments."[15] A disorganized attachment also lends itself to having some of the bleakest outcomes. Researchers have found that everything from math scores at nine to peer interactions in middle school to mental health and delinquency as a teenager are markedly worse for a child who was classified as having a disorganized attachment as a toddler.[16]

A Word about RAD

RAD is reactive attachment disorder, the most severe attachment result of childhood abuse and neglect. RAD, in its most severe form, is frightening and extremely difficult to work with. A person with severe RAD cannot connect with other people and form normal relationships. One researcher describes RAD as:

> *Affected children have difficulty forming emotional attachments to others, show a decreased ability to experience positive emotion, cannot seek or accept physical or emotional closeness, and may react violently when held, cuddled,*

or comforted. Behaviorally, affected children are unpredictable, difficult to console, and difficult to discipline. Moods fluctuate erratically, and children may seem to live in a "flight, fight, or freeze" mode. Most have a strong desire to control their environment and make their own decisions. Changes in routine, attempts to control, or unsolicited invitations to comfort may elicit rage, violence, or self-injurious behavior.[17]

Please don't Google RAD. When I get someone in my office that has Googled RAD, I feel that I need to do some soothing techniques for the parent before we can even discuss therapy. The problem with the diagnosis of RAD is that it is often misapplied, and I feel as if there's a lot of misinformation about RAD that can get people's anxiety pumping. One of the hallmarks of the Holding Therapies is an overemphasis and an overdiagnosis of RAD, and a related and nontechnical diagnosis of attachment disorder.

In my practice I don't diagnose RAD unless I have to. The only circumstance in which I talk about diagnosing RAD is if it is needed to get a child needed services. The reason I don't diagnose RAD is because many people see it as a death sentence—that RAD makes a foster child "unadoptable," and people believe that a child with RAD will never be able to attach. This may be true for the most severe form of RAD, but children that react to attachment can attach and go on to form meaningful adult relationships, but the road ahead in parenting them is not an easy one. I also think that for the most part PTSD is a much better diagnosis—because RAD is the product of trauma, and it is a direct result of what has been done to the child and the child's best attempt to survive. I feel like the diagnosis of RAD demonizes those attempts, making the child's survival strategy the problem rather than the trauma they survived.

All children with a disruption in attachment have some level of attachment difficulty, but that doesn't mean that they have RAD. When I took my first course in psychopathology, my professor cautioned us against overdiagnosis of ourselves and our family and friends, as often happens to first-year medical students when they first start studying new diseases. It's easy to look at a list of symptoms and see your child has everything. That being said, it can be helpful to see some of the symptoms of attachment difficulties so that the parent understands the source of the behaviors are coming from something deeper than just trying to drive their parents crazy.

Symptoms of attachment problems:

1. The child doesn't seek comfort when distressed.

2. The child doesn't accept comfort when distressed.

3. The child is rarely happy.

4. The child has episodes of unexplained irritability, sadness, or fearfulness that are present even during nonthreatening interactions with caregivers.[18]

5. The child exhibits excessive lying, even when caught in the act.

6. The child exhibits odd behavior around touch: either seeking too much or too little.

7. The child has shallow, easily replaced relationships, often being too friendly with strangers, or "parent shopping."

8. The child is aggressive to self through words or actions.

9. The child is uncomfortable with eye contact.

10. The child seems to have no conscience.

11. The child has a difficult time asking for help or admitting they can't do something.

HEALING
ATTACHMENT DAMAGE
What Is Broken in Relationship
Must Be Healed in Relationship

AFTER ALL OF THAT BAD NEWS, I offer you some good news. Damage that has been done to the brain and to attachment can be healed; it just takes time and patience. Wallin writes,

> *The amygdala's emotional memories are forever. Yet the fear response is a conditioned one, a product of associational learning. Past attachment trauma may well have created an association between closeness and danger (neurons that fire together wire together). . . . Recalling and reexperiencing childhood fears and hurts in a context of safety can gradually transform the patient's remembered past, and dampen in the process the automatic amygdala-based reactions it has long evoked. . . . As clinicians, we can be encouraged by research showing that the brain of the adult, like that of the developing child, can be reshaped by current experience that not*

only establishes new neural connections but also alters the actual physical structure of the brain.[1]

What Wallin is saying is that the brain is plastic, and that not only can our thought patterns change, but the actual brain structure itself can. When a child with a disordered attachment can actually get into a relationship with a loving, calm, and interested adult who can be a healthy attachment figure for that child, then magic can happen. Children (and adults) only need one real attachment figure where they experience real love and attachment, and it can change their entire lives.

What Doesn't Work: A Legacy of Bad Therapy

Before we get into what works, I would like to spend a little bit of time talking about what doesn't work. The reason why we need to do this is because in the 1980s and 1990s, there was a very popular trend that was called "attachment therapy," which included holding therapies and rebirthing. This therapy called itself attachment therapy but was not based on the theories of Bowlby and Ainsworth and the researchers that most of attachment theory had used up until this point. This type of therapy was based on a theory by psychologist Robert Zaslow (who is a Freudian, not an attachment therapist, for those keeping score at home), who had a radical idea to force attachment and to "cure" people with autism by holding them down while they raged, forcing eye contact. His theories resulted in injuries, his methods were debunked, and he was stripped of his medical license in 1974.

However, other therapists thought this might work for adopted kids with attachment problems, so they decided to try it with them. This therapy would involve inducing the child to rage while being pinned down or "held" by adults, have catharsis (get out all their rage), be reduced to an early stage to be "reparented" through rocking, holding, bottle feeding, and forced eye contact, and then the child complies. This type of attachment therapy focuses very heavily on the parent being very authoritarian and the child being very obedient, which this theory sees as a sign of attachment.[2]

Parents desperate to make a good connection to their kids are vulnerable to "experts," and it makes a lot of sense that parents were attracted to this. It sounds really good—you could "work through" the child's rage, get them to a place where they were tired and felt sweet, and everything was going to be peachy from there on out, right? The problem was that the people who theorized this were not as familiar with PTSD and did not look at this from the perspective of the traumatized children. Instead of feeling as if they were getting out their rage in a safe place, the child would actually feel trapped and triggered. Think about a child that has experienced abuse from their original family being held down—this is going to deeply trigger them. A child that is triggered isn't working through anything; they are in survival mode and will do anything they need to survive. A child will eventually tire and might even comply, but this isn't the sweet "reparenting" that sometimes a child will allow you to do on their terms; this is abusive and retraumatizing. Respected trauma researcher and psychiatrist Bruce Perry says that using force or coercion on children in this way simply retraumatizes them and produces obedience based on fear, which is also known as the trauma bond called Stockholm syndrome.[3]

Holding therapies are currently seen by most of the psychiatric community as unethical and are not generally practiced anymore. However, there is still very much a strain of thought out there that holds this theoretical model. This model tends to focus heavily on the diagnosis of reactive attachment disorder (RAD) and will say that gentler therapies don't work, that harsher things are needed to "break through the child's defenses." It might be easy to think that these theories are debunked and in the annals of history, but it would not be true. There are therapists currently operating that still use this modality, and they advocate for what they call "attachment therapy," which is very much in line with what holding therapy advocates—harshness to break through defenses, high authority of parents, absolute obedience, and very little discussion or work around things like caregiver sensitivity, triggers, or PTSD. This is not real attachment; this is Stockholm syndrome—or the trauma cycle when mistrust develops.

I've been surprised, however, to find that this is a commonly held myth. I have found myself having to speak to countless parents, caregivers, and even a preschool about how holding down a raging child with PTSD is not only counterproductive but can be really harmful. The only time it's okay to hold a child that's having a PTSD reaction is if there's imminent harm to themselves or others, and this needs to be seen as a psychiatric emergency, and you are talking about going to the hospital. Even if the child seems better afterward, this is often a false thing—triggering their PTSD isn't how we want them to be able to regulate.

So What Does Work?

That's the million-dollar question, isn't it? If I knew an easy, two-week program to fix attachment problems, I would be a millionaire. Researchers have actually found that they can accurately predict a child's attachment style at six years old by looking at the mother's attachment style during pregnancy; that's how predictable it is. But even more interesting for our purposes is that by the time a child was placed with a foster parent for three months, their attachment style starts shifting to reflect their foster mother's attachment style.[4] So an attachment style is something that is set pretty early, but it is something that can be changed by consistent, loving parenting. But fixing attachment problems is less of a one-time fix, like gluing a handle back on a cup, and more like growing a successful vegetable garden. It takes time, patience, and a lot of creating the right environment.

Imagine for a moment that you are a survivor of a Viking raid in medieval Scotland and have built a castle around yourself to keep yourself safe. Castles were great technology at the time—Edinburgh Castle was actually never taken by force, but only by stealth. Castles also take a great deal of time and resources to build; you only build something like them if it's absolutely necessary. You might be lonely in your castle by yourself, but at least you're safe. When the Vikings come back, you will simply pick up your drawbridge, man your turrets, and let the moat take care of the rest.

Now let's say that you have a visitor to your castle, someone that wants to come in and talk about an alliance. He looks a lot like the Vikings that have attacked before, and you are on your guard against him. The last thing you are interested in is an alliance.

"You don't need these walls now that I'm here," he tells you, looking at the walls in disgust. "I'm here to take care of you now. The king of all of Scotland has decided that we should have an alliance."

"My castle works just fine," you fire back. "Keep your distance."

"Nope, the king has decreed it, so it's time for us to be allies. So you either let me in now, or I'm going to lay siege to this castle and knock down your walls, and you'll be forced to let me in."

By this point any self-respecting castle owner is sharpening his arrows, boiling his tar, and doing some sort of medieval equivalent of "Make me."

But what if the person had approached differently?

"Wow, great walls," the visitor admires. "You must have had some run-ins with the Vikings. You sure know how to defend yourself."

"Well, thanks, I guess," the castle dweller begrudgingly answers.

"I know I sort of look like a Viking, but I want you to know that I'm not a Viking," the visitor informs him. "I'm actually from Ireland. I'd love to come into your castle when you're ready, but it's okay if you need to trust me more first."

"Why are you here?"

"The king of Scotland wants us to be allies to make this area safer for everyone, and I wanted to talk to you about that," he answers cheerfully. "You know, when you're ready."

"Where are you going to be?" he asks, suspiciously.

"I'm going to camp out here until you're ready for me to come in. Do you want to come and have a campfire with me for a bit tonight? You can share my dinner with me if you want."

The second person was much more enticing, giving the person space, and respecting why the walls were there. You get a lot further with traumatized kids, and people in general, if you respect where they are and the process that they had to go through to get there. And when you're trying to connect to a child that has built a castle wall to protect themselves, you have two choices— you can break out the siege engines, or you can try to entice the inhabitants. If you choose siege engines, you might one day break down the walls of the castle, but you won't win the inhabitant's heart—you will be seen as an occupying force, not a friend. Your only good option is to entice them, to convince them that you're harmless, and to let them gradually let down their drawbridge and respond in friendship.

> The first child to enter our lives in a nontraditional manner did so at the age of nearly eleven, and she was dangerously underweight. Her relatives knew this, and the meal we had together before she came home with us was mostly spent trying to pressure her and convince her to eat—as if every bite she took was a battle to win. Even though I was not a therapist at the time and was only in my first year of graduate school, I knew a dynamic I did not want to engage in when I saw it. So the first night she was home for dinner with us, she picked at her dinner as well. I ignored it. I wasn't going to battle with her over food.
>
> "Do I have to eat this?" she asked. "I'm not hungry."
>
> "Nope," I answered honestly. "We don't make kids eat here."
>
> "Good," she answered, relieved but suspicious.
>
> "That's too bad, though," I told her, taking a bite myself. "That you're full, I mean. I wanted to make popcorn after dinner for us, but I guess it's pointless because if you're too full to eat dinner, you'd be too full to eat popcorn."
>
> "How much dinner do I have to eat to get popcorn?" she asked, calculating. She had played these games before.
>
> "I don't know," I shrugged. "Just some dinner, I guess. Whatever you think is a good dinner. Maybe you're not so full, then? I'd love to make popcorn with you later."
>
> In all honesty, I was playing poker. She needed calories, and if those calories were going to be entirely popcorn for a little while, so be it. But she mostly needed protein and vitamins, and so I most wanted to get some of those into her before the popcorn. And, surprisingly, my strategy actually worked. Once I took the pressure off eating and instead tried to entice her into it, she gained nearly 10 percent of her original body weight in just the first month she was with us. That child is now an adult, and we laugh together about those first few months.

Felt Safety: The Fertilizer of Attachment

Children need to feel safe in order to attach. The perception of whether or not their world is safe can be very skewed, but they are not going to let the drawbridge down enough to let you come into the castle if they feel that there is any danger. Children learn felt safety over time when they see how you are with them over smaller things, when they see how you are with others, and when they have time to figure out how you feel about them.

Caregiver Sensitivity and Attunement

In order for a child to be able to attach, the caregiver must be able to attune to the child. Attunement means that the parent is able to understand the child's emotions and empathize with them at a deep level. In order to do that, the caregiver must be sensitive to the child's emotions and communication, and for a child with trauma, that communication can sometimes be more difficult to decipher.

When thinking about attunement, the first thing to remember is that all behavior communicates something. How we react to that communication can either shut the door to more communication or it can open it up. For example, when a child comes home and slams the door, kicking the frame as they come, what do you do? If you scold them for kicking the door, the conversation stops there. If, instead, you say, "Wow, you seem really upset. You normally don't kick the door like that. I wonder what's wrong." That's an invitation for your child to engage with you—and your attunement and reflection of their emotions and behavior around the emotions. Trying to understand how a child feels and being genuinely interested in them is what you are trying to communicate to them.

Children Need to Feel Enjoyed

Picture for a minute your next date night, where you are all dressed up and ready to try the new Italian place you've been wanting to try. Your partner comes home from work, looks you up and down, and sighs dramatically. "Well, I guess it's date night," they sigh unenthusiastically. "I suppose we're headed out, then. I hate the traffic and parking."

How does that feel for you? Nobody wants to feel like their date isn't excited about spending time with them, and that is true for children as well. Children want to feel enjoyed; feeling enjoyed is a major part of attachment for them. For a child, unconditional love feels like being enjoyed.

So what if your tanks are feeling dried up and you can't think of the last time you enjoyed something with your child? If you were in my office, I would jokingly write you a prescription for fun. Do something enjoyable together, even if you can muster no more than driving to get an ice cream cone together. Try anything with good sensory things to help your kid regulate—swimming, skateboarding, walking, biking—anything that you would think of as fun as well. And when they do something well, say, "I enjoyed so much watching your concert today!"

Regression on the Child's Terms

So much is said in the harmful holding therapy about regression that I almost hesitate to put this section here, but the truth is that for some kids, they will regress at different times, and it can really help with attachment. The key to regression is attunement—the parent must be reading the child's cues and following what they want. Some children never regress, and that's completely fine. But for kids that do, regression must always be on the child's terms and never forced, and must always be comfortable and fun for the child. Many children ask for regressed play with their parents, and confused parents don't engage in it because they're afraid that it might be harmful. So I decided to keep this section because this type of play actually is very helpful to children, and I wanted to let parents know how to engage with it if they have a child that regresses like this.

A child that regresses is a child that sometimes acts in a younger way, sometimes when triggered and sometimes just as a matter of course. For instance, if your four-year-old asks for a bottle or your six-year-old wants to be rocked like a baby or use a pacifier, these are all regressed behaviors. These behaviors are normal, natural, and can often be the brain trying to reshape and heal parts of the brain that were neglected during a child's traumatic early life. If your child wants to do these things, then by all means, participate! Especially if they want to do them on your lap, cuddled to you, or to have you participate in any way that feels like you're being a good parent in the scenario. Although there is a lot of pressure on parents of young children to push them through the stages of development, this can actually be harmful to a child with early trauma.

I was a new trauma therapist when my own traumatized four-year-old at home starting asking for a baby bottle. I was a bit disconcerted—wasn't she too old for this? What would other people think? So I talked to my supervisor at the time and I asked her advice, and she said that if she was willing to sit in my lap to take the bottle, then I should give her all the bottles she wanted. Though it felt odd, I complied, and soon my four-year-old was having a bottle any time she felt scared, triggered, or sad. She was a freeze type child, and every time she got triggered, she felt very young and became not verbal anyway, so it became really easy to just make the leap to treating her like a baby as well. After I got past the strangeness of how it felt to give a bottle to a child of that age, I realized that it did feel soothing and nice to do this for her, and I did feel like I got a little bit of insight into what her early years were like. As she grew she became less and less interested in the bottle, and it naturally and gradually fell to the wayside.

One form of regression that is often overlooked is when a child is sick. I tell parents that when a child is sick to view it as a golden opportunity to shower the child with love, affection, and attention, and to meet their needs when they don't feel well. Whatever your family protocol for sickness is, go for it—chicken soup, hot tea, movies, snuggles, comfort. Kids feel vulnerable when they are sick, and if you can meet their needs when they are vulnerable, it could be a good time to show them that you are trustworthy and that you care about them.

Physical Touch

Physical touch should of course never be used to harm, to hold a child against their will, or to coerce a child, but it is a very helpful tool for attachment when used well. If a child is able to tolerate it, activities such as cuddling, wrestling, hugging, rubbing backs, and any gentle, loving touching can be very attaching and loving. Be on the lookout for teens wanting to sit close when you watch television, young kids wanting to sit on your lap and wrestle, and games that involve touch. For kids that seem reticent around touch, it can build a sense of safety if you ask permission to touch, let them know that they are in control of who touches their body, and model good boundaries around touch. For instance, it's a good rule in your home to have a boundary that when a person says "Stop!" everyone stops touching, whether you're in a wrestling match, a tickle fight, or whatever. These boundaries reinforce safety for everyone, and make physical touch feel safer. If there are good boundaries, even kids that are reticent for touch can start to engage more.

The key to attachment is to focus on safety and attunement.

What to Do If You Feel That Attachment Is Failing

First, if you're in the place where you feel that attachment is failing with your child, I want to offer a lot of sympathy to you. Most parents I have met with that are in this stage feel hopeless and ashamed, and it is a miserable place to be. Nobody gets into the idea of parenting a traumatized child thinking that it will fail, and everyone thinks and hopes that love will be enough. Please be kind to yourself in this place. But here are also some practical, emergency-level interventions that you can do to help.

Get the best therapist you can find, ASAP. If you are in therapy that you don't think is working, try to get someone else on board. A good therapist should be able to give you specific recommendations that can help you grow in attachment.

Get a psych evaluation for your child. If there are other factors happening, like a possible other diagnosis, a psych evaluation is very important. Sometimes something as simple as a proper diagnosis of another disorder can significantly improve a parent's patience for the child, which can really help with attachment. In most of the cases that I've worked with where a parent is having an especially hard time attaching, particularly if the child came at a young age, there was a complicating diagnosis of something like ADHD or autism. Getting proper treatment for that condition helped a great deal for their relationship.

Get your own therapy. Oftentimes what interferes with attachment is the parent's trauma being brought up by the child's trauma, or the parent suffering from secondary trauma from the child, and this is treated by the parent being in therapy. Trauma therapists are usually in therapy to help deal with the stress of working with other people's trauma, and that's true for parents who are parenting kids with trauma as well.

If You Want to Read More About Healing Attachment

Deborah D. Gray, *Nurturing Adoptions: Creating Resilience after Neglect and Trauma* (London: Jessica Kingsley, 2012).

GOOD DISCIPLINE
STRATEGIES
Kids Are at Their Most Vulnerable
When They've Done Something Wrong

BEFORE WE TALK about good techniques, I want to talk a little bit about theory. Many books have been written about discipline strategies, for better or for worse. There are many great ones out there. There are also many out there that I throw in the garbage when I see them on a book table. But most books, even the great ones, aren't written with traumatized kids in mind, and traumatized kids are an entirely different ball game than typical kids. There are three big principles to remember when thinking about discipline strategies for traumatized children:

1. Strategies that work with typical kids won't work with traumatized kids.

2. Traumatized kids are at their most vulnerable when they've done something wrong.

3. When disciplining a traumatized kid, you want to work at being their ally, not their adversary. Stay out of power struggles.

For example, let's talk about strategies that work with typical kids. For example, let's look at the time-honored practice of a time-out. Done well and with a typical kid, this practice gives a child (and a parent) some time to cool down and re-regulate, and is usually followed by some good relational repair (apologies), and can be a useful tool for a parent. There has been a lot of press lately about how a time-out can be abusive and overly punitive, and of course it can be. But done well it can also be a great tool for parents and kids to develop emotional regulation, learn to take breaks when emotions are running high, and have some time to think.

For a traumatized child, however, this can be a catastrophe. First of all, most kids with early trauma are going to have trouble regulating their emotions by themselves, and if they are sent to their room or some other designated "time-out" spot in which to do so, they will likely just escalate. Second, for a child where their trauma revolves around abuse and abandonment, this begins to feel a lot like they're going to be abandoned. This triggers all those feelings of fear of abandonment, and this also escalates them further. Given these triggers, is it no wonder that a time-out that you assume would help a child calm down would instead escalate things even further?

Now let's mix in some of the complications of things like a child with a history of physical abuse or abandonment. Suddenly when you're talking to them about why they didn't take out the garbage, they're assuming they're going to get beaten. Or, if they're a fight kid, they might even be trying to provoke you into beating them, because this waiting for when you're finally going to be doing it is excruciating, and they are sick of waiting, and they want it to be on their own terms and get it over with already! Or if they've had multiple placements, is this where you're going to kick them out? Again, it could also be a child trying to provoke it as well, so it's on their own terms rather than feeling like someone else has control.

When a traumatized child has done something wrong, they often need more reassurance from their parents, and often it is at a time when the parents are more apt to be wanting to give them less because they are upset themselves. But this is a time when they are the most vulnerable, and when extra care is required.

As I said in the chapter about testing boundaries, every child has two basic questions: Am I loved? Are there boundaries? How we as parents answer those questions sets a child up for safety and attachment. The child should feel that the answer to both of those questions is a firm and kind yes.

How to Set a Boundary

It could be tempting at this stage to have no boundaries, then, but that would be a mistake. Kids need boundaries to feel safe just as surely as they need to feel loved. But the trick to disciplining traumatized kids is to make the boundaries the bad guys, not you. You want to be the good guy, the one helping them out to figure out how to follow the rule. You want to be the cheerleader hoping they can make it, the helpful one reminding them of the family policy, the one really hoping that the consequence doesn't have to fall. When you're the one the child is pushing against, the fight escalates. It can be helpful to picture the power struggle that your child is trying to get you to engage in as a hook with bait, and your job is to not take the bait, and to stay off the hook.

> *"I just noticed on the school website that you have a few late assignments in one of your classes. I just wanted to give you a friendly reminder of the family policy that there's no weekend activities if there are still missing assignments on Friday."*
>
> *"But Mom!" Betty protests. "That's so unfair! You know that that assignment is the one I'm doing with Mark. He forgot the thing at home he was supposed to bring."*
>
> *"That sounds frustrating," Dad empathizes. "It's Tuesday now, so good thing you've got some time before the deadline on Friday. I'm glad I warned you now. What's your plan for getting it done?"*
>
> *"Well, I guess I could text him and make sure he remembers it . . ."*
>
> *"Good thinking. Let me know if there's anything you need from me."*

Or for a younger child,

> *"I'm letting you know that it's bedtime in a half hour, so if you want some stories tonight, we're going to have to finish up with your bath quickly."*
>
> *"Don't want to finish bath!" Gus answers.*

"I get it," Mom answers. "Bath is lots of fun. I love the bath too. But we only have a half hour until bedtime, so the more time you spend here, the less time we have for reading. Which do you want to do?"

"Stories!"

"Great! Let's brush teeth and get the jammies on so we can have stories, then."

Those were both simplistic examples, but if a child feels that you're on their side, they are far more likely to comply. In both of these examples the family rules were the boundary, not the parent directly. The policy about homework was what to push against, and the parent got to be the helpful one that gave reminders and help. And the parent giving the bath got to enjoy baths and stories before the ominous bedtime rather than trying to order and rush the child through everything.

So how do you ally yourself with the child while setting a boundary?

1. **Empathy:** Empathize with their feelings or why they might be trying to do that behavior. Whatever feeling they're expressing, reflect it back to them. Is it frustration? Difficulty transitioning?

2. **Boundary:** Set the boundary. Set it kindly, set it firmly, and set it as a rule outside of yourself. The rule can be, "People aren't for hitting," "We speak kindly to people," or "In our house the policy is that peanut butter is not smeared on the dog."

3. **Choice:** Then let there be some choice the child makes. When you set a boundary, they feel disempowered, so it's best if there's a choice they can make at this juncture so they can feel more empowered.

You must do all three steps. Most of the time parents like to skip the first step and just set the boundary. But it is critically important that you express empathy for the child, because it makes setting the boundary feel less adversarial.

But what boundaries do you truly need to set? When setting boundaries, try to think about what is really necessary. Divide all the things that you would like to correct in your child into three boxes: critical box, good to work on box, and doesn't really matter box. What goes in each box is up to each family, but the fewest items in the critical box, the better. For example, when thinking about clothes for your child, the critical box is that the child is not naked. The good to work on box is that they follow the school's and the family's guidelines on appropriate dress. The doesn't really matter box is whether the clothes match. For dinner, the child eating dinner at the table is critical, sitting down to eat a balanced meal is good to work on, and using table manners doesn't really matter. For teenagers, maybe them not drinking at a party is critical, curfew adherence is good to work on, and which friends they hang out with doesn't really matter. The problem is that if we put too many of the "doesn't matter" and "good to work on" in the critical box, we are setting ourselves up for power struggles and an inability to set limits effectively on the critical matters.

Choice giving can also be a way to enforce the rules. For instance, if you have a family rule that toys need to be picked up by an 8 o'clock bedtime, then you can say, "If you choose to pick up the toys by 7:30, then we can watch a show before bed. If you don't choose to do that, then I'll understand you're choosing not to have a show." And you can be an ally by saying, "Well, it's time to start picking up to be done in time. I hope we make it because I love watching a show with you!"

There's some magic in how you give choices as well—rule number one is that you always want to give choices you're okay with. Don't say, "Your choices are to get dressed or go to school naked!" unless you're okay with them going to school naked. Try to give kids as much power over the choices as possible, but if they want something that simply cannot be a choice, just gently point them back to what are the choices. You can say things like, "Let me know when you've made up your mind," or help them calm down if triggered when they're having trouble choosing.

Consequences

For parenting typical kids, using consequences is a normal and accepted part of parenting. For children who have been traumatized, consequences can be triggering and an invitation to a power struggle. They are also not very effective. When boundaries are given and the child chooses not to respect those boundaries and use acceptable alternatives, then consequences can be used, but they must be used differently than for typical kids.

Here are guidelines for how to use consequences with traumatized kids:

1. Only give a consequence to a child that is calm and not in a triggered state. If they are agitated, giving them a consequence will likely make it worse. You can say that you will talk about consequences later when

things are calmer, or that there will be a consequence that will be decided later. If your child isn't calm, employ calming techniques to help them get there (reflective listening, sensory techniques, time-in, etc.)

2. Remember their trauma. Do not give consequences for PTSD reactions. Also think about the age they are developmentally and parent them for that age. If a two-year-old child throwing a tantrum would result in a cuddle and a nap, then a six-year-old who is mentally two should be treated the same way.

3. Stay out of the power struggle. Don't argue with your child, but you can negotiate if they are engaging you well. Find a good phrase to exit arguments, like, "I love you too much to argue with you," or "I'd be happy to talk about this more when we're both feeling calmer." The phrase "Nice try" can also be helpful for defusing power struggles.

4. Consequences should be natural, logical, non-shaming, and as short-lived as possible. So, if a child is having trouble following the rules at the playground, you can say she needs more practice at listening before she can go to the playground, and that it's time to leave. If a child is irresponsible with electronics, then the electronics might need a time-out for a few hours. If a child hurts another person, then the child needs to do something to repair the relationship and make it up to the other person. For instance, a good house rule is that if you hit your sibling, you do a chore for them that day.

5. Consequences should always be given calmly, firmly, and in a matter-of-fact voice. Be empathetic and try to ally yourself with the child as much as possible. So saying something like, "Wow, I'm sorry you made the choice to hit your sister. In our family, that means that you do a chore for her to make it up to her. So when would you like to organize the shoes by the front door?" or, "I'm sad that kids are making the choice to not put away their toys tonight, because that means that Dad has to put them away, and that means they have to go away for a few days. What a bummer." For a teenager, you can say, "So I see you've made the choice to text your friend past ten o'clock last night. What a bummer, that means your phone has to stay downstairs when you go to bed until you're ready to make the choice to follow the rule again."

6. Consequences should focus on repairing relationships. So, if your child gets in trouble at school, giving him extra chores is not as effective as saying, "Your teacher tells me that you wrote a note and signed my name on it. I can understand why you did that; you were worried about getting in trouble for not finishing your homework. But, we don't lie to people because then people don't trust us. You lying to her broke her trust in you and made her feel sad. What would you like to do to make it up to her?"

7. Let natural consequences in the world dictate things as much as possible. Often when a child gets in trouble at school, this really is enough of a consequence. And often having the child talk with you about things can often be enough of a consequence as well; don't feel like you have to add additional unrelated consequences.

8. Avoid power struggles as much as possible. If you have a child that is highly oppositional, do not give her consequences that she has to comply with. Giving a highly oppositional child something they have to comply with, like extra chores, is a recipe for failure. Instead focus on things that you control. Here's a chart to list some of the differences:

CHILD HAS TO COMPLY	CHILD DOESN'T HAVE TO COMPLY
extra chores	allowance
apology note	television privileges
going to bed early	Wi-Fi (you can turn it off)
time-in	you driving a child somewhere
giving you their electronic device	parent taking a time-out

9. If-then setups are the best for kids. Statements such as "Allowance is given to kids when their room is clean" and "We need to have a conversation about what happened at school before the TV is going to go on today" are setups for success. These statements give the child the control that they want, and avoid the power struggle.

10. With highly oppositional kids, say it and get out. You do not have to stick around for arguments. This kind of "drive-by" parenting works really well with teenagers. So as you're passing them on their way to school, you can say, "I'm sure you already know this, but your chores need to be done before you do fun stuff this weekend. Have a good day, honey!"

Time-in Versus Time-out

Time-outs are a common and accepted part of parenting today—nearly everyone does them! The idea behind them is great—your child has some time apart from the group to reflect on bad behavior, calm down, and get ready to rejoin the group. When done correctly and compassionately, a time-out can turn a hitting, truculent three-year-old into a more cooperative and apologetic youngster in just a few minutes with no parental anger. However, this discipline technique is one that is not as well translated for children with trauma. For children with attachment challenges, sending them away from the parent to calm down is not calming and will likely make their behavior worse. A good alternative to time-outs for a traumatized child is a time-in. The differences are described below:

TIME-OUTS	TIME-INS
The child is removed completely from the setting, either to a designated place or their room.	Child is removed but it doesn't have to be completely.
Child is left alone in their room or corner and told to "calm down."	The child is always with another person who is calm and loving. With time-ins, you aren't expecting the child to be able to comfort themselves.
Time-outs are often used as a substitute for spanking or other punishment, and are viewed as a punishment rather than for calming.	Time-ins are used for when a child needs to up- or down-regulate, not as an unrelated consequence.
Can often be dysregulating to attachment-challenged children.	Are comforting and calming to attachment-challenged children.
Say, "You're hitting your sister! There is no hitting in this house! You're in time-out for six minutes!"	Say, "I see you are angry and frustrated and are having trouble not hitting your sister right now. Please come sit by me and we can calm down together and feel better."
Seems very childish, not something an adult can do or model.	Can be modeled by an adult as good self-care. A parent can say, "I'm feeling so angry right now. I think I'm going to go sit and be quiet for a few minutes so I can feel better and not yell at people."

Thirty-Second Burst of Attention

The thirty-second burst of attention is a great tool to use for younger kids when they desperately want your attention. This can be utilized when you are on the phone, cooking dinner, doing work, or any of the other things that we need to do but that compete with your child's attention. Of course, if you have time to spend talking and engaging with your child for longer than thirty seconds, that is better. But for those times when you're in a rush and your child needs attention, use this tool.

The thirty-second burst of attention is simply that—you give your child your undivided attention for thirty seconds. If you are cooking, get to a place where you can take a thirty-second break, and get down on your child's level, look her in the face, and let her know that she has your attention for thirty seconds.[1] You can also say, "After dinner we can have some time snuggling on the couch, but for right now all I have is thirty seconds, so go! What would you like to talk to me about?"

For children with trauma, knowing that they can get attention from you when they need it is very reassuring. And try to give them what they need—some kids will need a hug for thirty seconds, some kids don't want to be touched. Don't be discouraged if your child meets with some dysregulation with this thirty-second burst of attention, especially when it's over. Being calm, consistent, and available will eventually give the child a sense of stability and safety, and the need for this intervention will eventually lessen.

The Magic of Redos

A redo is a great way of giving a child a chance to do something better, making a better choice. Karyn Purvis says of redos, "Remember when you were a kid on the playground and called for a 'do-over'? That same concept offers a great learning tool for kids."[2] They are meant to be playful and engaging, not a punishment. Here's what a redo looks like:

> *"Wow, Nathalie, I don't think you meant to say that to me that way. Want to try that again?"*
>
> *"Whoa, Nathan, we use walking feet indoors. Shall we redo that?"*
>
> *"Abi, wow, I don't think you meant that to happen! How about I help you clean that up and we'll try pouring that again?"*

"Miriam, I see that you just knocked down your brother's blocks. Let's redo that and build it for him again, okay?"

The keys to doing a redo:

1. Be non-shaming and do not assume ill intent, but rather assume either an accident or that the child needs more practice.

2. Phrase the redo as something you are helping with.

3. Be willing to help the child either by modeling or by cleaning up.

4. Keep your voice pleasant and playful as much as you can; your child will take the cue from you.

5. If you can, let them practice a few times.

Even teenagers can benefit from a redo. If your child asks for something in a really demanding way or says something disrespectful, a great response is, "I think what you just said is not what you meant. I'm going to pretend you didn't say that and give you a redo."

Make It a Game

One of the most effective disciplinary strategies is to make as much as you can into a game. Instead of repeating to your children to buckle their seatbelts, make it a game to see who can buckle theirs first. Instead of saying, "Do this right now!" say, "I'll bet you can't get that done before I count to ten." Kids love to beat their parents, and beating their parents at a countdown is very fun. Let them win as much as possible! Everyday stressors that you can turn into a game:

* Race to see who gets their seatbelt on first.

* Say, "I'll bet I can count to ten before you can get into bed. One, two, . . ."

* "Last one in the car is a rotten egg!"

* One summer camp tradition from my childhood is for other campers to "call you out" if you exhibited bad table manners (like putting your elbows on the table or not having a napkin on your lap). They would

recite a rhyme and make you walk around the table. Consider something fun like this to teach table manners. "Johnny, Johnny, strong and able, get your elbows off the table! 'Round the table you must go, you must go, you must go, 'round the table you must go, for your elbows!" If you do this, let the kids catch you sometimes and join in the laughing.

- For when Mom has a headache: "Let's have a quiet dinner and see if we can eat our whole dinner just whispering."

- Tell your children there is a bed fairy that brings treats to kids who keep their rooms tidy, beds made, and their laundry folded.

- One way to help your kids with math is to give them timed tests for addition, subtraction, multiplication, and division. Make sure they get a reward for every sheet they try, and special rewards when they beat their times.

Keeping Your Cool

We all know that parenting all kids is better done with a cool head, but with traumatized kids it is even more important. One trauma expert writes,

> *One thing is certain: Yelling at someone who is already out of control can only lead to further dysregulation. Just as your dog cowers if you shout and wags his tail when you speak in a high singsong, we humans respond to harsh voices with fear, anger, or shutdown and to playful tones by opening up and relaxing. We simply cannot help but respond to these indicators of safety or danger.*[3]

When a parent has trouble identifying if their child is fight, flight, or freeze, I ask what happens if someone yells at them, because this is the most reliable way to trigger someone. I talk to a lot of parents that have a lot of shame around how much they yell at their children, so my purpose here is not to increase shame on anyone. But I do want to reinforce that keeping your cool, counting to ten, and staying calm with your child is one of the most important parenting techniques you can have.

A Word about Spanking

My intention here is not to get into a debate about spanking when referring to typical kids. In some communities, particularly immigrant communities and communities with different cultural backgrounds, this particular issue is one of cultural identity, politics, racial tension, and one that I think would be arrogant and simplistic of me to simply say, "Read the literature and comply with the new norm!" About a third of the states in my country still allow corporal punishment in public schools, and I think that arguing over spanking in general is not the fight I want to have in this book.

The fight I want to have is the one over spanking traumatized kids. I have this talk with parents often in my office, and it is one that I will absolutely fight to the death about. There is absolutely no way to spank a traumatized child that will in any way be helpful and not harmful. It doesn't matter how calm you are and what method you use; it won't work. Any physical punishment that causes pain will immediately trigger their limbic system, causing their PTSD reaction to trigger, and they will immediately go into fight-flight-freeze. Triggering your child doesn't help them think or learn; it only retraumatizes them. Many parents don't believe me at first, but they usually come around to believing me when they see how much it doesn't work and how much harm it causes the child.

In my practice I have never seen a traumatized child improve behavior from corporal punishment, and if they were to, I would honestly worry about a trauma bond forming. A trauma bond is something like Stockholm syndrome—an unhealthy bond that's about survival. Basically, you can beat a person into submission and trigger their survival instinct, but sooner or later that child will turn seventeen or eighteen, and that bond is not real attachment, and that child will likely want little to do with you after that. In fact, often while corporal punishment is even a threat, it is very difficult for a child to even relax enough to do the important work of feeling safe and building attachments.

This is even more so if a child's particular trauma is that they have been hit or beaten before. But one of the difficulties that can happen if you are raising a child with this type of background is that sometimes you will feel as if they are trying to provoke this reaction in you—and you may feel as if they are trying to get you to hit them! This is very normal, and when those feelings come up, you should recognize them, name them, and realize that this is part of what therapists call an enactment—where you are being sucked into playing out a part between you and the child. The child is provoking you because their subconscious wants to know at what point you will beat them. Your subconscious is responding to that provocation by feeling the urge to hit them, even if you've never hit anyone in your life. When interpersonal therapists are trained, we are told to listen to the feelings that arise for us in our interactions, as that is important information about what the client presenting and what is happening in the therapeutic relationship. The same is true for you and your child—if you feel provoked, then use that information. And let the story that the child is trying to reenact with you have a different ending this time—one that ends with empathy and understanding rather than abuse and harm.

"You're going to hit me at some point," my then ten-year-old daughter informed me. She had just been caught doing something against the rules, and it had taken an hour of me assuring her that I loved her and that I wasn't going to hit her before we could have a conversation about it.

"I'm not," I told her, exasperated. "Look, I haven't hit any of your sisters, and they break rules all the time."

"It will happen," she told me with confidence.

"Look, how about we make a bet," I told her. "I'll bet you one hundred dollars that I'll never hit you. If I hit you for real, not like accidently bumping into you in the hall or playing slap-jack or something, but if I actually hit you, I will pay you one hundred dollars."

"Two hundred," she told me, her eyes narrowing.

"Two hundred," I agreed.

There was something about the bet that actually worked in a way that nothing else I had said before worked. We made that bet years ago, and even now if she gets scared that I might hit her, she just says something sassy like, "You'd hit me, but it's not worth two hundred dollars."

"Yep, not worth it," I agree.

If You Want to Learn More about Discipline Strategies

Daniel J. Siegel and Tina Payne Bryson, *No-Drama Discipline: The Whole-Brain Way to Calm the Chaos and Nurture Your Child's Developing Mind* (New York: Bantam, 2014).

Karyn B. Purvis, David R. Cross, and Wendy Lyons Sunshine, *The Connected Child: Bring Hope and Healing to Your Adoptive Family* (New York: McGraw-Hill, 2007).

Heather T. Forbes and B. Bryan Post, *Beyond Consequences, Logic, and Control: A Love-Based Approach to Helping Attachment-Challenged Children with Severe Behaviors* (Boulder, CO: Beyond Consequences Institute, 2009).

ROUTINES AND RITUALS

ROUTINES ARE THE THINGS that we do nearly every day, and rituals are things we do on special occasions. Brushing your teeth is a routine; wearing green on St. Patrick's Day is a ritual. Both are important to helping a child feel that their lives are safe and predictable, and both are part of a well-structured home. Without routine, a home doesn't have the day-to-day structure so vital to the predictability that a traumatized child needs, and without ritual a child can miss the magic and the traditions that defines what a family is.

Routines

It is very important to have established routines for children with trauma. One researcher writes,

> *Routines and rituals help children create expectations about the predictability of their external environment. Young children rely on their primary caregivers to help them organize their experiences and to guide them in exploration and mastery of new skills through practice and repetition. Children who have experienced complex trauma frequently have lived in an environment*

void of structure and routines. They form a perception that the world is an unpredictable and dangerous place, and their capacity for developing competencies through self-exploration and mastery becomes inhibited by fear. One of the key principles for restoring a sense of safety for a child is implementing predictable daily routines that establish safety, help children organize experience, and to develop mastery.[1]

All children like routines and rituals, but for children of trauma, especially those that have experienced a world where there has not been routine and structure, this is critical.

You most likely have routines that you are already doing. Routines are when we get up, what we eat for meals, when we have meals, when work gets done, when the house gets clean, when teeth are brushed, how parents interact with kids. Whatever routines you have established as a family are important to kids; you can also consider other routines that might make a difference to your traumatized child.

Routines can also be part of an emotional response. If the ritual in your house is that when someone cries, you offer them gum, or tea, or a lollipop, then your children will feel more empowered to know what to do if someone is having a hard time emotionally. One of my children in particular responds well to lollipops if she's upset, and one night we had a babysitter. While we were gone, she became upset, and the other children knew just what to do—they climbed up to the lollipop stash and got her one, assuring the babysitter that's what to do if she got upset. I loved their confidence in knowing how to care for their sister, and she appreciated their caring for her in that way too. It is good for kids to know how their parents will respond to a given situation and how they are to respond. Even such simple rituals as cuddling a child when they cry, or having simple tools to help them regulate, facilitate the organization of their experiences. When a child has that organization, then they feel safe enough to then begin mastering new skills.

Rituals

Rituals are the ties that bind a family together. Think about your own childhood. How did you know it was Christmas? How were grades or concerts celebrated? From our own childhoods, there are the large rituals that we remember, but also the smaller ones that are just as important. It's also important to have rituals around grief, loss, and stress.

Large Rituals. These are how you celebrate major holidays, family vacations, birthdays, and things like that. Think about the rituals that made these special to you as a child or young adult, or maybe what you wished could have been if you had a traumatic background. There are the foods we eat and the things we do during holidays that differ from other times of the year. Be very careful in the rituals you choose, however, because it only takes one year for your activity to become part of the approved canon of holiday activity that must be repeated every year.

I belong to a multiethnic and multicultural family. My husband is from New Zealand, I am from a rural area in eastern Washington, my two bio-children were born in Seattle, one daughter is from Ethiopia, and three of my daughters are from the Democratic Republic of Congo. Cross-cultural holiday celebrations have often ended in hilarity. We once had a birthday party for one of my daughters who turned twelve a month after she came into our home. She spoke very little English, and we spoke very little Swahili, so imagine her surprise when we told her we were going to light her cake on fire! And then we did. I treasure the picture we took of her looking uncertain and her two-year-old sister looking on with eyes as wide as saucers.

Our first Thanksgiving after the Congolese girls came to us was so strange for me as an American. My bio-daughter was only four, and with my husband's Kiwi parents in town, I felt like the sole arbiter of Thanksgiving tradition. My in-laws were horrified that I would make a pumpkin pie (they view pumpkin as savory; it would be sort of like someone making a sweet asparagus pie to an American). People kept asking why we were eating certain foods. My answer, "I don't know; I don't make the Thanksgiving rules. This is just what we do." Add to that the general chaos of trying to prepare the food. But the real fun happened when I took out the turkey giblets from the broth in which they had been simmering.

One of my African daughters asked, "What are those?"

I answered, distracted, "It's just the giblets. Like, there's the heart and the liver and neck and stuff. I boiled it to make gravy."

"What's gravy?"

"The sauce that goes on the turkey."

"Okay. What are you going to do with those parts?"

"Probably feed part to the dog and throw the rest away."

"Can I have them?"

"Why?"

"In my country we used to eat those."

"Sure, if you want. You might want to use some salt."

The others gathered, watching her. I encouraged her to share, and soon they were cutting up the heart in four pieces so each of the kids from Africa could have some, though my preschool daughter born in America wasn't interested. They carefully sprinkled each piece with salt and ate with gusto! I ended up trying a bit of the neck—it was better than I thought it would be after being boiled all day. But my daughter who initially asked for the parts ate it all with much pleasure—even the neck bones—assuring me that in Africa they say to eat the bones because it makes your bones strong.

Now on Thanksgiving day, my African daughters watch the pot that holds the simmering turkey parts, and they eagerly divide up the pieces when I bring them out to cool. The daughter who started it all says that the turkey parts are her favorite thing to eat on Thanksgiving Day.

The story above illustrates that the rituals that were important to me (having specific food on Thanksgiving Day) really were just based on how I thought things were supposed to be. They meant Thanksgiving to me. The addition of kids into our lives, especially kids that are old enough to bring a lot of their culture and rituals with them, expands our celebration of the holiday, and our enjoyment.

If you've adopted older kids, then they may bring some rituals with them. Encourage them to keep these rituals and participate with them as much as possible; it usually means a lot to have you participate with them. Because we have a family member from Ethiopia, we celebrate two Christmases and two Easters every year due to the difference in the Orthodox and Western calendars.

Ethiopian Christmas (celebrated in early January) in our family has evolved into a party that we throw for close friends to end the Christmas season. We make our best attempt at making some traditional Ethiopian dishes and even sing a few Christmas songs in Amharic.

If you have children from different ethnicities and cultures who were younger when you got them, then you have a little more homework to do. Find out the major celebrations and rituals from your child's birth culture or heritage and incorporate some of them into your life. Cinco de Mayo, Chinese New Year, Kwanzaa, St. Patrick's Day, Hanukkah, and so forth can be enjoyed by all.

One time one of my daughters came up to me and, in her preteen desperation to fit in, announced that she wanted to be solely American. I told her that I could see why she felt that way, that it was hard to be different at school. But I told her that our family was a quarter Kiwi because dad was Kiwi (we only had four people in our family at the time), so we did certain things because of that. And our family was a quarter Ethiopian because she was from there, so it affected how our family was as well. I told her, "Honey, you don't have to do anything Ethiopian until you're ready to; it's fine. But your dad and I really love the Ethiopian culture, and we'll continue celebrating even if you don't want to (we were involved in the local Ethiopian culture). When you're older, you'll probably come to appreciate your heritage more, but for right now, we can hold that for you." The idea of celebrating cross-cultural differences in your family isn't just about getting tacos on Cinco de Mayo, but rather about recognizing the reality that your family is now—however fractionally—part of another cultural heritage.

Large rituals aren't just about holidays; they're also about vacations, camping, and how different ages are treated in your family. Do you get a cell phone at thirteen? A driver's license at sixteen? These are all rituals that should be recognized and celebrated.

Small Rituals. These are another type of ritual to think about with your family. These are the rituals such as reading a book before bed, movie nights on Saturdays, or waffles for dinner on Sundays. One year on a whim I dyed the milk green for April Fool's Day, and the kids now race downstairs every April 1 to see what color I'm going to dye it this year. These can be part of your day-to-day life together.

Grief Rituals. We don't often think about this, but it is important to have rituals around grief and loss. We as a culture have funerals when people die, and we have ways of remembering and grieving together. Not all grief is as sad as losing a person, but make sure you've thought about rituals for when a pet dies, or what to do when mom or dad have to be out of town, or how to handle it when someone is sick. I have a very vivid memory of my dad cooking us waffles with strawberries whenever my mom had to be in the hospital with my younger sister (she had a lot of health problems). Knowing this was our ritual made it less scary that my sister was in the hospital and my mom was with her. In my own family, I alternate cooking either chicken curry or German pancakes when my husband is gone for dinner, and the kids keep track of which meal is next.

Having a funeral for a pet can really help a child cope with the grief of this loss as well as preparing her to grieve well when she inevitably loses a person. It can also help her grieve the breaks of attachment she has already had. When your child is showing what seems like out-of-proportion grief for something like a broken toy, be open to the idea that there might be other grief that she is processing at that time.

Having routines when someone is sick is also a great way to show caring and predictability. Whether it's Sprite or chicken soup, have a routine that shows kids how to care for themselves and for others when they're sick. Additionally, it is good to have a routine when children are emotionally unwell. Giving them practical ways to help themselves and others emotionally is always valuable.

PART 2

Emotional Regulation

ADOPTION (OR PLACEMENT) STAGES
How Children Grieve

BEFORE WE TALK ABOUT STAGES, I want to try a little thought experiment with you. Picture someone coming to your house tonight with a social worker and a few police officers, and telling you that someone has decided that you aren't safe in your home anymore and that they have found you a new place to live with very nice people to look after you. You are asked to come along quietly, and the police might even be there to arrest the people in your household that you love. You may be told you get to visit them soon, but you aren't told anything else. Then, you pack a quick bag and are driven to a new home, introduced to strangers, and are told that this is your new family and that they're very nice people.

How do you feel about these people? Police officers? Social workers? How would you adapt? Even kids coming from hard situations where they were subject to abuse and neglect are still very reluctant to change, and suddenly everything in their life has changed at once.

In the adoption world a lot of people have heard words like "honeymoon" and "boundary-testing phase" and many other terms like that. I've had frustrated parents say, "Was that the honeymoon?" incredulously because there was nothing honeymoonish about their first few months. I've had other parents wonder when the shoe was going to drop. The term *honeymoon* can also be a misnomer because many of these stages can happen while kids are still in foster care and not adopted, so really, these stages have more to do with placement changes rather than adoption per se. I usually see four clear stages when kids go through a placement change:

1. Feeling unsafe stage (some call this the honeymoon phase)

2. Boundary testing stage

3. Grief stage

4. Attachment stage

I'd also like to talk about the phases of adoption in the same way that we would talk about the stages of grief, with a lot of the same caveats. Children will progress through these stages in their own time, at their own pace. Kids can regress and go back to a stage that they have previously completed. Kids always start with stage 1 and always end with stage 4, but stages 2 and 3 can sometimes get swapped in their order. Just like with grief, it is a good thing when people move through these stages. It often feels bad to start with a kid that seems fun and nice (stage 1) and go to one that seems like a jerk (stage 2) to one that is suddenly remembering a bunch of things and is crying a lot (stage 3). It's easy to think, "Did I break him? Am I a bad parent?" But actually this means you're a good parent because they feel safe enough to go through the stages. A child can't grieve if they don't feel safe.

Feeling Unsafe Stage

"You're probably going to be happy about this," my client told me as she sat on my sofa, clearly exasperated.

"Am I?" I asked, completely confused.

"You said that he would start acting out," she told me. "I thought, well, if he hasn't been acting out in a year and a half, he wouldn't have started now."

"That's great news!" I beamed.

"I knew you would say that," she exclaimed, and then laughed a bit herself. "You're right, though. As rough as I know this is going to be to get used to him starting to test some boundaries, it's better than him still feeling unsafe and overly compliant."

"That is the longest honeymoon phase I have ever seen," I admitted. "A year and a half has got to be some sort of record."

In the story above, the client in question was a boy with extensive trauma adopted at twelve from the foster system. He was naturally a freeze kid and had developed a coping strategy of being overly compliant and pleasing people, which I saw as needing to come to an end if he was going to be able to actually test boundaries, grieve, and actually attach. But for a child in his position, trust doesn't come easily, and so he was sweet and compliant for a long time before the first cracks of boundary testing started rearing their heads in his relationship with his new adoptive family.

I really dislike calling this phase the "honeymoon" phase because it makes it seem positive and lovey, and I think it really can be from the parents' perspective. Oftentimes this is when they "fall in love" with their new child and have all those lovely feelings of how this placement was "meant to be." Not to disparage it for the child either; it can often feel good to them as well. But a real honeymoon is a time away to celebrate the culmination of attachment and love, and this phase is the reality that the child is on their best behavior because they don't feel safe yet.

Depending on the child's temperament and history, this period can last from a few hours to a year and a half, but typically it lasts at least a few weeks to a few months. During this time the child is gathering information on the new caregiver to see if they are safe, seeing how they meet their needs, and seeing how the household works. Ironically, the safer the household is, the shorter the time spent in this phase. For parents with a new placement, I advise them to be safe and predictable, and to try to meet the child's needs and felt needs as well as they can.

Boundary-Testing Stage

I like to think of this stage in the same way as I think of a two-year-old. The entire job of a two-year-old is to find the answer to two questions:

1. Do my parents love me?

2. Do I have boundaries?

The answer to those two questions set the stage for what type of household the child grows up in. If they feel unloved and have no boundaries, that is neglect. If they feel unloved and have boundaries, that is authoritarianism. If they feel loved and have no boundaries, that is permissiveness. If they feel loved and have boundaries, then that is authoritative parenting, which is the type that has the best outcome for children.

So when a child is testing boundaries, the thing you are trying to convey to them is that yes, they are loved, and yes, there are boundaries. This is frustrating when a child is two, and it can be even more so when the child is twelve and you can't just put them down for a nap when they are cranky. If you aren't sure about good trauma-informed ways to set a boundary with a child, look at the chapter about discipline strategies for help.

One of my daughters came from a country where physical discipline was common both in school and at home. She was on her best behavior for several months, watching to figure out when we were going to bring out the stick. One day when she came home, she finally asked the question she'd been too afraid to ask. "Mom? Are they going to hit me at school?"

"No, honey," I answered her, shocked to realize she was even worried about it. "No, schools here don't do that."

"There's no cane here?" she pressed. "What if I'm really naughty?"

"No cane," I assured her. "Not even if you're really naughty."

I could see her calculate a little, and she nodded a bit. A few days later, she decided she wasn't going to put away some things I had asked her to do. This was the first time she'd actually disobeyed me.

"I won't do it," she told me, her arms crossed.

"Okay," I told her. "That seems like a silly choice to me, but okay."

"Why is that a silly choice?" she asked.

"Well, because of course there's no TV until we get everything put away," I explained. "And I like watching that show with you too, so I'll be sad to miss our time together, if that's what you choose. Let me know when you get it done."

I still remember her tiny body standing there for several minutes, her arms crossed, furious at me but also ready to run in case I grabbed her to beat her for her defiance. Instead I sat, calmly doing something else, and eventually she sighed and then complied with what I had asked her to do.

The boundary testing phase usually lasts at least a few months, and can last up to a year or so. Kids that have experienced physical abuse will be especially bent on seeing at what point you will beat them, and will attempt to provoke you accordingly. It is especially important during this time that you remain calm and unprovoked, safe and available. Set boundaries in a kind and loving way—but it is really important that you set them.

Grief Stage

Hopefully, when kids are able to progress through the boundary-setting phase, they are able to do the grief stage. This stage can be very clear for some kids (lots of crying, disclosing abuse, memories) or very subtle. Grief can also look like lots of different things for different kids. Sometimes grief can look like anger at bio-family, anxiety about past events, memories surfacing (both good and bad), nightmares, and so on. It is not uncommon for a child to be removed from their bio-family and it to be several months later for them to be in this stage before they start disclosing abuse.

There are many definitions of grief, but for my purposes here, I'm going to say that grief is the internal processing of the emotions that come from loss and change in someone's life. Those feelings take a while for a child to work through, to internalize, and to make a real part of their story. And for a child that comes into your house directly out of a traumatizing situation, they will need even more time for their brain to calm down enough to be able to do that.

Grief is the internal processing of the emotions that come from loss and change in someone's life.

The grief stage usually takes at least a few months, and will be visited periodically throughout a child's life into adulthood. Grief is a natural and normal process, and will lead to better emotional health. I think the major work of therapists is to help people grieve, because usually we are just so bad at it.

I encourage families that anytime there is anything in your family to grieve, take advantage of the situation and institute rituals around it. If a pet dies, if a parent is out of town, or if someone is sick, you have the opportunity to teach your children rituals that can help them grieve and feel better. If mom is out of town, what do we do as a family? If our fish dies, how do we honor that pet? I see these as golden opportunities to engage grief collectively and to give children a place to grieve. And when they grieve for a pet, for instance, that is teaching them how to grieve deeper and more confusing hurts as well.

Disclosures: I wanted to add a note on how to handle when children disclose past abuse. Research shows that a major factor in how children are able to handle this abuse is in how caregivers handle it, and whether or not they are believed and supported. These are my guidelines for when a child discloses abuse:

1. Validate their experience and emotions. Say, "Wow, that was so wrong of that person to do," or "You were so little, it's so terrible that someone would do that." Do not tell a story of a time you felt that way. Focus on their emotional reality.

2. Do not grill them. You can ask gentle questions if appropriate or necessary, but emotional connection is more important. You are not a police officer.

3. Don't ask them how they feel directly; that can feel threatening. Instead, say, "I think if that happened to me, I'd be feeling scared (helpless, angry, hurt, worried). I wonder if you're feeling like that?" By phrasing it that way, the child can politely not answer, and you're not demanding an answer. You can also say, "I just want to check in with you about how you're feeling after being so brave in telling me that."

4. Ask what they would like to do about it, and if they'd like to report it. Realize that most victims don't want to report it, but also realize that for a lot of parents they don't have a choice. Foster parents and parents that work in a number of helping professions (teacher, social worker, medical professional, counselor, clergy) are mandatory reporters and legally must report any suspicion of child abuse.

For someone that discloses past abuse, the main thing they need from their caregiver is that they are believed, that their emotions are validated, and that they are still loved and cared for the same as before the disclosure. Many times in my office I work with adults that had made disclosures as children who were not believed or validated as children, and this can do as much damage as the abuse they are disclosing because it is a betrayal of someone the child has gone to for help.

Attachment Stage

Finally, the child is ready to get to the attachment stage. If the caregiver has been with them through the boundary-testing phase and the grief, then the child trusts them and will respond. Attachment can be a loaded term these days, with people thinking of Dr. Sears and co-sleeping, but what therapists mean when we talk about attachment is different. Attachment in this context means a deep and abiding trust between parent and child, something that is as much biological in nature as it is psychological. You can't just decide to be attached to someone—it's something that is the product of a long relationship, trust, and biochemistry.

Kids with trauma, even when they get to the attachment stage, will often still have challenges in attachment. It's hard not to when there's been attachment breaks along the way.

"Mom, I need to know if you're really serious that I will always get to live with you."

"Of course I am," I answered her. "Remember, we talked about this when you were hiding money in your room last year. I mean it: if I have a home, you have a home. You will always be welcome to live with me."

"I have to be sure," she told me seriously. "Because I'm going to tell Anna (birth-family member; not her real name) off and I need to know that I can depend on you if she disowns me."

"Oh, honey," I told her, nearly crying because I realized the significance of what she was saying. This family member had been trying for months if not years to try and get my then twelve-year-old daughter not to attach to us, and had been trying to force her to choose between us and her birth family. We had tried to protect her as much as we could, and try to work with the birth family not to make the children choose between us, but Anna had been relentless. "I promise, you can always live with Daddy and me. And you know I never lie to you."

"That's what I thought," she nodded, and went off to send her text that would start a text war.

I cried because at that moment I knew what my daughter had chosen—she had chosen attachment. It rarely looks like that clear of a choice, but that day it really did.

ATTUNEMENT AND MANIPULATION

All Behavior Communicates

CHILDREN WITH TRAUMA have a much harder time accessing and expressing their emotions than typical children, so they are going to need more help. Part of how parents can help them do this is to

1. Focus on emotion, not behavior

2. Think of behavior as communication

It is really easy with children to focus on behavior, as that is what is right in front of us, and usually what is bothering us the most. But when we focus just on behavior, we are focusing on the symptoms rather than what's causing the symptoms—sort of like giving a child Tylenol for a fever rather than treating an infection. It is much more effective to focus on emotions—or to treat the infection.

Verbal language is only a small part of what we communicate to others, and this is especially true for young children. If you have ever had the experience of being in a foreign country and being able to play with children there, you soon realize that you are able to function pretty well with them even without language. Body language, facial expressions, and gestures are universal language, and kids can get along well with very few words.

Trauma can severely impact how a child is able to express himself, especially verbally. For some kids, their PTSD reaction is to cut off their emotions, leaving them feeling frozen and numb. Others cannot regulate what feels like uncontrollable ups and downs, pushes and pulls. Because of these difficulties, parents of traumatized kids must learn how to effectively read body language and affect in order to understand what a child is communicating. Remember that all behavior is communicating something, so you always need to be asking what your child is trying to communicate. And the more you can reflect this communication and help the child identify the emotion, the better. Let's look at two different ways to handle the same scenario.

Scenario 1: A twelve-year-old boy comes in from school, slamming the door and throwing his backpack on the ground.

> "Stop slamming the door!" the mom tells him firmly. "We've talked about that before. And how many times do I need to tell you to stop putting your backpack on the ground?"
>
> "Do you think I care about your stupid door?"
>
> "Go to your room until you can behave yourself!"

Obviously, we can feel sympathy for this mother and every mom has been in this position before. But the scenario could have gone much differently:

> "Wow, Jake, you seem pretty mad. I wonder what happened at school today."
>
> "It was the stupid kids on the stupid bus. I'm not riding it ever again."
>
> "I can tell you are pretty upset. I would love to hear all about it. Why don't you come here and I'll get you a snack."

In the second scenario the mom looked at slamming the door as an expression of emotion. If she wanted to, she could address not slamming the door or throwing his backpack on the ground later, but when a child is upset is not the time to do that. She also didn't rise to the bait of Jake telling her that he would never ride the bus again—instead of arguing, she viewed this as another expression at the frustration Jake was feeling. Later in the conversation she would help him identify the feelings that he was having, but right now she's reflecting back to him his behavior as well as his words, and offering him reassurance that she wants to enter his world, and also to provide nurturing (through a snack).

Attunement

Attunement is the word we use to describe a caregiver's ability to read the child's cues and to be able to respond in a way that helps her manage her emotions and make good choices. When a caregiver is attuned, it is easier to focus on what the child is trying to say rather than just the behavior. Few situations in parenting are as straightforward as the previous example, and no parent is going to be able to be perfectly attuned all the time. Sometimes caregivers just get tired of the door being slammed. But if parents can increase the amount of attunement with their child, and more often than not understand the emotions driving the behavior, then the child is able to learn to express their feelings better. This can also help with parental frustration with behaviors.

Every child has cues that help caregivers understand what's happening. Here are some things to look for:

1. Body position and language: Is she curled up? Stomping? Frozen? Are her hands clenched or flailing?

2. Tone of voice: Is it softer or louder than usual? Is he being nonverbal? Is she yelling and storming?

3. Regression: Does the child seem younger than usual? Is he wanting to curl up and be held?

4. Withdrawal: Is your child withdrawing and avoiding? Is he clingy?

Scenario 2: A six-year-old girl is becoming slower and slower as the time comes for the bus to pick her up.

"Hurry up, Aisha, or you will miss the bus."

Aisha is silent, but sits on the stairs.

"Here, get your shoes on, and hurry! I don't understand why you aren't going faster!"

"I don't know where they are," she whimpers quietly.

"Here they are. Take them, and get going!"

Obviously there will be times when we are in a rush, and it can be really hard to think and to be attuned at those times. But this scenario was also a situation for the mom to attune to the child.

"Hurry, Aisha, your bus is coming."

Aisha is silent, sitting on the stairs.

"I see that you're quiet this morning and not wanting to move very fast. I wonder if you're feeling a little stressed out."

"I don't want to go to school."

"It can be hard sometimes, I know."

"I miss you, Mama." (body language very young)

"I can see you're having a hard time today. You're feeling sad."

"I just miss you."

"I have an idea. Why don't I get something for you to take to school with you while you're putting your shoes on? It's a surprise."

(child puts shoes on)

"Here you go, Aisha, here's a picture of our whole family from Christmas. Let's put it in your bag, and if you miss me today, you can look at it."

"Thanks, Mama."

In the second version, the mom is able to focus on her child's emotions, recognize that the child was having separation anxiety (and was regressed), and parented her how she would parent a two-year-old. Both scenarios took almost equal time, only one was attuned to the child's needs.

Nope, They're Not Manipulating You

I'm sitting in my office, doing an intake for what looks like a very nice couple who are coming in because they are very concerned about their five-year-old adopted son. I listen to the facts that are sadly so familiar to me—two years of trauma with his bio-mom before his removal, a few different foster homes, and then adoption by this family who earnestly wants the best for him. But then they say the "M" word and I find myself nearly flinching.

"Everything he does is just trying to get attention," the mom insisted. "He's trying to manipulate me."

"How do we deal with him trying to manipulate us all the time?" the dad asked. "It's like we don't want to do anything for him because everything is about manipulation."

"I understand," I tell them. "But you're not going to like what I tell you."

The truth is that children aren't capable of manipulation until adolescence, because to be able to manipulate, you need a more developed prefrontal cortex. The dictionary defines manipulation as "to control or play upon by artful, unfair, or insidious means, especially to one's own advantage."[1] This means that in order for one person to manipulate another, an action has to be done to control another with clear purpose by unfair or artful means. So, in order to manipulate, a child needs to be able to

- have cause-and-effect thinking

- have empathy to the point of anticipating your reaction

- be able to think ahead several steps

- use hypothetical thinking

- possess and use impulse control

Most children that have been traumatized just don't have the developmental maturity to be able to do this. Even typical children can't do this until at least early adolescence (around nine or ten), and generally speaking, children with trauma tend to have developmental delays in the areas of emotional and social maturity.

So, if it's not manipulation, what is it when a child does things to get certain reactions, leaving us feeling manipulated? These actions are survival strategies for the child; strategies that they've had to learn to survive very difficult circumstances. And when we as adults see these strategies, we often interpret them through our lens and ascribe adult meanings and motivations to the behavior.

For example, let's say that our five-year-old really wants his mom to be in his bedroom as he's falling asleep. The mom says that any time she tries to leave he cries, but she doesn't feel that the emotion is real because there aren't any tears associated with the crying, and he's able to instantly stop when she returns to his room. She's feeling resentful and manipulated, and also feeling like she's a bad mother because she's not setting the right limits, and her five-year-old is taking advantage of her.

It can be a very sad state of affairs when parents get locked into this mind-set, and it's a very easy one to get into with traumatized kids. This mind-set can very much foster an "us against them" mentality. Parents can get so paranoid and worried about being taken advantage of that it can completely break down the trust they're hoping to build with their child. Remember the attachment cycle: responding to a child's needs builds attachment, and not responding to a child's needs builds mistrust.

So how can we handle these situations that feel manipulative in a way that builds trust rather than mistrust? One of the keys can be looking at it from the child's perspective, and asking what need they're trying to meet with the behavior. Let's go back to the couple in my office with the "manipulative" five-year-old that seems to be doing everything to be getting attention. Turns out he has a real need—for attention. He also has a need for security, stimulation, and affection. He just might be really bad at getting those needs met, and so his attempts at getting those needs met results in irritation from his caregivers rather than what he really wants.

When thinking about a child's behavior, if you focus on the behavior, you're going to feel like you're running in circles. It's important to focus on the emotion behind the behavior first, because that is what is driving the behavior. Allow me to demonstrate:

"Mom? Can I have a glass of water?"

"But that's the third time you've asked!" an exasperated mom answers. "You're just trying to manipulate me and not go to bed."

"But I want water!"

"Go straight to bed and stop asking for water!" she tells the child sternly.

Here's another option:

"Mom? Can I have a glass of water?"

"That's the third time you've asked," the mom observes. "I'm wondering if you've got some other emotions coming up for you."

"No, I'm just thirsty."

"Usually when a kid asks three times, they're feeling scared, or worried, or lonely. I'm wondering if you're feeling any of those things?"

"I'm a little scared," the child answers. "I don't like sleeping in a room by myself."

"I thought you might be," the mom answers. "What can we do to help you feel less scared?"

This is a very simplistic example, but it shows that observing the exact same behavior—asking multiple times for a glass of water—can be interpreted two radically different ways. In one scenario the mother is protective of herself, thinking that she needs to protect against getting manipulated by the child. Thus, her response is guarded and exasperated. In the second scenario, the mother is curious, not guarded, and focused on the child's emotional reality. This is a much better posture to be able to help figure out why a child might be engaging in a certain behavior and even helping them get their needs met in a better way.

REFLECTIVE LISTENING AND EMOTIONAL MODELING

REFLECTIVE LISTENING is an incredibly useful tool for a child of any age. The main idea in reflective listening is to express that you are hearing what the child is saying, and this can be a very powerful component of attachment and regulation for children. Many strategies we have only work when a child is regulated; reflective listening is something that works during times of regulation and dysregulation. In fact, it is often one of the few things that can work when a child is highly dysregulated.

Reflective listening sounds deceptively simple. It is simply that you are reflecting back what a child says to you in a way that is meaningful to them. Here are the steps:

1. Accept and respect all of a child's feelings. Feelings are not good or bad; they are just there. Never approach your child with the words or attitude that she does not have a right to her feelings or that she isn't allowed to express them. In fact, a child expressing highly negative feelings with words is a sign of mental health—words are a lot better than behavior. Often children will stop doing destructive physical behaviors if they can start expressing them with words.

2. Show your child that you are listening. Use your body language (including eye contact and body position) to express to your child that you are listening to her. You can nod and give verbal assent as she is talking, if that helps. If it doesn't trigger your child, touching her hand or back can be helpful too.

3. Reflect back to your child what you hear. This can be the tricky part. You want to reflect back what you hear without correction or judgment. You want to validate her feelings even if you don't agree with them. For example, you could find yourself reflecting, "I hear that you're saying that you hate me. I hear that you think I ruined your life. Wow, that must be really difficult to feel that way." Or, on a less dramatic note, "It sounds like you're saying that you had a really hard time when your teacher assumed that you were involved in stealing. I could see how that would be really hard."

4. Help the child identify the emotion. Once you have conveyed that you are hearing the child, then you can reflect back an emotion. Don't ask the child what he is feeling; instead, guess. Also, try to do it without asking a question if you can. Say something like, "I wonder if you're feeling really angry," or "I think I would feel really disappointed if that were me. I wonder if that's how you're feeling." If the child doesn't agree with the emotion you named, then you can talk about the cues that led you to think that. For example, if your child shouts, "I'm not angry!" then you can say, "Wow, I hear that you are saying that you're not angry. I thought you might have been because your fists are clenched and you're yelling, and that's how I am when I'm feeling angry. I think it's pretty understandable to feel angry in this situation. I wonder what you might be feeling if you aren't angry?"

5. Offer advice, suggestions, or reassurance only after doing the previous steps and helping the child express emotions verbally. It can be very tempting to jump into the advice mode, but you have to resist. Look at every opportunity to do reflective listening as a space for your child to learn more about her emotions to be able to identify, regulate, and express them. It is more important that children learn the skills to deal with their strong emotions than it is to fix whatever particular problem has arisen. Children don't feel heard (and neither do adults!) if the person is far more focused on the solution than on the problem. Also, you may inadvertently communicate that you think the child is incapable of finding solutions herself by jumping in too quickly.

> *For example: Katy comes back from a visitation with a bio-relative and she looks really unhappy. Mom says, "I'm so glad you're home! How was your visit with your aunt?"*
>
> *"Fine," Katy answers, stomping her feet.*
>
> *"It looks like your body might be saying that it wasn't fine."*
>
> *"Well, it is just stupid. I don't see why I can't just live with her."*
>
> *"I hear you say that you wish you could live with her."*
>
> *"Yes! If stupid CPS wasn't involved, then I could live with my real family! I hate this!"*
>
> *"Wow, I can hear how hard this is for you. I would be so hard to have CPS dictating where you can live."*
>
> *"Why can't I just go back?"*
>
> *"It sounds like you're really missing your aunt. I would feel pretty sad if I were missing my aunt like that."*
>
> *"Of course I miss her. Why can't she just stop taking the drugs so I can be with her? The social worker said if she went to rehab then maybe I could be with her."*
>
> *"It sounds like you might be a little angry with her too."*
>
> *"I am angry! She loves the drugs more than me!"*
>
> *"I can tell how angry you are, and kids in your situation have every right to feel that way. It's so hard when adults can't do what they need to do to take care of kids."*

This scenario is likely far from over, but you can get the idea. This mom is allying herself with her foster daughter, providing the reflective listening to help the child name her emotions. Notice how she didn't ask questions but that her daughter felt invited to respond anyway. And in this type of situation, suggestions and advice probably wouldn't be very effective at all.

Emotional Modeling

Another really helpful thing parents can do to help with emotional regulation is called emotional modeling. Kids learn how to deal with their emotions through watching grown-ups deal with theirs, so you're on deck with being very clear with how you deal with yours. And part of modeling is in being extremely clear and verbal with how you're dealing with an internal reality that you're probably not used to verbalizing. Here's what's important to convey about your emotions:

Identification. It's very important that you identify your emotions very clearly for your child. This can be as simple as, "I'm feeling sad right now," or "Wow, I sure feel happy to get all that work done!" If your child is at a complete loss, you can watch the movie *Inside Out* together and at least get the basic five emotions to start with—joy, anger, fear, sadness, and disgust.

Self-care. This is especially good for the harder emotions. If you can verbalize your self-care, your kids will start picking it up. Sample things you can say:

I feel so sad when I think about my friend who's sick; I'm going to text her.

I am so stressed about my day; I think a cup of tea will help me feel better.

I am so angry and I want to yell, but I'm going to count to ten instead.

I am frustrated, and I'm going to take a break and walk the dog until I feel better.

Children are far more likely to begin to identify and to care for their emotions if they see their parents doing it and if it becomes a normal thing to do.

A Word about Anger

I would like to write a section specific to anger, as that is a very common struggle with traumatized kids, especially fight kids. Anger is the easiest emotion to feel, and it feels powerful. For some kids, it can be the only emotion they can feel, or perhaps just angry and happy. Anger is what we call a secondary emotion, which means that there is always something else fueling it; it can never be just a feeling on its own. Anger is a lot like a volcano, where the anger spews out on top, but the things under the surface fueling it can be a lot of different emotions:

A child's anger doesn't get easier to control until they are able to identify, express, and care for the other emotions under the surface of the volcano. Depending on which feelings it is that are fueling the anger dictates what tack to take. In my experience, for most kids with trauma, fear is a large component of what's fueling the anger. So, whatever else you do, focusing on felt safety and emotional awareness is going to be key.

SENSORY SUCCESS

KIDS WITH COMPLEX TRAUMA often have a very difficult time with their five senses integrating into their thinking brains. When a child develops without trauma, her brain grows and integrates the senses. As she grows, her reactions to sensations become more mature and complex, and she learns how to regulate sensory input overall. But for children that have either overwhelmingly traumatic experiences or neglect, their brains develop differently. These differences have been shown to negatively impact emotional and self-regulation.[1] One researcher writes that if a child's brain is either so overwhelmed that they need to dissociate or if it's so neglected that pathways don't form, this affects the child's sensory development as well as their relational one. This lack of sensory stimulation can make the baby not learn how to "accept comfort, think positively, and have hope."[2] This damage goes so hand in hand with early childhood trauma that it is very rare that I see a child that has had early childhood trauma that doesn't register as having some level of sensory integration disorder.

So what can you do with a child with sensory problems? You need to take a multifaceted approach—part of it is that you need to set up their world to suit them, and the other part of it is specific interventions to help them cope with their sensory deficits and build tolerances to live in this world.

First and foremost, however, kids that have moderate to severe sensory issues will have the best chance of success working with an occupational therapist who specializes in sensory disorders. It is beyond the scope of this book to fully address sensory processing disorders, but I wanted to give you an idea of the different areas it affects and hopefully enough of an idea if this is a major area of concern for your child. If you have concerns about sensory issues with your child, consult with your therapist to decide if a referral is necessary. That said, the suggestions made in this chapter will help with mild to moderate sensory issues and support you in creating a home helpful to children with sensory processing disorders.

Creating Safe Places

Kids with sensory processing disorders need to have safe places where they can retreat to avoid sensory overload and unwanted behavior and to recover when feeling agitated. There should be things on hand to help de-escalate a hyperaroused child and stimulating activities for children who struggle with low arousal. If your child struggles with sensory issues at school, work with his teacher to develop strategies to give him a safe place at school. Often if the teacher doesn't have a safe place in her classroom, the nurse's office, counselor's office, or a resource room can be made a safe place. If they have a few sensory tools with them to help the child, and the child knows they can go there to recover, then that can be a safe place.

At home, a safe place can be a corner of the child's bedroom, a tent with soft blankets, or—for a teen—a place to listen to music in peace. Safe places should never be used as a punishment, but rather a time and space where kids can recover. For a child that seeks stimulation, a safe place is often with a trusted adult, either cuddling on the couch or even doing something more active. Depending on the child, a safe place can be on a bean bag reading a book, a trampoline, or on the couch cuddling with a trusted adult.

Part of creating safe places is setting up the child's environment. Children with trauma and sensory issues don't always receive accurate information from their senses; they could really thrive with more predictability and control.

Therefore, it is up to caregivers to give the child an environment in which they are able to have as much predictability and control as possible. Parents should avoid overscheduling their child, allowing enough space for the child to thrive; sticking to a reliable schedule is going to be key.

Ideally, every child should be screened for sensory integration disorder, and you can check off which of these issues your child has. I give each of my incoming clients something called the Short Sensory Profile, which neatly measures and categorizes these things. Unfortunately I cannot include a copy of this profile in this book, but what I can do is tell you what each of these types of sensory issues looks like and see if it rings true for your child. If this is an issue that seems to be overwhelming for your child, then it is an area that might be good to get checked out by an occupational therapist or a trained trauma therapist.[3]

In this next section, there will be a description of each type of sensory integration category, and then there are suggestions for both soothing and increasing your child's skills. Be slow and careful in building skills, however. Biel writes, "Never, ever force sensory stimulation on a child, teen, or adult. Watch out for signs of physiological overload, such as increased distractibility, disorientation, nausea, skin reddening or paleness, breathing changes, and unexpected behaviors."[4]

Tactile or Sensation Seeking

Children who have sensation-seeking processing disorder are always touching, feeling, and bumping things. These children are often misdiagnosed with ADHD because they are always moving and touching things. These children love to wrestle and play rough, and they love being touched. In my office these are the children that come through the door and throw themselves head-first into the bean bag or the life-size stuffed bear; I feel like Big Bear is nearly a diagnostic tool.

For children that are sensation-seeking, they need a certain level of sensory input to help regulate themselves. They need big muscle input—like the trampoline and the yoga ball—as well as small muscle input—like the sand and the weighted blanket. They will absolutely love water play, water beads, foot massage, and anything like this. Most of their misbehavior will often boil down to them trying to get their sensory needs met in bad ways, so if you can get their needs met in good ways, they will be in much better shape. The interventions here are endless, but a word of caution: these will cease working if the child doesn't think they're fun or they feel good. Make sure the child continues to have fun, and change up what you're doing with them.

INTERVENTIONS:

worry stones or marbles for children to play with

clay or Play-Doh to smash or to handle

firm massage

tummy drum—patting the tummy firmly, pretending it's a drum

games that involve touching, such as tag or red rover

bear hugs

wrestling

sandbox or sensory bin with rice, dry beans, or sand

vibrating toys or toothbrush

Weighted blanket

trampoline

yoga ball

water beads in a water table or large bowl

a bowl full of sudsy water in the sink

Example: You have a child that is sensation-seeking and you take him on an airplane. He keeps kicking the seat in front of him even though you have games and crayons to distract him. A good strategy is to recognize that his kicking is sensation-seeking, and you can rub lotion on his feet to meet that need in a way that doesn't disturb other passengers.

Building skills: Building skills in this area is tricky, because the need for sensory input is real, and the more input a child gets, the more regulated they will become. As the child improves and grows, their need for sensory input will grow less desperate.

Auditory Filtering

Children with this sensitivity have a very difficult time coping with loud and extraneous sounds. They tend to get dysregulated by certain sounds, and are highly distractible. One of the keys to addressing auditory sensitivities is to create a good environment. When a child needs to concentrate on homework, things should be as quiet as possible. Headphones with soothing music can be really helpful in the car or other places. Protect children from loud noises as much as possible. A white-noise machine can be extremely helpful to help the child sleep.

INTERVENTIONS FOR SOOTHING:

Soothing music or quiet

Listen to the sounds of nature, including water and wind.

If you must be somewhere loud, use noise-cancelling headphones or white noise.

In school, you can request headphones for the child if they would find them helpful for taking tests.

INTERVENTIONS FOR BUILDING SKILLS:

Let the child have control over skill building with noise.

Use a kazoo, recorder, ukulele, or other musical instrument.

Bang pots and pans or drums.

Sing songs together.

Example: You do all the obvious things, like having a quiet homework space and a white-noise machine for the child to sleep, but there is still the issue of the noise of the car when you travel. So, you get the child noise-cancelling headphones, and have them help you choose the music to put on for their special car music.

Vision and Auditory Sensitivity

Researchers have found that people that score "sensitive" on the sensory profiles and have PTSD tend to have a much harder time interacting with others socially and can have impaired social relationships.[5] Sensation-sensitive people are also linked to having higher overall anxiety as well.[6] Children with vision sensitivities tend to be very stimulated by visual cues. They especially will need a safe place, and one that is less visually stimulating.

Turn off bright overhead lights in favor of soft lamps.

Have a relaxing photo or picture on the wall to gaze at when dysregulated.

Use sunglasses to reduce input.

Use a soft nightlight or complete darkness.

Use a fish tank, glitter jar, or lava lamp to watch to de-escalate.

Smell or Taste Sensitivities

When children have smell and taste sensitivities, they are often very averse to tastes and smells. Children with taste sensitivities will sometimes have a very limited menu that they will eat, and may refuse to try anything new. If your child has taste sensitivities, do not try to force her to eat foods she's resistant to. Instead, try to introduce foods in a low-key way, and follow the guidelines set up under the food and sleep section of this book. Taste and smell sensitivities can overlap because the two senses are linked, so try some of the interventions for both. If you try some of the suggestions in this book and really can't get anywhere, then there are registered dietitians that specialize in helping children with these types of sensitivities.

INTERVENTIONS FOR SOOTHING:

Have foods that the child will eat served with other foods at the table.

Use smells that the child finds soothing, such as scented lotions and candles.

Using oral soothing, such as blowing bubbles or using gum.

Drinking water

INTERVENTIONS FOR BUILDING SKILLS:

Explore new scents with essential oils, such as peppermint, vanilla, and orange.

Find a food similar to something they will eat, and try changing it a little. For instance, if your child will eat bananas, try freezing and blending them (have your child help you). If your child eats chicken nuggets, try dipping them in different sauces; then try chopped chicken with sauces.

Drink carbonated beverages.

Try different textures, such as chewy, crunchy, and soft.

Movement and Body Awareness Sensitivities

Children with movement and body awareness sensitivities are often very dys-regulated by movement that they don't control. These are children that dislike rides at amusement parks, don't like riding bikes, and will often have trouble with being in cars for long distances. If this is your child, then one of the keys is to make sure the interventions you do are fun and that the child feels in control of them.

INTERVENTIONS FOR SOOTHING:

Quiet, still, safe place

Limit car rides, parks, and amusement parks.

Meditation

INTERVENTIONS FOR SKILL BUILDING:

Let the child explore movement in a swimming pool.

Learn to ride a bike.

Car rides in short bursts

Sports, gymnastics, dance, karate, yoga

Bounce on a yoga ball.

Blanket swing—parents hold the corners of a blanket that the child is sitting on and swing it gently. Always stop when the child says stop. You can even make it a game—stop and start when the child says so.

Sensory Diet

A Sensory Diet is simply a way of talking about the sensory needs of your particular child. Just like you think about if your child is getting enough vegetables or enough protein, you also think about getting their sensory needs met. And just like you wouldn't want your child to get all of their nutrients in one meal, you also don't want them to get all of their sensory input all at one time either. Spread it out during the day. With each of the different types of sensory issues, you can think through what works best for your child, and what will help them be more successful. Integrating those things into their everyday life would be what a sensory diet would look like.

EXAMPLES:

For a child that is sensation-seeking and auditory filtering (probably one of the most common configurations I see), this would be a common sensory diet I would work out with the parent:

Morning before school: ten minutes active play

In school: active recess play; never miss recess as a consequence

After school: active play for twenty minutes on trampoline (or similar), or karate on Mondays and Wednesdays

Homework time: thirty minutes, no music or noise during homework time

Before dinner: tactile play with sand or beanbags

After dinner: yoga ball time, ten minutes family yoga

Bedtime: warm bath, lotion rubbed on feet

For a child that is vision and auditory sensitive:

Morning before school: slow, quiet morning with soft music

In school: plan in place to visit the nurse for quiet time if overwhelmed

After school: quiet time in safe place as needed

Before dinner: karate class twice a week (to build skills)

After dinner: fun skill-building exercises

Before bed: warm bath, calm story, soft music

To Learn More about Sensory Processing Disorder

Lindsey Biel and Nancy Peske, *Raising a Sensory Smart Child: The Definitive Handbook for Helping Your Child with Sensory Processing Issues* (New York: Penguin, 2005).

Carol Kranowitz and Lucy Jane Miller, *The Out-of-Sync Child: Recognizing and Coping with Sensory Processing Disorder* (New York: Tarcher Perigee, 2005).

PART 3

Identity

TRANSRACIAL AND
TRANSETHNIC ADOPTION

I AM WHITE, and I often tell my children that I don't get as cold as they do because my ancestors ran around the north of Scotland wearing kilts. My ancestors came to America fleeing persecution in the Highlands after monstrous oppression and persecution by the English. My husband is a more recent immigrant from New Zealand and has ancestry that is Jewish, Welsh, and Irish. Four of our children are black and were born in two different African countries. These racial differences present their own parenting challenges, and they are challenges that we hadn't really thought much about when we met those sweet faces for the first time. The truth is that between us and our black children, our experience in society is different, the privilege we experience is different, and even issues of hair care have surprised me by how different it has been. So how do two white parents raise four black children?

This is a really good question, and something every parent that is involved in a transracial adoption needs to ask, and ask continually. This is also incredibly relevant to our time, as the number of adopted kids being raised transracially has increased 50 percent over the past 10 years[1] and actually accounts for about 40 percent of all adoptions.[2] This is one of those areas that you never become an expert in, and you have to be learning all the time. I have not done this perfectly, but I can tell you where I've screwed up and some of the things that have helped me along the way. This chapter is going to talk more at the beginning about white parents adopting children of color because that is currently the majority of the transracial adoption that happens in the United States, though I would like to recognize that this is changing. I have worked with families of color adopting white children as well as other ethnicities different than themselves. I will have a section at the end discussing nonwhite parents in transracial adoptions.

The worst thing a well-intentioned parent can do in transracial adoptions is to completely ignore the issue. Parents, especially white parents, can often feel uncomfortable discussing race openly and freely with their children. Parents can often feel uncomfortable discussing puberty and sex with their children, but we still do it because we know that we have to—because we know that if kids don't get information from us, they get misinformation from other sources. We also want to foster intimacy with our children, communicate positive messages about their bodies, convey our family and cultural values, and so on, which are all things that we also accomplish talking about race and ethnicity with our children. And the same thing that happens when we don't talk about sex with our children happens when we don't talk about race—the child learns through our cues that it is a topic that is off-limits, and will not bring it up, and will search for answers elsewhere. We don't want our children looking for answers about sex from their peers and the internet first, and we don't want them to learn about a topic like race and ethnicity there as well. But it surprises me how many families I see that have adopted children of a different race that have never had a conversation with the child about the fact that the child is of a different race, let alone asked how that has been for the child, or checked in with them about peers, school, or any discrimination they may have encountered.

Before we get into talking to kids, let's agree on some basics. Race and ethnicity are different but similar things. Race refers to physical characteristics such as skin color and bone structure, and ethnicity refers to cultural and historical ancestry. So, my race is white, I have auburn hair and blue eyes with pale pinkish skin. But my ethnicity is Scottish American, and all the history and culture that entails. I'm mostly going to use the term *transracial* when referring to these adoptions, but in actuality, *transethnic* would be a more appropriate term. And it is also possible to adopt a child of the same racial background and come from different ethnicities—an African American family adopting a child from Ethiopia, for example.

There has been much controversy over the years about transracial adoptions, and for many years they were very rare. But as attitudes about race in our country started changing, so did some of the norms for adoption, and transracial adoption started becoming more common in the 1960s and early 1970s. Then, the National Association of Black Social Workers came out with a statement in 1972 condemning the practice of black children being adopted by or placed with white parents for any reason, with the president of the organization even going so far as to say that it would be better for children to be institutionalized than for them to be adopted by a white family. They were worried that a family that wasn't black couldn't properly prepare a black child for surviving systemic racism present in the culture nor nurture a child's identity as a black person. They also worried about a child growing up in a family as a minority within the family, and cultural assimilation.[3] These were and are, of course, valid concerns. Other African American organizations took a different tack, such as the NAACP, and came out in support of transracial adoption when no suitable black family could be found.[4] Despite this, transracial adoption numbers plummeted, bringing transracial adoptions to a virtual halt within just a few years, especially of black children. The unfortunate result of this was that many black children weren't getting adopted and were aging out of the system. Facing mounting pressure and increasing percentages of black children in foster care for longer and longer periods of time, in 1994 Congress passed a law that any adoption agency that receives federal funds cannot consider race as a factor in adoptions at all, and since that time, transracial adoptions have increased dramatically.

So what does the research say about all these transracial adoptions? For the most part, research says things are pretty good.[5] By most markers transracially adopted kids do almost the same as children adopted by parents who match their ethnicity, with a few exceptions here and there. One noted exception is about communication about race, and about differentiating reports on how the parents and children report on this communication.[6] Research has shown that how parents raise their transracially adopted children can greatly affect their racial identity, their self-identification, and their self-esteem. Adoptive parents have the greatest impact on their child's psychological well-being if they are able to engage their child around these issues.[7]

Here are some of the best suggestions for how to adopt transracially and transethnically:

Make sure you adopt from an ethnic group that you respect and are excited about participating with. This is not the time to be the "great white savior" adopting the less fortunate. If you go into adoption without having dealt with your issues of white supremacy, then it will be a disaster. You will be the person teaching your child about their culture and race of origin, and you cannot be that person if you believe that culture or race is inferior to your own. This is the place to be honest with yourself, and do not enter into a transracial adoption if you haven't worked on this area of your life.

Have a good relationship with your child's culture of origin. Children have the best outcomes and the best cultural development when they sense harmony between their original culture and their adopted culture.[8] They are, in effect, becoming bicultural, and if those cultures feel like they are at war, it will make their internal life much harder.

Make sure you're comfortable in spaces where you're the only person of your ethnicity. You should have regular places in your life where you are in the minority, if for no other reason than this is likely the experience your child is going to have a lot of the time. For our family we have a regular weekly commitment where we are part of a community where we are the only white people, and this has taught us a great deal about communication and humility, and it has also given us good connections with nonwhite people.

Think about your own privilege. If you are unfamiliar with the concept of privilege, you have some reading to do. Anything by Brenda Salter McNeil or Robin DiAngelo will work pretty well, although there is a lot currently written about this topic. Becoming educated in these areas is vitally important. You are the one teaching your children about these topics, so you need to know what you're talking about.

Own your own stuff. All of us bring racial history, identity, prejudice, family history, and *stuff* into parenting. Pretending it doesn't exist doesn't help anyone. It is much better to own what is there. Think carefully about your family history and messaging growing up—even if you disagree with it, it is still part of your story and it affects you. Nobody is free of all racial prejudice and privilege; it is much better to be aware of where yours is than to pretend it doesn't exist.

Learn to recognize racism. Part of the privilege of being white is that we can go through our lives pretending that racism doesn't exist, or at least minimizing its impact. But when you start actually seeing it, and seeing how it impacts people you love, suddenly you have skin in the game that you never had before. Suddenly when it's your child being followed in a store or your child being a victim of a racist taunt on the bus, you enter into a place where you cannot be complacent anymore. And you realize that part of becoming an aware parent is repenting for how you've been complacent in the past, and knowing that complacency is no longer an option in the future.

Join an organization that works to help advocate for people of the same race or ethnicity as your child. There are many out there—the National Association for the Advancement of Colored People (NAACP), for instance, is a well-respected one that has been around for many years. But there are others that help other ethnicities as well, such as Asiafamilies.org; the Hispanic Heritage Foundation; NALEO, a Hispanic advocacy organization, UnidosUS; OCA Asian Pacific American Advocates; and the Arab American Institute. These are just a few of the many out there. You should be able to find one that fits your family.

Be able to enter the conversation. If you are a parent adopting a child of any ethnicity that is different from your own, there needs to be conversation. I have noticed that white parents often find themselves particularly paralyzed. If you are a white parent adopting kids of color, talking about these issues is critical. You might find this intensely uncomfortable, and you might be tempted to try to make the world seem as if color doesn't matter, but your kids need you to be an educated, "woke" person who understands these issues and not only is able to talk about them but actually brings up the conversation.

I sat frozen to my seat, not knowing how to answer. All of my cross-cultural training was supposed to have prepared me for this, but somehow I sat there feeling completely unprepared—a mouthy teenager had just said my worst nightmare to me, without me even realizing what my worst nightmare would be. I sat there, a Sunday school teacher in a room full of Ethiopian immigrant teenagers, looking at me to see how I would respond. How was I going to respond?

"Why should we listen to you about race?" the boy had spat at me. "Your ancestors probably owned slaves."

Later I would reflect on the irony of the son of an Ethiopian immigrant saying such a thing to me, co-opting the African American culture as he was from the only country in Africa to escape the scourge of colonization. But at that moment I was frozen. Part of me wanted to defend myself—saying how my ancestors didn't own slaves, and how dare he judge me based on the color of my skin? Didn't he know that my ancestors were the victims of the English and run out of their own country to have to settle in the United States?

But there was also the white guilt—maybe this teenager was right. What right did I have to talk about race? Was I being a white savior being in this space teaching? Should I slink away with my tail between my legs? Gone was my teaching about how the church should speak across racial divides, and present was a racial divide that I wish had never existed. I found myself wishing for someone, anyone to rescue me in that moment, to not have to confront this teenager so confident in his own anger at me, and I was completely flustered.

I don't remember how I got through the rest of my lesson, but I eagerly awaited an already scheduled lunch date with a friend of mine a few days later. Lois was a friend that was visiting from her home in New York, and we had become friends while she had gotten her PhD in Seattle. More importantly, she was a black woman of incredible insight and had taught teenagers before. In fact, while she had lived in Seattle, she had run a tutoring program through her church for children in a disadvantaged area of Tacoma.

Settling into our lunches, I quickly spilled the story about what had happened in Sunday school, of my fear and paralysis. I sort of expected her to tell me to engage with the young man better with his feelings, maybe have a talk with the group about racial tensions.

"He was being rude, Barbara," she told me confidently in her thick Brooklyn accent. "You need to handle that like you would handle any rudeness in your class."

"But it was about racial issues . . ." I began.

"He said that to get your goat," she told me. "Do you think a black woman would have put up with that in her class? Don't let your white guilt paralyze you. Engage with the kids how they need you to do it. They need to know you're not afraid of these issues."

"But I'm white . . ."

"They know you're white," my friend patiently agreed. "And the elders asked you to teach, didn't they? They came to your church and asked your church for teachers, right? It wasn't a secret to anybody that you weren't Ethiopian. But you can't pretend that your color doesn't exist."

In the story above, I took what my friend said to heart, and I think this is very true with kids as well. It's important to talk to kids about race, and it's important for it not to paralyze you. A lot of parents wait for transracially adopted kids to bring up the topic, but this is exactly the wrong tactic to take—they need you to bring it up! Parents should lead on bringing up this topic, and they should feel comfortable. Become educated without becoming too much of an "expert;" you need to be able to converse about these topics but not be lecturing. Whatever the issues are for the race of your child, you should know about—whether it's the history of the country they're from, the particulars on how to do their ethnic-specific hair, or at least a few phrases in their language of origin.

I have spoken with several adult adoptees that felt that their parents were great in so many areas but didn't address the issues of race with them. Either the parents didn't learn how to do their hair properly, they didn't ever talk about race (making it a taboo topic), or the parents told the adoptees that they were being too sensitive if they ever brought up the topic of race. Race will come up—either by a teacher putting them on the spot during black history week, someone on the street assuming they speak Chinese or Spanish, or at a Black Lives Matter rally at your child's high school. It's better to be in conversation before something happens.

> Remember not to go overboard. When my five-year-old African daughter asked for a white doll for her birthday, I thought I'd failed. Why was I not communicating that black is beautiful? I had bought her beautiful African dolls; did she not like them? How had I failed in messaging to her that only white dolls are beautiful? I then felt much chagrined when she went on to explain, "With blue eyes and brown hair. I want her to look just like you, Mommy."

Live in a diverse area. This is the suggestion that people are most likely to dismiss out of hand, but hear me out. If your kid is the only kid of color in the school, it's going to be hard for them. I have heard countless stories from adult adoptees about how intensely uncomfortable it was being the only child of color in their school or town, and how much they longed to see someone else that looked like them. This can be a very hard choice to make, but research shows that transracially adopted kids feel more comfortable about their appearance if there are kids in their community that look like them.[9] One writer puts it, "You can celebrate Kwanzaa. You can learn how to twist and box-braid your daughter's hair. You can make #BlackLivesMatter your Facebook profile picture. But for many white adoptive parents, the act of raising kids in a diverse environment is too hard, or too inconvenient, or too easy to trade off for better schools or safer neighborhoods."[10]

When There Is Little Diversity

Research has shown that black and brown kids do best in schools and communities when there are other black and brown kids. My best advice is that if you are transracially adopting black and brown kids, live somewhere that they are able to have diverse friends at school and in their community. However, that is not always possible, and I wanted to write a section about some helpful hints if you are raising a child where they are one of the few, if not the only, black or brown face at their school.

First off, it's always important to talk about it with your child. Talk specifically about it, and often. Recognize how it must be for them to be in the minority for most of their lives. Having you as a sympathetic listener is an important resource for them.

Look for opportunities for them to interact with their racial community. Think summer camps, weekend trips to a nearby city, vacations somewhere culturally appropriate. I've seen families make traditions of celebrating Chinese New Year at a nearby city with an international district, or maybe make their own Chinese New Year party and invite friends. Celebrate what makes your family unique! Whatever cultural and ethnic traditions your child brings to the family, celebrate and invite others into celebrating as well. You could be the cool family that has the Ethiopian Christmas party or the awesome Cinco de Mayo party; embrace!

A vacation in a larger city with more diversity can be a good choice, or if you have the means, even a country where they can interact and be with people of a similar culture or racial background. For an international adoption, going to the child's country of origin can be really fraught with many different issues, so please do this thoughtfully. But any trip you can take with some interaction with a child's culture of origin is usually positive.

Watch movies and television shows that have characters that reflect your child's ethnicity. Engage and speak about the characters and their issues, and make sure that the character's ethnicity is part of the conversation. Talk about politicians and celebrities that share your child's ethnicity, especially if they're people that you respect. Think about who can be role models for your child, even if they're not someone that your child will likely ever meet. It's better if there are role models in your everyday lives that your child does meet, but if there are no possibilities of them in your community, at least provide some virtually. And television and movies can be powerful tools to show representation and what's "cool." I will never forget the moment in the theater when one of my daughters leaned over to whisper to me in the middle of watching the movie *Black Panther,* "The girls have hair like me!" The choice of the makers of that movie to star dark-skinned African women with natural hairstyles not only as the best-friend types but as the romantic leads shouldn't have felt so progressive at the time, but it was one of the first movies of its kind to do so.

White Privilege

A lot has been said about white privilege, and one very important essay in this conversation was an essay called "White Privilege: Unpacking the Invisible Knapsack" written in 1989 by Peggy McIntosh. Here is some of what she says:

> I think whites are carefully taught not to recognize white privilege, as males are taught not to recognize male privilege. So I have begun in an untutored way to ask what it is like to have white privilege. I have come to see white privilege as an invisible package of unearned assets that I can count on cashing in each day, but about which I was "meant" to remain oblivious. White privilege is like an invisible weightless knapsack of special provisions, maps, passports, codebooks, visas, clothes, tools, and blank checks.[11]

White privilege is something that is unearned and mostly unrecognized until we learn to recognize it. Last year my family and I went on vacation. We had a stopover in Los Angeles, and we stopped at a Walmart to get some supplies. We were in an area of LA that was a lower socioeconomic area, and I was a little surprised by some of the security measures. I needed a pair of tweezers, and so I went into the area of Walmart where they had all of the makeup and such, and realized that it was set up differently than the stores in Seattle. There was a checkout in the makeup area, and everybody was lining up to pay for their items before they left the area. It was set up in a way that it was clear that you were meant to pay for your makeup purchases before you left the area. I looked at the line and did not want to wait in it, and I didn't see a sign that said I needed to. So, I skipped the line, walked confidently to my waiting cart, plopped the tweezers in the cart, and went about my business, leaving the tweezers to be paid for at the front of the store with all of our other purchases.

"White privilege!" my husband laughed at me. "Did you really just skip that line?"

"There were no signs!" I defended myself. "I figured if it was a rule they would have just asked me to pay."

He was right, though; it was white privilege. I was confident in my ability to be treated fairly by the store personnel, and if I was supposed to have paid, I wouldn't have been accused of shoplifting. If I were black or Hispanic, would I have been that confident?

How does white privilege work itself into adoption? In many ways, I'm afraid. Here are the ways I've seen it and experienced it:

* In the mechanics of things like the home study, in many cases due to unconscious bias from the social worker, white parents usually have somewhat of an advantage.

* In many adoption agencies, the fees for adopting white children are higher than for black children. Even lighter-skinned mixed race babies are more "expensive" than black children.[12]

* White parents can be "color blind" and not engage issues of race and culture, not recognizing distinctness and differences between races and cultures.

* White parents have the privilege of not thinking about having to talk to their children about how to interact with law enforcement, assuming that law enforcement will treat everyone fairly. This can be counterproductive if their children need to be prepared for how to interact with law enforcement.

* White parents will often choose a "good school" over a more ethnically diverse school because they want their children to "achieve."

* White parents assume that schools and systems will work for them—and they often do.

* White parents have the privilege of being assumed to be an adoptive parent. Nonwhite parents of differently raced children are often typed as the babysitter at best, and it can get much worse. I know a social worker, a black woman, that, when babysitting a friend's white child, had a neighbor call the police to do a welfare check on the child in her care. And this was in liberal Seattle.

* White parents have a reasonable expectation that the people they come across in the foster care and adoption system, especially the people with the most power such as judges, will share their ethnicity.

- White parents and white children have to worry about their hair and clothes less with regard to how they present themselves to the world. For a white child, a sloppy ponytail looks like a lazy Saturday, and a hoodie looks just like a cozy way to stay warm; these mean very different things for black children.

- White parents have the luxury of not wondering if a home study, a judge's decision, a placement decision, or a birth parent's decision was based on their race.

Your experience of white privilege might be very different than what I experience in my corner of the world in Seattle, but thinking about white privilege is a good exercise if you're a white person in our society, especially one that wants to parent a child of another race. And thinking of your white privilege isn't an exercise designed to make you feel guilty, but it is designed to help you see how the world isn't going to be as easy for your child as it has been for you.

There are also ways that you can use your white privilege to help make the world more just for your child and for other children like your child. If you view your white privilege as unearned power, then you can take the Spider-Man route and think that with great power comes great responsibility. A white person speaking up about racial inequalities can sometimes be heard louder than others, and you can also use your knowledge of the system. You were given an unearned gift with white privilege, one that hopefully future generations will share more with people of other races. But for now, how can you use that power for the good of the world you live in? Where are the places you can lay it down to encourage power in others?

We were standing outside with a group of Ethiopian teenagers from our class, enjoying the summer sunshine and joking about my husband's new car. A few of the boys were trying to talk him into a ride, but he was laughing and saying that he'd given them a ride before and they didn't need another one.

Suddenly, a white woman came out from one of the neighboring houses and began yelling at the teens about stealing her credit cards.

When we realized what was happening, my husband and I and the other teacher (all white) moved to where we would be easily visible to the person, so that she would see that there were adults here, and she should leave the teens alone. We moved between her and the teens, ignoring her statements and hoping our body language would be enough. She persisted with her yelling, and I detected some paranoid delusion in her words, which reminded me of my first job out of college working with a group of paranoid schizophrenics. So I actually tried to approach her, calmly asking if she'd like to talk to me about what was bothering her. I told her I was a safe person to talk to and would like to hear what she was worried about. As I approached, she ran inside her house and slammed the door. I stopped approaching the house, but I was close enough to see that her window was covered with conspiracy theory sort of propaganda. I went back to where we were standing, told the kids she probably was mentally ill, her ranting had nothing to do with them, and to pay her no mind.

When I talked to another adult that was more in charge, I suggested that if it happened again they could call the police.

"We wouldn't want to do," she replied, worried. "We wouldn't want to get anyone in trouble."

"I didn't mean calling the police to get her in trouble," I explained, realizing I had assumed the police were a helpful presence that this Ethiopian community would not have assumed. "I meant to do a welfare check. She's not doing well, and if she's screaming at a bunch of teenagers, it might not be a bad idea to have someone check on her. It's a way for her to be able to get help if she needs it."

In this story I used my white privilege to protect the teens in my class, by moving physically to where we were between the person and the teenagers, hoping that our presence would be enough to dissuade her. I have several white friends that go to marches and protests and use their bodies in the same sort of way, knowing that if there are large groups of white people at protests and rallies, then police are far more likely to treat people fairly. But then when

I talked to the other adult about calling the police, not only did I not think about what calling the police would be like for the black community but also for people from Ethiopia, where the police were often the enforcers of an oppressive government and not agents of any help whatsoever. In my privilege and my history of working with paranoid schizophrenics, I knew that that is one way that people who are having a major episode can access help. But I didn't think to explain that's what I meant, so of course I sounded like I wanted her to get arrested.

Nonwhite Parents in a Transracial Adoption

Thirty years ago, it was unheard of for nonwhite parents to be placed with a transracial adoption, because current thinking of the time was to try and match the ethnicity of the child with the parents as much as possible. There were more white adoptive parents than nonwhite parents, so most nonwhite adoptive parents were matched with a child of the same ethnicity. Today, adoption agencies are barred by federal law from considering race in adoption placements at all, so more and more transracial adoptions are happening with nonwhite parents. In my practice, I work with a significant number of parents of color that are raising children of a different ethnicity than themselves.

For parents of color, most of the suggestions I make in this book apply to them as well, but with perhaps some interpretation. Race still needs to be talked about, and still geared toward questions about why they don't look like Mommy. There may be less privilege to unpack, but parents still need to truly respect and care about the culture of the child that they are raising, and find opportunities for the child to connect with people from that ethnicity and culture.

And it is always important, no matter what your race and ethnic background, to know and own your stuff. What has race meant to your family? Extended family can be a source of great support or cultural and racial prejudice. And nonwhite parents have to do their homework as well when placed with a white child. I worked with a family that had mixed-race members that was placed with a freckled white child, and their introduction to how easily such a child could get sunburned was eye opening for them. An afternoon jaunt to the park—something they wouldn't think twice about for their other children—suddenly had to always be proceeded with appropriate sunscreen and a hat or the child would get blisters.

Hair and Body Care

When you adopt transracially, your child will have different hair and skin than you do. This may seem like not that big of an issue, but let me tell you right now how much of a big deal it really is. When we received our first transracial child, she had hair curlier than mine, but not so much so that I couldn't braid it or style it similar to how I braided and styled my own hair, or the hair of my bio-daughter. She came from Ethiopia and had a looser curl than many children from Africa. However, I was very much in for an education on how African hair is substantively different than white hair, even if the curl doesn't look that much different. Luckily, I had some black women in my circle that were able to educate me on how to care for my new daughter's hair, which included only weekly or even bi-weekly shampoo with ethnic shampoo, and the addition of leave-in hair conditioner daily when I brushed and braided her hair before bed. White people continually shampoo their hair, usually daily or every other day, to keep the oil under control; and here I was adding oil to my daughter's hair! But we developed a rhythm, found products we liked, and basically figured out how it worked.

I was perhaps overconfident and didn't think it would be a big deal when we then received three girls from the Democratic Republic of Congo, but let me tell you that hair and body care was a completely different story than what I had known before. Their hair was what is called 4c in the black-hair world, which requires an education for someone with no experience, like me. My girls with their 4c hair got a lot of messages that their hair wasn't acceptable, and I wanted so much to communicate to them that their hair was beautiful and unique in its own way. So I read blogs, searched YouTube, experimented with products, consulted with natural black hair stylists, and was determined to figure out how to do the majority of their hair care myself. I learned that their hair was better washed with a special conditioner called co-wash and apple cider vinegar, and how to comb it gently to avoid breakage. I have always paid braiders to do special hairstyles, but I have also worked hard to learn to do the basic ones. I started on the youngest daughter first, learning to do little puffs in her baby-soft fuzzy hair. Then I graduated to doing box braids, putting a colorful clip at the end of each one. When my older girls saw my progress, they encouraged me to try beads, which a kind hairdresser at the black beauty supply store showed me how to install. Then, my older daughter said if I could do box braids, I could do extensions, and a few tutorials on YouTube later I figured it out. But the holy grail for me—cornrows—took me a few years to be able to accomplish. Finally I was able to get that skill under my belt, and along with those came crochet braids. And when I couldn't find a skin lotion that worked well enough, I made one with coconut oil and shea butter that finally tackled their dry skin after swimming lessons.

Why did I tell you this whole story? To try to tell you that it is a process to learn, and if you adopt transracially, you will have a lot to learn. Do not assume that the child you have will be just like you in skin and body care, or things you take for granted like shampooing will be the same. You will need to get help—and for this you will need input from people who have the same skin and hair as your child. If you do not have immediate access to adults of the same ethnicity as your child, go online and find other parents that have adopted, or try to find a hairdresser of the child's ethnicity. Educate, educate, educate—there is a lot out there to read and to learn. One of our children has even decided to try microlocs to fit her more sporty lifestyle (as well as her strong dislike of having her hair brushed) and we were able to do that research together, find a person to install them, and learn how to maintain them.

How to Talk about Race with Your Child

There was an incredible documentary project called *Side by Side* done about Korean adoptees, who were mostly adopted by white parents, starting in the 1950s and peaking in the 1980s and 1990s. This documentary project interviewed adult adoptees in different stages in their lives, and specifically asked very pointed questions about many areas of their lives. This is what they had to say about how their parents talked about race:

> *Most interviewees were reluctant to discuss race with their adoptive parents. This feeling started as kids, with a first attempt to discuss racial experiences gone awry, and continues today. It seems most often rooted in the parents' dismissal of racial experiences as unimportant or something to be ignored.*

"Color-blindness" or "We don't think of you as Korean" is taken as a denial of race. Refusal to discuss or acknowledge race results in a sense of shame. Attempts to discuss race by the adult adoptee might have been rebuffed by the parent, as offensive or disrespectful.[13]

This answer is very sobering. It doesn't take much to shut down a child's desire to discuss race, and parents pretending that race doesn't matter is one of the easiest ways. This is a position of privilege to pretend that race doesn't matter; it matters to your child. Every time someone assumes that your child isn't yours because they're a different race, your child feels it. Every time someone at school assumes they speak Chinese or Spanish, know how to use chopsticks, or can speak for the African American experience during the school's celebration of Martin Luther King Jr. Day, race matters to your child. You don't necessarily want to ask your child about race every day, but when they do talk about it, be sympathetic and engaged. Or when racial issues come up in the news or in your community, talk about it. Be very clear in public, saying loudly that you are the child's parent if there's ever any question. Many adult adoptees report getting frustrated about not being identified as a family member.

Some ideas to bring up the topic with your child:

- China was in the news today for this new discovery they made. What does it mean to you that you were born in China?

- Sometimes I wonder what it must be like for you to have white parents and be Hispanic. What are some good things and some hard things about that? (Kids often are better about saying hard things if they can say some good things first.)

- What is it like for you during MLK week at your school? Do people ask you questions?

Here are some scenarios from my own family. How would you handle them?

- teenager using the N word on Facebook

- our black teenager realizing that she was being followed in a store, probably due to her race

- freshman in high school's new African American friend telling her she's not "black enough" because she has white parents

- a grade school child being teased on the bus for having white parents

- a black man approaching our family in a store and angrily yelling at us that a white mother cannot parent children of color

- a middle school student from Ethiopia being put on the spot in a social studies class during a unit on slavery being asked about the African American experience

- a black teen posting "all lives matter" on her Facebook page

- a neighbor not believing that a black child was my white child's sister

- discussing with our teens how to handle being pulled over by police

"Aisha said my name is too white," my daughter complained when she came home from school. Her name was a relatively common English name with French spelling, as she came from the French-speaking Democratic Republic of Congo. Think a name similar to "Franchesca."

"Really?" I asked. "How do you feel about that?"

"I'm mad at her," Franchesca replied. "She's stupid."

"It must be frustrating to have someone judge what's 'black' enough."

"I don't see how she gets off on it anyway," my daughter ranted. "I mean, she was born here, but her parents weren't. She's not better just because her parents are black."

"You usually like your name."

"I still do," she affirmed. "But she's right, it doesn't sound as black as her name."

"Okay, so just so I can get this straight," I smirked. "Your African mother, in Africa, who doesn't speak English, gave you this name—and your friend has deemed it too white? Seriously?"

My daughter, seeing the humor in the situation, started to smile herself. "I guess that is pretty stupid."

"Honey, do your other black friends give you a bad time about your name?"

"Nope, they're fine with it," she answered. "They don't really care about stuff like that."

"So, the thing is," I told her, "you get to decide for yourself what being black means to you. Aisha doesn't get to dictate that, that's something you get to decide for yourself. Aisha is just being mean and trying to control you. We've talked before about how she does this."

"I wish I didn't care about what she thought."

"Yeah, that does sound hard. What do you want to do regarding Aisha? Any ideas?"

Medical Care and Counseling

Medical care is an area where you could introduce a person of a different ethnicity to your child's life. It might be a little more difficult to find a provider that is ethnically similar to your child, but this is a great natural person in your child's life. If possible, also try and find a therapist that is culturally appropriate as well. This can be difficult, and if the therapist isn't culturally similar to your child, then you should at least ask the therapist their views on how to address transracial adoptions. I have had a few clients ask me about this, and I appreciate their candor and that they realize how much of an issue this is for their child. Unfortunately I only have a few referrals for when people want a therapist that is similar to the ethnicity of their child, something I wish wasn't the case in my area.

Law Enforcement

It saddens me when I watch the news and realize that there has been another needless shooting of a young person, and there has been much said in the past few years about how black parents prepare their kids to interact with law enforcement. As much as I wish it were not the case, I think it would be irresponsible for any parent of a child of color to not prepare them for how to interact with law enforcement. The empirical evidence shows that the victims of police shootings are overwhelmingly poor and minority, with black individuals being dramatically overrepresented given their percentage of the population.[14] One analysis found young black males twenty-one times more likely to be shot dead by police than their white counterparts.[15] I have known families to install dash cams on their children's cars just for this reason. These are the rules we tell our children:

1. Always stay polite and respectful. Answer what is asked. Do not volunteer information.

2. Keep your hands on the wheel of the car. When the police ask for your license, registration, and insurance, tell them that you are getting them and where you are reaching: "I'm getting my license from my purse."

3. Do not get into an argument. If the police are doing something unfair, we will address it later.

4. If you are arrested, do not resist. Ask for a lawyer and to talk to your parents.

5. If they ask to search something, politely decline. Tell them you want to call your dad or your lawyer before you consent to a search.

There can also be an added complication if your child has had some bad experiences with law enforcement before they came into your home. We had had our first child from Ethiopia only a few months when we went to a pancake breakfast fund-raiser for a local fire department. She had come from Ethiopia, and when she saw some men in uniform and a few police officers with guns at the breakfast, she had a panicked PTSD reaction. Luckily I had a high school friend who had become a firefighter, so he showed us around the station and a firetruck later that day so she'd feel more comfortable. We also had a situation with our children on the school bus a few years ago when there was a person with a gun on one of the school campuses. They had police officers in full tactical gear carrying an assault rifle board the school bus with my child, who had survived a war zone in the Democratic Republic of Congo. She was triggered, in full fight, flight, and freeze mode, and panicking. But with the help of my other daughter, who was also on the bus, she managed to survive until they got to the designated safety pickup point where I could pick her up.

Multicultural Family

I was talking to a coworker of Korean descent one time about race in America. We were talking about how race should work and what model has been there in the past. He rejected the idea of the "melting pot" that America has had for so much of its history. He was proud of his Korean heritage and didn't like the idea of it melting into the uniformity that a melting pot represented. "But I don't like the idea of ethnic groups existing completely unchanged and separate either, like a salad," he commented. "Because I am American, and I am different than Koreans in Korea. I think we exist more like a stir fry in a wok—we each have our own identity as who we are, but we flavor and are changed by the other ingredients."

Being in a multicultural marriage, I can't agree more. I am thoroughly American and nearly twenty years ago I married someone who was thoroughly a New Zealander. At first I didn't even realize how multicultural my marriage would feel in the long run—after all, we were both from rural farming communities. We actually joked that we had a lot more in common than if I'd married someone from New York. But then things started cropping up—like how he was shocked when I didn't think it was a big deal to mention a scholarship I'd received, or when I realized I'd have to coach him to actually sell himself at a job interview. You see, if a New Zealander won the Nobel Prize for Physics and you asked them if they knew anything about physics, they might answer, "I know a bit about physics." Where Americans think it's no big deal to talk about accomplishments but have hang-ups in other areas, such as talking about your salary, in other countries people have no trouble discussing it. Through marriage we have worked out these minor differences, and a few major ones, to realize that I have become a little bit Kiwi and my husband has become a little bit American in the process. He is different than the Kiwis back home, and I am different than the Americans I grew up around; we have "flavored" each other.

The same thing happens with kids. You should always love the culture from which you adopt a child, because you are going to become part of that culture in the process of raising that child. Your DNA might not change, but in loving a child of that culture and having a person in your family from that culture, that culture enters your family and your story in a powerful way. As our family grew and we added a child from Ethiopia, and then children from the Democratic Republic of Congo, not only did the cultural makeup of our family change, but so did we as people. We were in the wok of our family, and that is what being a multicultural family means together.

I saw this beautifully demonstrated in a family that I worked with that had the rare formulation of parents of Hispanic origin adopting white children. When the topic of what their new last name would be, the family was flummoxed. The children wanted to change their last name to the family's last name, much to the surprise of the adoptive family. They were worried about giving their blond-haired children such obviously Hispanic names. Would it set them up for a life of explaining?

"But you realize that they will be a part of your family," I told them.

"But they won't be Mexican," the mom objected. "Won't it be hard for them to have names they will always have to explain?"

"Their DNA won't be Mexican," I agreed. "But let me put it this way: though they look white and will know white culture, when they go to college and meet someone with Mexican ancestry, will they feel a little bit of affinity for them? Will they want to find a good place to get tamales together, or maybe take Spanish in high school to be able to practice with you at home? How much will it rub off on them that they are being raised by parents with Mexican heritage, visiting relatives in Mexico every summer?"

When the kids were adopted, they kept the original Scandinavian last name as their middle name and proudly sported their new Hispanic last name.

And lastly, celebrate your cultural heritage. This may seem like a strange one, but I firmly believe that celebrating your cultural heritage is setting the example for celebrating everyone's cultural heritage. "White" isn't a cultural heritage—but Scottish, English, Norwegian, Russian, and Irish sure are. Don't know your cultural heritage? Celebrate what you do know—what are family traditions that your family does? Look up your last name and find out what country it comes from—what are the traditions from that country? Celebrating within your family the cultural heritage from different members is a great way to make everyone's cultural heritage not only okay but something special and good about them. Maybe in your family you eat a special meal to honor a holiday to celebrate Dad's Swedish grandmother, or you learn to make tamales to honor a great-aunt. Though not of German descent myself, a family favorite in my family was a dish from my German aunt (by marriage), whom we talked about fondly every time we made it. And having a husband from New Zealand and kids from Ethiopia and the Democratic Republic of Congo, I have learned to make many dishes that, although I am not proficient yet at making them, can at least pass enough as being okay for nostalgic purposes.

To Learn More

The Adopted Life (www.theadoptedlife.com): This is done by Angela Tucker, an adult transracially adopted person, my former colleague, and the person behind the movie *Closure,* which I also very much recommended.

Jane Hoyt-Oliver, Hope Haslam Straughan, and Jayne E. Schooler, *Parenting in Transracial Adoption* (Santa Barbara, CA: ABC-CLIO, 2016).

OLDER CHILD ADOPTION

MOST CHILDREN ARE ADOPTED before the age of three, so when you are talking about older child adoption, you are talking about children over the age of three at the age of adoption.

Adoption of children over the age of three is more complicated than the adoption of infants on many fronts. Certainly anxiety about attachment increases exponentially for the adoptive parents with the increased age of the child. Studies have found there is good reason for this anxiety. One researcher found that when they looked at sixteen-year-old teens that had been adopted, 83 percent of teens that had been adopted at a young age reported a constructive relationship with their parents. For children adopted at an older age, only 38 percent reported a constructive relationship with their adoptive parents. This study went on to show that an increase in the adoptee's age at adoption can hinder a child forming a strong attachment to their adoptive family.[1]

Dissolution is the equivalent of divorce in the adoption world—it's the disruption of an adoption, and a failure of attachment. This happens at a rate of 4.6 percent for children adopted between the ages of three and five, and increases steadily with age until it is at a rate of 26.1 percent for children adopted between the ages of fifteen to eighteen.[2] One researcher identified five main areas that older adoptive children dealt with: "developing a sense of belonging, getting along with siblings in the adoptive family, establishing his or her identity, dealing with loss and grief, and making the adoption successful, stable, and permanent."[3] It's easy to see how these areas would be tougher the older a child was upon joining a family.

To understand some of these dynamics, let's revisit a thought exercise we did back in chapter 10, about the stages of adoption. We pretended to be in a place in our adult lives where someone removed us from our normal lives, as happens to children who are removed from their lives and placed in foster care. Someone comes to your house right now and tells you to pack a bag, that your house isn't safe, and that you're going to live somewhere else with a nice family. Even if there are problems where you're living, this is still shocking and horrifying. For me, as a fully functioning adult with coping skills, I would have a very hard time coping with a complete change of life like that—how much harder is this for a child? I would worry about my dog, my plants, my family that I left behind—just like a child does. Even if the person taking you away assures you that the new family will be very nice and that they have a nice house, you will probably insist you prefer your current family, thank you very much. Can you understand the helpless feelings a child would have in that situation? And what if the person explained you would have to change jobs too because your new home was too far away, and we'll see if you can visit your friends sometimes? This type of loss is catastrophic for older children, as they have more connections with people outside the home—friends, school, and in the neighborhood.

So that's the bad news; and if you're interested in adopting an older child, you should go into it knowing the odds. But if you're interested in an older child adoption, you should also know that there is a lot of hope as well, as many families have welcomed older children successfully into their home. My "nontraditional" children came to me mostly at older ages—they were two, seven, ten, and twelve upon placement in our home. There are a few things that are more complicated to navigate, however, and this is not the place to enter with naïveté. Every child deserves a home, but homes that accept older children need a few more skills. Here are some of the areas in which foster and adoptive homes need special skills:

Think about the situation from the child's perspective. The child has probably had several foster homes and disruptions in their past, and probably a lot of people promising things that haven't happened. It's going to take them some time to learn to trust. Focus on building a relationship with them with positive memories and enjoyment; go slowly. Trust takes time to build—it's not something that can be demanded quickly. It takes awhile to let their guard down. One teen said that her entire first year at her adoptive home was "complete paranoia."

Respect their story and relationships, even if that seems really hard to do. It can be really hard to respect a story where the good guy might be a grandmother who drank too much or a mother who makes endless bad choices, but that could be the only option of attachment for the child up until now. Safe people can often be a relative option—a drunk grandma might be a better attachment option to a young child than an abusive father or an absent mother. When kids develop healthy attachments with healthier adults, they can then evaluate other relationships for themselves. But this is certainly not for you to point out—this is something for the child to process, and something they will likely process in young adulthood. It's better to accept now that part of adopting an older child is that you will "share" that child with their family of origin, and come to peace with it now.

"I wouldn't want to adopt kids," one of my non-bio-kids told me one day out of the blue. She was a child that had come at an older age.

"Really?" I responded, as neutrally as I could. "That surprises me. I've quite enjoyed it myself. But I understand it's not for everybody."

"I know you're going to say how you love me and all that," she waves her hand, dismissing my platitudes. "But honestly, how could you want to raise a child you always have to share with other people? Any child you adopt has other parents."

"I went into it knowing that," I told her. "I figured sharing you was better than no part of you at all."

"Hmm," she replied, not convinced.

"I do love you," I told her, smiling a little mischievously.

"I knew you were going to say that," she shot back, smiling a bit herself.

They may have more issues with things like names and other parts of adoption. Some of the time-honored traditions of adoption, such as changing the adoptee's name to match that of the adoptive family, can be particularly difficult for some kids. You have to decide how important this is to you—can you raise a child with a different name than yours? Professionally, I don't recommend changing any part of a child's name without their permission if they are old enough to register an opinion about it. I've seen potential adoptions not happen over issues such as a name change, and it is heartbreakingly unnecessary. For a child who has lost so many things about their past and their family, something like a name can mean the world to them—why not give them power around what happens to it? I've also seen parents change a child's name against their will—only to have the child fight it for the next ten years and then change it back when they're of age. There are many more important things to fight about; if a child doesn't consent to a name change, it's not going to go anywhere good—first names or last names. I have also seen beautiful things come out of name changes that the child chooses—where the child chooses a family name of the adoptive family, or to honor a grandmother from their bio-family, or even an author they admire. If you think about it, how names are incredibly personal and a daily part of your life forever, it makes sense how meaningful it is.

For kids approaching adolescence, it's tricky to be attaching to a child at the same time that developmentally they're trying to differentiate. Adolescence is a time when children are supposed to separate from their parents and begin to become more independent—moving toward adulthood. This can cause a lot of problems even with typical kids, and it can be tricky for kids and parents to navigate. But for kids with trauma, this can be extra tricky—especially as you're trying to attach at the same time as they're trying to separate in this way. This can definitely still be successful, and lots of families successfully navigate this, but this dynamic can get tricky. Successful parents recognize the need for differentiation in the face of attachment, and look for good opportunities to attach. Get a therapist involved sooner rather than later if problems develop.

Attachment can look different for children that come to you older, and that's okay. Many parents I see feel guilty that the attachment they feel for a child adopted at an older age feels different than a child they gave birth to or adopted at birth. Please know that this is okay, and very normal. If you'd given birth to ten children, your relationship would feel different with all ten of them! Attachment, love, and family are for the long haul—over decades of relationship. Feelings and attachment take years to develop. You don't have to force or push anything. Enjoy your child, connect with them, work on attunement, and attachment will take care of itself.

16

WORKING WITH
BIRTH FAMILY

FOSTER AND ADOPTIVE PARENTS have wildly different views and ideas of working with birth families. Some foster and adoptive parents come into the relationship with birth families assuming that they are fostering a larger, wider family, and I have seen relationships with the birth family enter something that looks nearly like coparenting. And I have seen other foster and adoptive parents that are completely against any contact with bio-family whatsoever.

> I grew up with a younger sister whom we adopted at two. She knew next to nothing about her birth family, and the prevailing wisdom of the time was to tell children nothing until they were eighteen. So my parents, who honestly knew very little about the birth family themselves, told her that they would tell her everything they knew when she turned eighteen, and even help her find her birth parents at that age if she wished.

One nugget of information that my sister did manage to glean about her birth family was that they had moved back to California after leaving her in Washington State, where she entered the foster system and was eventually adopted. So when we went to Disneyland when she was ten, I was excited about the roller coasters, but my sister was sure that she would be able to meet her parents somehow in California. Her eyes scanned every crowd, and it wasn't until we were headed back home that she broke down crying because she hadn't seen them.

She spent her childhood wondering about her birth family, and making up what she didn't know. By the time eighteen rolled around, the fantasies that she had created about her birth family were not only completely unrealistic but unhelpful for when she did finally make contact with her birth family and they were nothing like the dreams she had held all those years.

There are three main benefits to adopted children having contact with birth family:

1. **It helps with identity formation.** Kids often have a lot of questions about who they are as they grow up, and for adopted kids this extends to who their bio-family is.

2. **Real information is important.** In the absence of real information, children will invent information, so it's very important that they get real information.

3. **Your children seeing you embrace their bio-family makes them feel better having you identify that part of them.** Your adopted and foster kids will, for better or worse, identify with their bio-family as part of themselves. How you treat their bio-family gives them a road map on how to treat themselves.

There are some caveats, however. There are times when bio-family isn't safe, or the parent has psychological problems that create a higher than tolerable level of anxiety with the child. Many times bio-family has some problems;

otherwise they would be caring for the child themselves. But if visiting is causing psychological harm and efforts to remedy it haven't helped (including getting a professional involved), then don't insist on it. Sometimes if bio-mom or
bio-dad isn't safe, there can at least be a grandma or an aunt that is, and that
can be helpful too.

Fifty years ago most adoptions were closed, and there were very few mech-
anisms for adopted children to make contact with bio-family. Nowadays, there
has been a definite shift toward the model of open adoption, with children
having regular contact with bio-family where possible. There are pros and
cons to this shift, however. And the adoptive parents have to be dedicated to
the contact with the bio-family; if they are not on board, the contact won't
happen. In the group I work with, some of my colleagues run a group for birth
mothers, and the most common situation for the birth moms is no contact
with the child they placed for adoption, even if there is a legal adoption agreement in place. This is so sad, as this is something that is truly a benefit for the
adopted child.

Adoptive parents that do see the value of their child having a relationship
with birth parents have a lot of hoops to jump through to get there—both
logistically and emotionally.[1] Here are some ways that adoptive and foster parents can help make visits with bio-family easier and better for kids:

1. Insist on common adoption or foster care language. Language really
   matters, and it's important that the terms are consistent. The implications for calling someone a "real mother" versus a "birth mother" can
   be painful for everyone involved, and it's a hurt that doesn't need to
   happen. See chapter 17 for a handy chart for some of the most common
   terms.

2. Help facilitate an activity. Often bio-family might not know how to
   interact with the child in an age-appropriate way, so provide an activity
   or game for them to do. Even over Skype this is an option, or have a list
   of things the child wants to tell them about. For young children they
   can read a story or sing a song that they liked as a child as well.

3. Agree ahead of time what topics will be off limits if there's been a history of problematic behavior. Topics such as placement changes, court
   cases, abuse allegations, and so on can all be a part of this list that

is agreed upon. Also agree what happens if these topics come up—generally, the visit ends.

4. Timeliness can be a struggle when the visits start. A good solution to this is to have the visit somewhere fun so the child can play and have fun and not fret if someone is late.

5. If your child becomes dysregulated with the visit, pay attention to when it is and troubleshoot it. A common time for dysregulation is at the end. Is there a way to make good-byes better? Can you end the visit with something sensory and fun like popsicles or blowing bubbles? Help model happy good-byes, but also state that it's okay to be sad as well. If you know when, talk about the next time you will see bio-family.

6. Have an aftercare plan if your child dysregulates during the visit. Usually an evening of movies, snuggles, and popcorn can regulate almost any kid, or maybe some good sweaty time on the trampoline or in a swimming pool. Make a plan ahead of time, let your child know what the plan is, and then execute it. Also have an emergency backup plan for if the visit was particularly dysregulating.

For several years our kids were required to do visits with bio-family that were very dysregulating for them, and it took us a few years to find the magic formula to make them the best possible scenario. If it was a particularly bad visit, I would go and sit with the kids, sometimes for hours, just letting them regulate and talk and cry until they felt like they could return home. The aftercare often involved milk shakes. Our job was to help them regulate, to be their ally, and to provide comfort and support. Often when children are in the system, their voices aren't being taken seriously, as I have seen in my practice when children are forced to visit parents who have abused them and will sometimes continue to threaten them during mandated visits. As a foster parent it can be frustrating because it feels as if there's nothing we can do. The truth is there's a great deal we can do, but what we do has to do more with support and aftercare.

TALKING WITH
YOUR CHILD ABOUT
ADOPTION

HOPEFULLY GONE IS the expectation of old that the child grows up in ignorance of their adoption and at some point around eighteen there's a serious talk where information is revealed. Study after study has shown that the best thing for a child is to be raised with full knowledge of their adoption and to reveal details in an age-appropriate manner. But there are still a lot of questions parents usually have about when and how much and how to do it, so this chapter is designed to help with some of those practical details.

First of all, adoption should always be talked about in adoption-positive language. Language is important, which you will feel if someone asks your child who their "real" mother is or if your child hears you tell the doctor something about them compared to "your own" child. This language can also change over time—my child who came at two differentiated me as "pink mama" as compared to "brown mama" at the time, and now in her tween world she uses what she sees as more dignified terminology. Here's a chart with some ideas and language that other people use to get you started thinking:

INSTEAD OF SAYING:	ADOPTION-POSITIVE TERM:
"give up for adoption"	"place for adoption" or "make an adoption plan"
"real parents" or "real family"	"birth family," "bio-family," "first family," "tummy mommy"
"Your mom lost you because of her addiction."	"Your mom struggled with addiction, so a judge decided that you needed somewhere safer to live."
"natural child," "my own child"	"birth child," "bio-child"
"keep her child"	"choose to parent her child"
"is adopted"	"was adopted"
"reunion"	"make contact with"
"adoptive parent"	"parent, mom, or dad"
"take away"	"terminate parental rights"
"My kids are adopted," or "These are my foster kids."	"I am an adoptive (or foster) parent."

It's important that kids know the story that you bring to adoption. Tell how excited you were when you first found out your child was coming, when you first met them, and how much you had hoped and dreamed for them. It's sort of like recounting dating and your wedding in your marriage; those early feelings can be very powerful and make the child feel very wanted. If there's pain of infertility as part of the story, when the child gets older, you can be honest about some of that pain. If the story doesn't involve infertility but involves a desire to adopt for other reasons, be age-appropriate but honest about those too.

For babies adopted at birth with an adoption plan created by their bio-parents, it's important for them to know that the plan was made by their parents in love. This is easier if they have some contact with bio-parents and know them to be loving people. The basic information should be something along the lines of, "Your parents didn't feel that they could take care of you very well, and wanted you to have a happy life with good parents. They (or she) carefully selected the parents they (or she) thought would be best for you."

For children adopted at an older age, things are a bit more complicated. Kids in this position will sometimes feel stolen or kidnapped, and this can complicate their ability to attach to foster and adoptive parents. It's very important that the story that they hear follows this basic pattern (change as appropriate for their situation), "People were concerned that your parents weren't able to care for you very well, so police and social workers checked on you. A judge had to decide if your parents were able to take care of you, and she (or he) decided that you weren't safe, and needed to be removed. The judge then gave your parents a list of things to do in order to get custody of you again. They weren't able to do this because of their addiction, so the judge decided that the best thing for you was to be adopted by a family that could be your forever family." It's important that the child realize that the judge makes the decisions about placement, not the parents. And that decision is made before they find potential adoptive parents.

It is really helpful for children to have a reason why they are in foster care, because if they don't know why, they will make up their own reasons. I've worked in several cases where the child doesn't know about the reason why they are in foster care, and they tend to blame themselves. Instead of blaming their parent's drug addiction, the child will think they're a bad kid or blame the fact that they get in trouble at school, told someone about the abuse, or that they struggle with encopresis. It can often be a relief for a child to find out that their being in foster care is not their fault at all, and is decided by a judge that has nothing to do with them.

Whatever you tell your child, they should know everything by the age of twelve. Share age-appropriate details with the child as they grow, but by age twelve, they should know everything you know. There are very few exceptions to this rule, and those are usually in the interests of the child's safety. For example, I worked with a family that didn't tell a child a birth father's name because of his involvement with a dangerous gang, and they were worried for the child's safety if he impulsively tried to contact him. There are several reasons for telling children information by twelve, one being that you want your child to know the information before they reach the angsty age of differentiation that is thirteen and fourteen. Eleven- and twelve-year-olds still trust their parents and will process with their parents more than their friends, making this the ideal age. So, if you know that the child was the baby of a prostitute that took meth, then when they are little, you explain that their birth mom had a lot of problems and wanted her baby to be somewhere safe. As they get older you can explain that she didn't have good support and maybe start explaining drug use. But by eleven or twelve, you should give them all the details, emphasizing that though she did make bad choices (drugs), she was also in a really difficult position. Convey compassion for the birth mom, but don't sugarcoat reality to the point of obscuring the truth.

Explaining addiction can be pretty challenging to children sometimes, but it is vitally important. Here's how I usually do it: Sometimes people take drugs because they're sad or hurt and they're trying to feel better. Drugs sometimes make you feel better for a little while, but when you take them, something happens called addiction. When someone is addicted to a drug, that drug becomes more important than anything else in their life—more than the people they love, more than eating, more than anything. The problem when someone who has an addiction becomes a parent is that it's impossible to be a good parent when you have an addiction. When you're addicted, it's incredibly hard to stop using the drug, and you can't stop using it without a lot of help from doctors; this help is called rehab.

Another thing to be thinking about in the grand scheme of working with birth family is thinking about social media. Facebook has changed the level of privacy even available or expected in adoption. Every parent needs to be realistic about this, because it's much better to be realistic about this rather than let it catch you off guard. It's not an uncommon scenario for my practice to have a family bring an adolescent into my office because the child is having some behavioral problems, and they swear that the child has no access to social media. It doesn't usually surprise me when I'm talking to the teenager that they not only have a Facebook account that they made on their friend's phone on the bus, but that they've made contact with several members of their bio-family. Many kids tend to be intensely curious about bio-family, and often they are more curious about siblings than they are about parents. And be prepared for more relatives than just parents—there could be cousins, aunts, and uncles looking for the child on social media.

18

LIFEBOOKS
Not Just for the Crafty

IF YOU ARE THE TYPE of person who is waiting with bated breath and seven different types of dye-cut shapes and a stack of scrapbooking paper, then this is the chapter for you. If you don't know what exactly archival paper is and can't remember the last time you printed out an actual paper copy of a photograph, this chapter is for you as well. This is the chapter where we talk about lifebooks, and the many forms they come in, and the functions they perform for adopted and foster kids.

A lifebook is a physical record for a child of their life—usually from birth to either present or to adoption. A lifebook isn't something that is meant to be kept on a shelf—it is meant to be handled and for a child to use as a reference to help make sense of their lives and their story. The lifebook should be accessible to the child, preferably on a shelf in their bedroom if they can be trusted not to destroy books. It's better if they don't have to ask for it, but can bring it out any time they have a question or want to see the pictures.

There are several ways to go about this, and only really a few essential ingredients that must be there. The first decision about a lifebook is whether you make the book for them or whether the child participates in making it with you. It sounds like it would be a good craft project to do with your child, and many people attempt to make it with their child if they have an older child. Then, when things become difficult, they don't understand why. But let me put it into another context: picture yourself after the death of a spouse. Let's say you had a friend that was chipper and happy and wanted to make a scrapbook about your spouse's life. Do you feel the fear and the grief? Now imagine a friend handing you a book they had made about your spouse, saying that they had made you a gift of pictures of your spouse, and you can look at them when you were ready. Now doing a lifebook isn't exactly the same as doing a scrapbook of your deceased spouse, but it is something to do with grief as well. Doing a lifebook can be triggering; I've done them in therapy with children many times and have worked through the emotions that arose from them.

The next decision you need to make is what kind you want to make. Here are some options:

Scrapbook-style: If you are a crafty person and like scrapbooking, then doing one in that style will seem pretty fun. Make it fun and colorful; it's easy to include memorabilia and trinkets as well.

Pros: It can include memorabilia; very customizable; fun and colorful; you can add pages.

Cons: It can be expensive if you don't have proper equipment already; not easily replaceable; takes a long time to make.

Tips: Don't use original documents; scan or copy things instead, laminate pages, or use plastic sleeves on pages to protect them.

Printed book: This is a book that you can have printed anywhere, from Shutterfly to Costco Photo, and making it is a matter of downloading some photos, clicking and moving some photos around, and sending it off to print.

Pros: Expenses vary; fairly inexpensive for Costco, and prices go up from there, although layouts are easier on other formats. It is relatively fast and easy, and if one gets destroyed, it's easy to print a backup.

Cons: You can't add memorabilia.

Tips: Prices vary widely; shop around for the best price.

Low-key creation: If money is more of a concern, you can create a low-key sort of book with very little money invested, with just a printer and copying some pictures. You can use predesigned pages and just fill them out and paste pictures on them, or just create some pages based on my suggestions here. Then you can clip the pages in a three-ring binder or have them bound together at FedEx Office. There's a lot of great Web pages to help. Here's one I really like, from the Iowa Foster & Adoptive Parents Association: https://tinyurl.com/rjcexkz.

Pros: The least expensive option, very flexible, can add pages.

Cons: Cheaper looking, less sturdy.

Tips: Laminate or cover with plastic sleeves to make it more sturdy; don't use original documents, but scan or copy instead.

Contents of a Lifebook

Contents of a lifebook will vary for the child. For instance, a child adopted at birth will have a much different lifebook than a child who has been in ten foster homes before adoption. Sometimes lifebooks can be tricky if significant information isn't known about the child, as is sometimes the case with international adoptions. So read the list of contents of a lifebook as a list of suggestions, and customize it to your family and your needs.

Birth family tree: This can be a great way to help the child sort out who is who in the birth family. You don't have to go back beyond grandparents unless it's helpful. Sometimes the existence of siblings or other information like that is information parents wait to share until the child is older, or sometimes there is a lack of information. It's okay to skip this one if you're uncomfortable.

Birth family pictures: Any pictures you have of birth family are great to have in here. A lot of adoptive families find Facebook can be a great source of pictures for this purpose. Make sure you use neutral language descriptions, such as "But Timothy's first mom wasn't able to care for him, so she made a plan for him to be adopted and raised in a safe and loving family."

Birth page: List information about the child's birth—things like their weight, length, where they were born, and a birth certificate or footprint if you have it. Again, don't use originals; use copies.

Coming home page: If adopted at birth, put in pictures of what it was like at first when the child came home.

Official adoption day: If adopted at birth, there is usually a day where it becomes official after birth. Include pictures!

Foster story: For a child who was not adopted at birth, try to track their story as best as you can. If there is a foster home that you cannot find a picture for, the child can draw a picture. Try as well as you can to represent their journey through the foster system. Always make sure that you portray that it is the judge that is making decisions about where a child is placed, and it's always about the child being safe. For instance, this is how you could phrase a removal: "When Sarah was two, the judge decided that where she lived wasn't safe, and she was placed with Bob and Maryanne, a foster family, where she lived for a year. They lived in a green house and had a brown dog named Oreo."

Tips:

* Make sure that the book is easily available to the child, and don't try to limit their viewing of it.

* The content is more important than the artistic nature, but having some fun colors and stickers will make it more engaging for the child.

* Make sure you use adoption-positive language in how you describe events (see chapter 17 for talking with your children about adoption or questions). Don't sugarcoat events, but be kind as well.

* Never write anything that isn't true or use confusing euphemisms. It's better to use the word *addiction* than to use the word *sick* because if you use the word *sick* for why a parent couldn't take care of a child, if you catch pneumonia, the child could think a social worker might take them away.

Examples:

These are example scripts you can use in a lifebook. You would normally use a sentence or two per page, along with pictures—either digitally taken or drawn. In writing a newspaper article, the six questions you are trying to answer are *who, what, where, when, why,* and *how.* Think of those questions when you are writing your child's lifebook.

For an easily triggered child or if the story is really horrific: If the story is really traumatic and you think the child might be really triggered, or if you just can't figure out how to make the story work, it's okay to not have much of a storyline, and just have pictures of people and places. For this type of story, you tell it more as you look through it together. You can edit people out if they are not the primary parent and if they were a primary abuser. If Uncle Joe raped your child, there is no reason to include his picture. If Mom or Dad was an abuser, ask your child if they'd like their picture in the book, but don't be surprised if the answer is yes. The book is a safe place for a picture like that to be—it is closed most of the time, and can be picked up when they are ready. You can also tape a flap of paper over pictures—let kids move the paper up when they're ready. You can also not have a picture of a person altogether, though it is rarer that that's what a child wants.

Baby born addicted: This is an example of what the text could be for a child:

> *Cheyenne was born on June 25, 2011, at Swedish Hospital in Seattle to her first mom, Brenda. She weighed 5 pounds, 3 ounces. When she was born, she was born sick because her mom was addicted to drugs, and a judge decided for her to go to a special type of foster home that helps kids that are born to addicted mothers. Cheyenne's first foster mother was Mama Katie, who was a nurse and took care of babies in her home. Cheyenne stayed there for three months. When she was there, she learned to use a bottle like other babies, and she grew strong. Then, when she was ready, she moved to her forever home with Mommy and Daddy. Mommy and Daddy were so excited to have Cheyenne come home to them, but they weren't sure if they were going to be able to adopt Cheyenne. Cheyenne had visits with Mama Brenda for a year, and then the judge made the decision that he thought it would be best for Cheyenne to be adopted. Mama Brenda agreed to the adoption because she realized that she wasn't going to be able to take care of Cheyenne, and Mama Brenda, Mommy, and Daddy agreed that she could have visits, phone calls, and letters as Cheyenne grows up. Mommy and Daddy adopted Cheyenne on September 19, 2012, and they changed her middle name to Ella after Daddy's grandmother.*

Now, there has to be interpretation for her as some of the terms, like *addiction*, might be complicated, but this is a basic construct for telling the child her story.

A child with extensive foster care experience: The biggest key here is that the story explains the movements and removes the shame behind them. Here's an example of how to do it:

> Carson was born on Nov. 14, 2011, at Mary Bridge Hospital in Tacoma. He was 6 pounds, 5 ounces at birth. Carson went home from the hospital with his first mother, Tina, and his first father, Jonathan. Carson's family moved around a lot when he was little, and sometimes lived with his mother's mother, his grandmother Aimee. Sometimes he would stay with Grandma Aimee when his parents left. Then, when Grandma Aimee died when he was two, Carson's parents started having more trouble.
>
> When Carson was three, a judge decided that it wasn't safe for Carson to live with his family anymore, so he was placed with Scott and Jamie Smith. He lived with them for a few months, but they are a special foster home that only has kids for a short time to get them ready for a longer home. Carson then moved to live with Andrew and Alissa Brown, who lived in a white house. Andrew and Alissa had two daughters who were older than Carson, and they all played together on a trampoline. Carson lived with the Browns for a year, and during that time he visited his parents.
>
> Sadly, Andrew and Alissa had to move away because of Andrew's job, and they couldn't take Carson with them because they couldn't adopt Carson yet. Everyone was very sad; the girls cried a lot and the Browns wished they could take Carson with them. Carson went to live with Beth Angelo, who lived in an apartment by a really fun park. Carson was very sad about the Browns, so he felt sad and angry sometimes, and it was hard for him to like Beth very much, even though she seemed nice. He was with Beth about six months when his social worker, Michael, said that they had found an aunt that wanted to try having him.
>
> Carson moved in with his Aunt Miriam and was there for one year. Sadly his Aunt Miriam dated a man named Tim who was not a safe person for Carson. Carson was very brave and told his teacher at school that Tim was hurting him, and so a judge decided that Carson should go live with Katherine and Pat.
>
> While Carson lived with Katherine and Pat, the judge decided that Carson should be adopted because mama Tina and daddy Jonathan were not going to be able to care for him. Katherine and Pat decided that they wanted to

adopt Carson, so they became his forever family. Katherine and Pat had two other children older than Carson, a boy and a girl, so Carson is now the youngest in his family!

AN INTERNATIONAL ADOPTION:

When Faith was born, she was born in Addis Ababa, Ethiopia, on August 27, 2015. Faith was found on the porch of a police station when she was newly born. Her birth parents did not leave any notes, but left her somewhere safe where they knew she would be found quickly. We don't know why they weren't able to parent her, but we know that they cared for her because she was left somewhere safe where she would be found quickly, and she was found wrapped carefully in a soft blanket so she would be comfortable. The police officer who found her named her Emnet, which means "faith" in Amharic.

Faith was taken to the orphanage, where she lived for about a year. In the orphanage she was taken care of by nannies, and she especially liked a nanny named Hana. When Faith was a year old, Mommy and Daddy met her for the first time! They flew to Ethiopia and stayed for two weeks, filling out paperwork and spending time with their new daughter. Mommy and Daddy felt really sad when they had to go back to the US without Faith, but the law said they couldn't take her home yet.

Four months later, Mommy and Daddy were able to come back, and this time when it was time for them to leave, they brought Faith home with them! These are pictures of their driver, Baraket, who helped them while they were in Addis Ababa, and here's a picture of the orphanage director, Saron. This is a picture of the police station where Faith was found, and a picture of Faven, another child Faith's age that she liked to play with in the orphanage. Faven was adopted by a family that lives in Texas.

When Faith returned home with her new mommy and daddy, Grandma and Grandpa met them at the airport with snacks and warm blankets, because it was February and Faith wasn't used to cold weather! But Faith soon got used to her new home.

A lifebook is a great gift to give your child, something they can tangibly look at and use to make sense of their life and their story. It's also a way to show that you are at peace with their story, you welcome conversation about their trauma and their past, and that it is safe to talk about.

If you don't have enough information for a lifebook, you can do something with whatever you do have—whether it's a framed picture, a poster, or a time-line. The point is to make their story safe to talk about and accessible to them. It's less about whether or not you are good at making a scrapbook.

PART 4

Living and Thriving with PTSD

19

THE CHILD YOU HAVE

THIS IS GOING to be the most controversial chapter in the book, so if you're easily offended, maybe give this one a pass. Whether you are conservative, liberal, or some wacky hybrid of the two, these can be touchy issues. While I have tried very hard to address them with gentleness and dignity, it is a little bit like trying to tiptoe through a mousetrap factory. At the very least, before reading this chapter, take a deep breath, center yourself, and say whatever calming mantra helps you through hard situations. My goal is not to offend but to prepare. Trust me, in the art of raising children, there is much greater offense lying in wait for you. And we are about to talk about everything my mother said not to bring up in polite company.

There is a difference between the child you dream about and the child that ends up in your house, and this is true whether you adopt, foster, or give birth. I remember when I first had the dream of adopting from Ethiopia—I dreamed of a snuggly baby with fluffy hair and round cheeks. Instead, our Ethiopian child was a nearly eleven years old with wide eyes and a ready smile. When I dreamed of the children coming from the Democratic Republic of Congo, I thought of children who would be scared and need comfort and reassurance—I had not dreamed that that fear would express itself in yelling at us and barricading themselves in their room. I expected a starving child to eat everything given to them, not to be picky about what I served.

What was your dreams about the child coming into your home? Was it of a frightened foster kid that needed hugs and love? Was it of a baby you could cuddle and nurture? Was it of a child who would grow up to be just like you?

A big part of raising our children can be wanting them to be like us. One of my children, a daughter I gave birth to, had broken the training wheels on her bike. She seemed to be doing really well on her bike, her balance was good, so instead of getting her new training wheels, we decided to have her try her bike without training wheels. The other kids had learned relatively quickly and without training wheels, so we thought she'd do the same. My husband and I also enjoy riding, so we thought it would be easy. With some instruction and a bit of a push, we figured she would take to it easily. How incredibly wrong we were. She rode down the gentle slope by our house, completely terrified, and crashed at the bottom. It took us two years to get her on a bike again, and this time we were much more careful to recognize the child we actually have—one that was a bit more nervous about riding a bike—rather than the one we thought we had.

In any relationship, be it marriage, friendship, or partnership, maturity comes when you can recognize the person for who they really are and not who you want them to be. The same is even truer and even trickier when you think about your child. We have a very false idea that we can mold and shape our children into exactly what we want—although hopefully this gets disabused sometime in the terrible twos. Children are people with their own personalities, likes, dislikes, experiences, and perspectives. Yes, our role as parents is to shape and to guide; but more importantly our role is to help them to become the best one of them they can become, not something else entirely. If you have an anxious child, you cannot parent them out of being anxious—your job is to give them tools and strategies to help with their anxiety. If you have a dream of coaching soccer and your child is far more interested in karate, you have to come to terms with the fact that your child is not there to fulfill your dream of coaching their soccer team. You can still coach soccer; their participation is not necessary. But you can't force your child to love soccer to fulfill your dream of coaching soccer—you need to not only let them do karate, but show up at tournaments and cheer for them. Even if it makes you very sad—you dreamed about coaching your child's soccer team since you were a kid!—there really is very little alternative that's going to work. If you try to bribe or force them to play soccer, they will end up resenting you, and soccer, and you won't get what you want anyway. It's better, as gracefully as you can, to let them choose the sport they want to play.

The psychological term for this idea of recognizing a person for who they are, separate from you, is called differentiation. Differentiation is healthy; it is necessary for healthy identity formation for children; and it will take a lot out of you as a parent. You have the opinions you have as opinions because you think they're right—so it is irksome when someone has another opinion or belief structure, and you want them to agree with you. And so much of parenting is about instilling better information into the belief system of your child—no, jellybeans are not a good breakfast option. People aren't for hitting. Always tell the truth even if it gets you in trouble. So it can be hard to let the child develop their own identity separate from your own.

When you enter into adoption, foster care, and trauma, these issues become even trickier because often kids come from backgrounds and cultures different than your own. There are areas that feel like morality, right and wrong, politics, religion, background, culture, and identity all rolled into one. How do you differentiate as a parent which are areas you insist upon and which are areas that you let children sort out their own identities? This is not as easy as it sounds. Some choices might be easy for you; others might push your buttons. They might even fish for options that would push your buttons. But the single most important tool that a foster and adoptive parent can bring to the table is a radical sense of differentiation and acceptance—the idea that this child is their own person, and that you will accept and love whomever this child is meant to be.

"Will you still love me if I rob a bank?" my sixteen-year-old daughter asks. It's a game we play sometimes, where she asks questions to see if there's any situation that would make me not love her. It makes her feel safer, so I play along.

"I'll come visit you in prison," I promise her. "I'll bring you cookies."

"What if I kill someone?"

"Well, I'll be pretty sad," I admit. "But I'll still visit you. I don't think they'll let me bring you cookies in maximum security."

"What about if I'm gay?" she asks. "What if I marry a woman?"

I was surprised by this question, but I wanted to make sure that I handled it appropriately. She had never given me a hint that she was gay, but if this was a precursor to coming out, then I wanted to make sure she felt supported. She comes from an African culture that has very low tolerance for homosexuality, and she has enough contact with that culture to recognize that.

"I'll always love you no matter what," I assured her.

"Will you still help pay for my wedding?" she asked.

Ah, the real question. She dreamed of weddings, planned her wedding dress, and couldn't wait to be a bride despite her young age.

My husband jumped into the conversation: "Only under certain circumstances."

"Which are?" she pressed. "Do I have to marry a man?"

"We never said that," my husband answered firmly. "We've always said the same thing: that we have to meet the person you marry, and they have to treat you well. We won't help pay for a wedding for anybody who doesn't treat you with respect. It doesn't matter if they are a man or a woman; it matters how they treat you."

She thought for a few minutes, then said, "I'm not gay, just so you know. I just wanted to know if you were homophobic."

"Okay," I answered, trying not to be offended that she thought we were homophobic. "But Dad was serious: the thing we want the most for you guys with a future spouse is someone that respects and loves you. We've seen people we love marry people who were abusive, and that would break our hearts if that happened to you."

In that story, my daughter wanted to see in which scenario we would not accept her, and if there were boundaries on her developing identity. We were clear that there were boundaries—but the boundaries weren't around the gender of who she dated, but rather what kind of person they were. She's seen the heartbreak of people we love and abusive spouses; she knows what we're talking about when we reference them, and why we would take a stance as drastic as not paying for her wedding to try and keep her from making that mistake.

In the end, with your children, you don't get to choose the lifestyle they lead but rather you choose how much relationship you have with them. And there are of course boundaries that would make it hard for you to be in relationship with your child—perhaps drug use or illegal activities. But what about the others? If you are completely fine with your child coming out as gay, how would you feel about them coming out as a Republican or a member of the NRA? I once sat with a very stereotypically liberal family who were baffled at decisions their son was making, saying, "We would be fine if he wanted to buy a van and play his guitar as he drove around the country finding himself for a few years, but why did he want to join the military?"

I have a list of scenarios, and I've purposely left out the age of the child. Think about what this would be like for you as the parent at different stages, at different places in the child's life. Think about how you would handle each of the following scenarios:

- Child decides they want to become a vegetarian.

- Child decides they want to go on a calorie restrictive diet.

- Child decides they want to get a Mohawk.

- Child decides they want to cut their hair short or grow their hair long.

- Child wants to dye their hair green.

- Child decides they support a political candidate you detest.

- Child posts "black lives matter" on their Facebook page.

- Child posts "all lives matter" on their Facebook page.

- Child decides that they want to quit all sports.

- Child decides they want to quit all activities.

- Child decides they want to start dating someone.

- Child decides they don't want to have children.

- Child decides they want to join the NRA.
- Child decides they want to join another religion.

Those were some ideas to get you thinking, but for most kids there will be many, many scenarios in which there will be differentiation happening that you will have to adapt to. There may be grief for you as the parent in this, and recognizing that grief as your grief and not putting that burden on the child is critical to allowing the child to form their own identity.

"Mom, I don't want to do dance anymore," my daughter told me.

"Really?" I answered, a bit surprised. She had been in so many different dance options, from ballet to jazz to Scottish Highland dancing, that I was surprised it would actually come down to her not doing it any more.

"Yeah," she answered. "I think after this recital I'm done."

"That makes me kind of sad," I acknowledged, feeling it surprisingly acutely. "I've enjoyed watching you dance over the years. But I can understand. I've seen that you've enjoyed it less this year."

"Yeah," she agreed.

"Is there any other dance that you want to try?" I ask, probably a little too hopeful.

"Why do you want me to do dance?" she asked.

"Well, I told you before," I answered honestly. "When I was a girl I wanted to take dance lessons, and my parents wouldn't let me. So I guess that I wanted you to have them because I wanted them. But that's kind of silly if you don't really want them, so you don't have to have them if you don't want them."

"Good."

"Well, you know our family policy about doing some activity that trains your body," I reminded her. "What were you thinking about trying next?"

"Fencing?" she asked hopefully.

"Um, I don't know where to find that," I laughed. "If you can find where to do that, we can talk about it. Otherwise, do you want to join

> the tae kwon do class that your brother is doing, at least for now? It looks pretty fun."
>
> "Okay, I'll try it."

This story illustrates the basic conflicts that happen whenever a child starts establishing interests and identity different than what the parent has planned for them. There's the parent's desire, the child's resistance, the discussion of feelings, and hopefully some sort of resolution. How else could it have gone as a parent? If she wanted to quit that week, I could have reasonably insisted that she wait until after the recital, or to the end of the sports season. But insisting that she continue with dance when it's clearly not her love would harm both our relationship in forcing her to go, and her relationship with dance—she would grow to hate it. If my desire is for her to like dance, forcing her into it would not be the way to go about it. It's important to acknowledge your own grief in the differentiation, as well as your story and what you have brought to the interaction. In the rest of this chapter I'll highlight some of the hot-button situations that tend to hit this button harder than most others.

Ethics Versus Identity

One really helpful way to think about differentiation is that our job as parents is to teach ethics and responsibility; our child's job is to form their identity. There are many external factors that help a child form their identity—where they live, what friends they have, what interests they end up exploring—but how they eventually identify is actually going to be up to them. We as parents need to decide what is identity and what is ethics and responsibility. Some of it is pretty easy—nobody reasonable would think their child's identity is now as someone who doesn't shower, or doesn't do homework. And some identities are easy to identify—such as if your child wants to become a vegetarian. One good rule of thumb for an identity is if there's room for ethics and responsibility within the identity—such as teaching a budding vegetarian about getting the proper protein combinations and adequate vitamins. Your child who is exploring her identity as an anime artist may need help with not letting it interfere with her homework or being able to take criticism. You can also recognize the child's emerging identity and help them get there in a healthier way, such as "I see that you are wanting to work on having a healthier body. So that celebrity fad Master Cleanse thing is probably not a good idea unless the doctor okays it. But I'm happy to help you figure out how to get more exercise into your day. And I'd love to be buying more fruits and veggies if you'd eat them. Would you like to come to the fruit market with me and pick some out?"

When something is a question of ethics, you can have influence and help your child make a better, more ethical choice. When it is a question of identity, then it is not something that you can change for your child, and it would be harmful if you tried. For example, a study found that for LGBTQ children whose parents sought what is called "conversion therapy"—or therapy to change their sexual orientation or identity—when compared to their LGBTQ peers that did not undergo this type of therapy, they had three to five times the rate of suicide, higher rates of depression, lower educational attainment, and as adults, lower weekly income.[1] This was a study done with typical kids, not foster or adopted kids, and clearly trying to change their core identity didn't change anything—it just caused them distress and harm. This is why conversion therapy has been banned in many states, and most health and psychological organizations have made statements against both its effectiveness and the ethics of using it. When you try to change someone's core identity, you end up not changing anything, but instead making them feel depressed and anxious about who they are.

A really extreme example of this is in my first job out of college, which was working with schizophrenics. The first rule of working with schizophrenics is to not correct their delusions, which can be really hard when, say, a person believes that there are micro-persons living in his collarbone. It is natural to want to "correct" the person, to help them see "reality" and assume that they will get "better" if they learn to recognize their delusion. But the thing is, their delusions are so real to them, and the experience of this person's micro-persons living in his collar bone is so irrefutable, that if you call into question his reality, he won't question his micro-persons, he will question you and not trust you. So, instead of telling the person, "You're wrong, what you're experiencing isn't real," you say, "Wow, tell me more about what it's like to have micro-persons living in your collarbone." Obviously schizophrenia is a psychological pathology, and the other examples I'm using in this chapter aren't, but I used this example to show how important it is to respect other's identity and how it's possible to have a respectful and supportive conversation even if you don't experience the same reality as the other person.

This seems great as long as the child's identity is something reasonably compatible with the family's existing culture, but what about when the child seems to be forming an identity that can be at serious odds with their family culture? Here are four areas I have seen in my practice and in my family where the forming of identity in a kid has been challenging for the parent.

LGBTQ

Lesbian, gay, bisexual, transgender, queer, and questioning (LGBTQ) kids are one of the most vulnerable populations currently in foster care. I understand if this section is not for you, either for religious or personal reasons, so feel free to skip ahead. But if you're able to tolerate thinking and reading about this issue, what our world needs is more caregivers that are sensitive to the needs of children with this identity. Before we start, it might be a good idea to think about what you bring to the table with this topic—is this an area where you harbor feelings of judgment, fear, misgivings, and worry? It's always better to be honest about your feelings; you can't make feelings go away by ignoring them, but instead by acknowledging and working through them. And you can't be a good ally for your LGBTQ child if your feelings of fear and judgment hold you back from being able to fully engage with them.

A child's sexual orientation and identity are areas where a parent's upbringing, religious background, political beliefs, and culture can all come together and make for one really complicated intersection. This is definitely where the child you had dreamed about and the child you have can come into sharp relief—and for some parents the process of grief can be very real. If you are wanting to be a parent, let alone a foster or adoptive parent, you have to grapple deeply with the idea that the child you are raising is a person separate from you and may differ from you in key areas, sexuality included. And this work should be done before a child is in your house, because the child in your house needs you to be present and supportive to them rather than paralyzed or judgmental. To adopt or foster a child in your home is opening yourself to taking a child and choosing to be supportive and loving to them no matter what.

This particular intersection of politics, religion and culture has been very hard on traumatized kids in care. Kids in foster care or other unstable housing between the ages of ten and eighteen identify as LGBTQ at about three times the rate as kids in the general population.[2] Twenty percent of homeless youth identify as LGBTQ, with the majority of them (75 percent) citing family rejection over their sexual identity as the reason for their homelessness, and for transgender youth that percentage jumps to 90 percent.[3] Though homeless youth are not always the same population as those in foster care, their populations overlap. And for children in foster care, their sexuality or identity has been part of their story of why they are in care (such as rejection by their bio-family), and sometimes their identity has been a source of abuse by family members, their community, and even previous foster homes. LGBTQ youth in care receive fewer options for permanent placements, which means that more end up in group homes and aging out of the system.[4] And when they do get foster homes, it might not be that great either—one study based in New York even found that an incredible 78 percent of LGBTQ teens have been removed or ran away from a foster placement due to anti-LGBTQ violence or harassment from their foster parents.[5] This is horrifying to read—it is truly shocking that trained caregivers would inflict harassment on kids that are already so vulnerable. One study found,

> *LGBTQ youth in care experience the same vulnerabilities as other youth. But their vulnerabilities are compounded by the high levels of abuse and rejection they often experience in their families, their placements, among their peers, in their schools, and in their communities. This can have profound consequences for their mental and physical health.[6]*

But research has also identified the one thing that LGBTQ youth in foster care need the most—and that's the care and support of their foster or adoptive parents. One researcher writes, "Findings suggest that foster family acceptance plays a pivotal role in creating an affirming and inclusive environment for LGBTQ youth."[7] Children that identify as LGBTQ that are in care need kind, understanding, and supportive foster and adoptive parents. Research shows that LGBTQ kids have the best outcome when their parents monitor their behavior and communicate with them just as with their more typical peers, but also when they are aware of and support their identity, providing accurate health information. "Supportive and accepting parent-child relationships that are characterized by open, mutual, and low-conflict communication have been found to be associated with better health outcomes, specifically in reducing sexual risk among young gay and bisexual men."[8] For children with trauma and disrupted placements, this can be especially difficult, but it is critical to realize how much they need this support and connection from their caregivers.

So what does care look like for LGBTQ children? Unsurprisingly, it looks very much like good parenting in many other areas. LGBTQ children are people just like other children, and desire dignity, relationship, connection, and to be listened to and understood by their caregivers. PFLAG, an organization that exists to help friends and family of LGBTQ people, suggests for parents of LGBTQ children during the "coming out" process to lead with love (hugs if you can't manage words), listen with intention (asking leading questions to help), and show support to LGBTQ people, either in subtle ways or overtly.[9] Educate yourself and learn more about LGBTQ issues and terminology, and look to sources and people that you trust (you can start with such basic resources as the American Academy of Pediatrics). Also be curious with your child, and don't assume they know that much more than you do—they have probably gotten a lot of their information from friends at school.

But just as it is not the transracially adopted child's job to teach the parents about what it means to be a racial minority, it is also not the LGBTQ child's responsibility to educate the parents on what it means to be a sexual minority either. The child is just learning this too! Parents should seek education and support from other people, and if possible be curious with the child and learn with them. One writer says,

> *Adolescence is a time of exploration. To facilitate healthy identity development, youth need the emotional, psychological, and physical space and support to explore who they are and who they can become. When a foster or adoptive parent accepts a youth into their home, this acceptance means they are willing to fully care for the youth and their needs, which includes accepting their sexual and gender self-expression and identity.*[10]

LGBTQ kids in foster care need what other kids need—connection with a caregiver, safety, stability, and to be loved and enjoyed. It's not their needs that are different than other kids, it is the ability of the system to provide them with parents that are able to give them what they need, and the ability of parents to meet those needs. Every child needs a family, and how a child identifies doesn't change that need.

Gender Expansive and Transgender Kids

It is normal and typical for children to engage in what is called "gender expansive" play, especially in the preschool and early elementary years. This play often looks like a boy wanting pink shoes or to paint his nails, a girl deciding she won't wear dresses, a boy wanting to play princess, a girl saying she wished she could play football or wanting to cut her hair "like a boy," and so on. This is really typical, and the best way to parent it is to simply let it be and let children be children without pressuring them to conform to the mold we have for them.

But for a very small percentage of children, their play isn't just this gender expansive play, but rather something else. They don't say things like, "I wish I was a boy so that I could be on that particular soccer team with Justin," but rather, "I am a boy." If this happens, the child might be transgendered, and this is something else altogether and needs the advice of a professional that specializes in it.[11] It is beyond the scope of this book to deal with the complexities of what to do if you find yourself in that situation, but please seek help if you're concerned that this might be an issue for your child. Transgendered kids need supportive counseling and specific health care.

Adding an interesting twist to this fact is that people self-identifying as transgendered or nonbinary score higher than typical on measurements designed to measure autism and are often undiagnosed with autism, particularly those assigned the female gender at birth.[12] Children in foster care tend to have about double the rate of autism spectrum disorder as the typical population, so this might be part of the reason that the *T* in LGBTQ is over-represented in the foster care system. Not only are transgendered children overrepresented in foster care, they are also particularly vulnerable in it, as they are far more likely to be victimized by their foster family and unfamiliar peers as they move schools—a common cost of foster care. They also report nearly double the rate of suicidal ideation as their non-LGBTQ peers in foster care.[13] Supportive, protective care from an understanding caregiver is critical to these kids, and they are far less likely to get it than their gender-normative peers.

Adopted and foster children identifying as LGBTQ need support, care, and connection just as any other of their peers, as well as caregivers that are able to respect and accept them for who they are.

Religion and Spirituality

My mother always told me that when you were in polite company (anybody who's not your relatives) you should never talk about politics or religion. Those topics were taboo; people were likely to disagree, and there was no way to have a conversation without someone getting offended. Given the reality of politics and religion in our current day and age, this advice seems quaint, but it also does highlight the potential for offense and hurt when you talk about religion. Religion is a tough issue in a lot of ways, because so much of family culture is tied up in religion. This is also a way that children will differentiate from their parents, often to their parents' heartbreak. There's a very old movie called *Mermaids* in which the mom describes her seeking her freedom from her Jewish family on her eighteenth birthday as "holding a cigarette in one hand and a ham sandwich in the other." Children have been eating ham sandwiches for centuries, and seeking out their own spiritual realities and truths is often a part of growing up.

The Amish, a strict Christian sect, allow for their young people to have a season of what they call Rumspringa, when their children aged fourteen to eighteen are allowed freedoms usually not allowed people in their closed community, in order for them to decide, when they reach adulthood, whether they want to be baptized and join the sect or whether they want to leave the community. There is a lot of wisdom in letting children and young adults have some freedom in making these choices for themselves. I don't think it's an accident that in the Jewish religion, age thirteen marks the coming of age with a bat or a bar mitzvah, and the young person's faith becomes their own responsibility. This is the age that kids are able to engage faith, spirituality, and have opinions of their own.

But how do you engage those issues with a child that may be from a different background and culture? Or who may be rejecting your religion and values? These are hard issues to address, and ones that should be done carefully. Part of that also depends on how your family addresses spirituality and how you practice. Are you a family that goes to church, temple, or mosque once a week? Do you do yoga and hike in the woods as your spiritual practice? Do you write "Jedi" on a form that asks you your religion? Do you not have a specific religion and instead think of spiritual practice as altruism? What conversations do you have with your child? Whatever your religion, spirituality, or practice, it is important to communicate that to your child, but also to respect that they might have opinions and ideas too, especially if they are coming to you as an older child.

Being flexible and being in ongoing conversation are going to be key in this process. I have known atheist foster parents to foster devout Ethiopian Orthodox foster children and become somewhat part of that community in support of their foster children. I have seen Christian parents foster Muslim children and talk with local Muslim leaders and parents on how to best support their children's spiritual needs. And I've seen devout parents work out a deal with their doubting teenager that they could volunteer at a food bank instead of attending services with the rest of the family.

The family I was working with was loving, warm, and excited about adopting a young teenager. The only problem they had was that the family was devoutly Christian, and the teenager was devoutly not. The family was trying to be flexible in their thinking, but fretted over expectations, worry, family culture, and how they were going to set expectations with the younger children in the family. Having a slothful teenager stay in bed on Sunday mornings was making the other kids say, "No fair!" and giving him household tasks to do while they were at church felt like punishing him. This placement was moving toward adoption, but the parents were hesitating because of this one issue. They didn't want the child to feel that he had to convert to be adopted, but going to church was a huge part of what they did as a family; so they were torn on how they wanted to handle the situation. We talked about it in session, and the parents went home to do some soul-searching.

The next week, the parents returned, completely changed. "We've figured it out!" they told me excitedly.

"What did you figure out?" I asked, confused.

"The Bible talks about this," the mother explained. "Well, not exactly. But the Bible talks about when you're married to an unbeliever. It says that if the unbeliever is willing to stay married to you and live with you, then you should live with them, and that your job as a Christian is to show them love and your reverence for God. If we just think about Corey as we would think about a nonbelieving spouse, it's kind of the same thing. If he's willing to live with us, then our only job is to love him and practice our faith as best we know how."

"So what does that look like for you guys?" I asked.

"We talked to Corey," they explained. "And basically we're going to go on like we are now, and while we're at church things, he's going to do something for his spiritual life, like take a hike or volunteering or something; whatever feels meaningful to him. And we'll meet up after for lunch."

In the story above, this thought process shows good differentiation, mutual respect, and compassionate compromises for this mixed-faith family. Even though religion is a hot-button issue, it doesn't have to be in your family as long as it's one that is of continued conversation and mutual respect. And here's the real truth—attachment issues make children more prone to reject a family's religion, even if the child has spent the majority of their life with the family. Some families feel a lot of guilt over this, but this guilt is misplaced. It is not your fault, but likely a necessary process. Instead, patient and loving differentiation as described by the family above is a much better way to stay connected with the child.

College, Career, Future

Another area that you may not have thought about hitting a differentiation area for you is college and career. This one hit my husband and me surprisingly hard, even though we'd been previously warned about it. I remember having a conversation with another mom who had fostered international refugees like we do, and she told me about one of her daughters who had struggled a lot in school with various learning difficulties. "She's a nurse's aide now," the mom explained. "She's happy, and the old folks she works with just love her. It's the perfect job for her." I was happy for her, but I knew that was never going to be my children. They were all going to go to college and have professional jobs.

In my family, going to college was a hard-fought battle. My father grew up in a dysfunctional blue-collar family and joined the Navy mainly to escape. He decided his goal was to be able to buy a new car and not a used one, so he then went to college to secure a job that paid well enough to do so. His was the first generation to go to college, and he and his brother both secured middle-class lifestyles. My mother's father grew up on a log cabin in West Virginia, rode the rails west to Washington State at fifteen years of age, found work, and eventually found a program at a college that gave him enough of an accounting and business degree that let him open his own business. College in my family has always been held up as "the thing successful people do." I was focused on going to college from a young age; I took every college prep and AP class I could, happily accepted great scholarships to college, and very much enjoyed college and then eventually (much later) graduate school. To be honest, I would get a PhD if I could figure out how to make it work in my already insanely busy life. So, of course, I assumed each of my kids would get a degree as well, wouldn't they? Even as other members of my family didn't go to college, surely my kids would, of course.

Enter my eldest child, who had come to us at nearly eleven. She was of course capable of it—she struggled a bit in high school but acquitted herself well enough to get into a private college in our city of Seattle. And when my husband and I went through the new student orientation with her, with the parent campus tours and the parent weekends, we were so excited. I had tears in my eyes as I helped her set up her dorm room and left her there for the first time. They were tears of sadness of missing her, but also tears of joy and hope—thinking of her future and dreaming dreams for her.

As you have probably guessed by now, this all came crashing spectacularly down. I will spare you the details, but several of my friends told me during the next several months that "college isn't for everyone" and I found myself hating that phrase. It may not be for everyone, but surely it was for my precious daughter! I wanted her to have the great experiences I had and to have the start in life it would give her! But, as my husband and I became painfully aware, by the time a child is in college, it is also not your choice anymore; and that dream ended. The differentiation was hard and painful, and it made us examine our own thoughts around college and expectations. We didn't realize how much expectation we really had, and how much we wanted this for her. But college couldn't be just our dream, it had to be hers as well; it couldn't be a dream we forced onto her. Maybe that dream will happen again sometime; she will occasionally take a class or think about going back, but I have learned the painful lesson that the power of this dream has to be on her own shoulders and not on mine. And there is truth in that annoying adage that college isn't for everyone. So we celebrate the job she has, we commiserate with her about the job she wants and isn't qualified to have without a degree without saying "I told you so," and we let her choose what she wants to pursue her goals.

What are your expectations and dreams that you bring to your child about their future? Maybe college isn't the hill you stake your dreams on, but how about being a grandparent? You won't be able to force your child to have a child if they don't want to, but you can sure do a lot of damage to your relationship. What are your dreams that are hard to give up in respect to your child? College? Career? Marriage? Parenthood? Body image? Many a parent has wanted their offspring to have at least as good if not better a body, career, marriage, and life than we have. It is far better to be honest to yourself before these dreams cause damage in the relationship to your child.

The good news is that there is a child you think you want and a child that you have. The child that we think we want, however, isn't a real person at all, but more like you're playing with a doll. The child you have is a real, breathing, thinking person that will teach you more than you ever thought you'd learn from them. The child you have will certainly be more of a challenge, of course, but that challenge comes with the sweetness of knowing and connecting with a real person on the other end, not a creation of our own agendas. If your child right now is an infant and you think you are the most liberal and open-minded person imaginable and can't imagine how this differentiation will be painful, I really do wish you the best for the journey. Because the journey is not about surviving the terrible twos or the dramatic thirteens or them learning how to drive or going to college—it's about a special connection you're going to have to another person for the rest of your lives. Right now you can be focused on diapers or peewee soccer or any of the myriad things that take our attention, but what we're really doing is attaching and building family—and that doesn't end at eighteen.

> *There are only two lasting bequests we can hope to give our children. One of these is roots; the other, wings.*
>
> —JOHANN WOLFGANG VON GOETHE

> *There are two gifts we give our children, whether born to us or arriving in more nontraditional ways—one is attachment, and the other is differentiation.*
>
> —BARBARA CUMMINS TANTRUM

20

SLEEP AND FOOD STRATEGIES

Sleep

When therapists are assessing how much a child's trauma has impacted daily living skills, they often look at the child's eating and sleeping. Often children with trauma have difficulty going to sleep, staying asleep, getting good restful sleep, or sleeping too much. One researcher writes:

> Bedtime and other transition times are a frequent target of intervention with young children who have experienced interpersonal trauma. In normative development, children commonly experience some anxiety and distress at bedtime, which is managed through consistent co-regulation provided by their caregivers. Children who have experienced abuse or neglect have a high incidence of sleep disturbance; they may feel particularly vulnerable at night and may not trust that their primary caregiver will keep them safe. These children may demonstrate hypervigilance, intrusive thoughts, nightmares, bed-wetting, excessive clinginess, inconsolable crying, and severe tantrums.[1]

So, what are some good strategies to deal with some of these difficulties? Here are some ideas:

1. Get a good routine. Routines and rituals make kids feel safe, and bedtime is a good time for the family to spend a few minutes together. Try to make the last thirty minutes before bed as calm as you can; watching television together or reading a story together are all good things to do. Then, have some sort of before bedtime ritual such as family prayer, roses and thorns (where each person says one good thing and one bad thing from their day), or singing together. Brushing teeth, getting changed, and other rituals are key. This signals your body that it's time to sleep.

2. Treat clinginess and separation anxiety as you would with a young child. Try giving the child something of yours to snuggle with, or perhaps sit in his room for a few minutes as he is getting settled down. Leave a nightlight on if she wants that, and make sure she has transitional objects that she likes. Remove anything from her room she finds frightening.

3. For kids where it's triggering, especially if you suspect a history of sexual abuse, make sure the father of the family does not go into their rooms after bedtime. If you find out more information about the sexual abuse, and the perpetrator was a woman or a sibling, you can adjust this rule to fit those triggers, but it's a good rule of thumb, as about 90 percent of child sexual perpetrators are men.[2]

4. Exercise patience. This can be very difficult because it's the end of the day and you're tired too, but be as patient with your children as you can. As they feel safer, bedtime will go better.

5. For bedwetting past the age of five, be non-shaming and let the older child be in charge of keeping pull-ups in their room. Also talk to your doctor about bedwetting; there are some medical interventions that could help.

6. Let the child know he can come get you if he needs you. If your child has frequent nightmares or needs a lot of reassurance at night, consider having a small area in your bedroom with a mat and blanket where he can come during the night and sleep. It might allow your whole family to get better sleep!

Food

Food is another common area where parents get frustrated with their traumatized kids. Kids that come from backgrounds of neglect can sometimes have difficulty regulating their intake of food, either wanting too much or too little. Often kids that have been raised on fast food have a difficult time adjusting their palates to healthier foods, and it often surprises parents how picky children who had been previously starving can be.

Food Hoarding

Kids that have had neglect in their background and had a time when food wasn't available regularly can often develop food hoarding. This can happen even if the child was an infant during the time when food wasn't available. Food hoarding can be seen when the child "collects" food from everywhere they go and hides it in their room. Parents of food hoarders are often disgusted at finding moldy sandwiches, rotten fruit, and packets of sugar hidden all over the child's room.

This sounds counterintuitive, but one of the best ways to deal with food hoarding is to give the child a box to keep some nonperishable snacks in their room that they can eat any time they want. This will often reduce their anxiety and help them not be "collecting" all the time.

Food Availability

When feeding typical children, do not let them graze all day. This is true of the traumatized child as well, but the traumatized child has a greater emotional need to know that food will always be available to them. Keep snacks that the child can get themselves and have them available at all times. These can be healthy snacks like fruit and carrot sticks. Even if you are cooking dinner, do not say no when your child asks for food. If you are cooking dinner and you know that you're having carrots for dinner, go ahead and let your child start on the vegetable.

So many parents get into power struggles with their children over how much and what they eat. Many parents feel like failures if their kids don't eagerly eat organic vegetables and multicultural options. The best advice to deal with food struggles is not to engage with it as much as possible. Your job as the parent is to provide healthy foods that taste good, and your child decides how much to eat. Often, kids are really hungry one day and not the next, so let them choose how much they want to eat.

> Our kids had difficulty adapting to the radically different food in the United States when they first came. We decided to serve rice and oranges at every meal, so the kids had familiar foods to eat, and then they were able to experiment with other foods as they grew accustomed to it. We even ate rice with pizza! One of the children asked, when being introduced to tacos, "Don't you have anything normal to eat, like goat?"

Also, remember cultural and background issues that come with food. If your child has eaten nothing but fast food for their whole lives, do not expect them to enjoy your organic sweet potato and kale casserole right away. Put several things on the table and let them choose among those options. What you think of as normal food may not be what your child thinks of as normal food.

Cultural norms can come into play with cross-culturally adopting families. In some cultures, it's a large insult to refuse food; in others it's considered a sin to waste food. Be attuned to these differences. You could inadvertently make kids from these backgrounds overeat if you encourage eating too much.

> One foster family was eager to have their new children in their home. The father of the family was from India and loved to cook as a stress relief from his day-to-day job, and enjoyed making traditional family recipes from his childhood—aromatic rice, perfectly seasoned lentils, and tender, marinated chicken. Never would frozen chicken nuggets or pizza have been in their house. But the children they received into their home had had little exposure to food beyond breakfast cereal and chicken nuggets, and the foods their new foster father carefully prepared for them were confusing, unfamiliar, and unwelcome. The father's dreams of loving his new children through sharing his love of food was met with children who

would only eat the familiar—and for them the familiar was McDonald's and Froot Loops.

The father was nearly to the point of tears in frustration as the feasts he prepared were met with tears and resistance to even trying it. But through therapy, he began to see that the children weren't rejecting him and his culture through rejecting the food; they had just never been exposed to it before. They had never eaten rice before, let alone saffron-scented basmati rice. My advice to him was to go as slow as possible, incorporate familiar foods, and to have the kids help him cook whenever possible. He took my advice, and made simpler dishes that were similar to dishes the kids had had before—like homemade pizza the kids helped to make and grilled chicken chunks they could dip like nuggets in different flavors of sauces they made. Dipping a chicken nugget in coconut curry sauce is a good way to try curry for the first time! With patience and time, the kids were on their way to eating a more varied diet and enjoying their new foster father's gift of cooking.

HOW TO CHOOSE THE
RIGHT THERAPIST

THIS IS A QUESTION that I get asked a lot, especially if I'm speaking somewhere far enough away that the person can't see someone in my practice. In the early years of my practice I thought that most therapists would do things mostly the same as I had been trained and that most therapy would be helpful, with maybe some techniques better than others. And then during my practice I worked with kids that had seen other therapists that had actually done harm, and I had to work to build trust with kids that had been broken due to punitive and shaming therapists, and to help build trust with parents who had been involved in improper alliances with therapists. A lot of this harm was done unintentionally by people that were ill-equipped to work with children with attachment disorders, and they didn't understand how a therapist is a very tempting target for a child with indiscriminate attachment to do what we call "parent shopping."

I had to come to the realization that just like there are mechanics of differing skill levels, there are also therapists of different skill levels as well. And just as you might need a specialist for your antique Ford Model T rather than just a regular mechanic at your local shop, so a child with the specific trauma that comes with adoption and foster care might need a specialist as well. I am certainly not trying to knock the many good-hearted and well-meaning therapists out there that are just inexperienced with issues of these types of trauma in children; there is certainly a very needed place for a good general child therapist. But I have also seen enough harm in this area that I hope that in writing this chapter I will help to demystify therapy and educate parents on how therapy can help, as well as identify some of the common pitfalls for children with early trauma when they go to therapy.

When Should a Family Go to Therapy?

The answer to this simple question is both simple and incredibly individualized and complex. Anybody that feels that they need help should go to therapy. If you are feeling overwhelmed, tired, confused, ashamed with how you're parenting, frustrated and worried about your attachment, then you should go to therapy. If you personally are having trouble managing your own emotional reactions, particularly if you have a history of trauma yourself, then you should think about going to individual therapy yourself. And, of course, if raising a traumatized child is putting a strain on your marriage or partnership, then couples therapy is enormously helpful.

How Does Therapy Help?

There are three major ways that I see therapy helping kids with trauma. There are a lot of smaller things that can happen in therapy as well, but these are the three that I see happen in therapy that are hard to happen elsewhere.

1. Most kids do work out their trauma and issues in therapy. Not all, but most. For younger kids I have seen crazy things happen in filial play therapy, where kids act out scenes of abuse, resolve issues of ambivalence, and process in their current mind subconscious trauma and memory. Teens often do this with telling stories, art, or sometimes the sand tray. It is amazing to watch it happen, and it is usually followed by a major reduction in problematic behavior. Sometimes it can take a lot

of work in identifying and expressing moments to get kids to the place where they are able to do this work of thinking about and processing and integrating their story into their life, however. Even if kids only get to identifying and expressing emotions, where they recognize that others have emotions as well, that's not a bad place to be.

2. Learning skills—kids can learn skills in therapy that can help them manage their emotions. In my office we make sensory boxes, take five-minute vacations, blow up balloons, practice yoga, and use all sorts of different ways to help our bodies engage in sensory practices to help ourselves regulate PTSD responses. These are a learned skill, and that's one of the things a therapist helps teach.

3. Parental education and support—this is a really big one. Parenting kids with trauma requires a different skill set than parenting typical kids, so parents need a great deal of information as well as help emotionally interpreting their kid and their play. I see myself as setting parents up for a lifetime of relationship with their child, and the teaching I do today influences the relationship they have forever. Parents that come into my office are also often tired and discouraged, and I want to give them hope and encouragement that their love for their child is not in vain; that there is hope that their child will heal. In reality kids are in my office for one hour a week, and it's actually unhealthy for them to attach to me, so I feel that supporting parents who are doing the majority of the heavy lifting on helping a kid feel safe and attached is time very well spent.

The Most Important Building Block for Therapy: Safety

The biggest requirement that a therapist must create for their clients is felt safety, which simply means that everyone feels safe. This became really clear to me when I was in graduate school to become a therapist, but not in the way that you might think. When I was in grad school, I had two classes where I had to visually record myself being a therapist; the first one was with a classmate, and the second one with clients in my internship. I had two professors overseeing these classes; I'll call them Professor A and Professor B. In Professor

A's class, the atmosphere was very critical and shaming, and I found myself dreading class every week. When I had to choose a clip to show the class to get feedback, I would try to choose the clip I thought I had done the best to escape critical comments and the shame that followed—all the time shoving down my doubt and fear that I would never be a good therapist. My classmates had the same experience; we were just trying to keep our heads down and survive the course. There was none of the sense of learning, encouragement, of openness or exploration that should have been present in that class. To me, Professor A felt capricious and unknowable—I had no idea what would receive censure, what would trigger her fairly stern reprimands, and what would make us flunk the class. And the stakes would be high if I did flunk that class, which wasn't an unreasonable fear because about half that class didn't pass—some took it again, and some dropped out of the school entirely.

Thankfully I did pass Professor A's class, and I believe she was surprised at my exit interview at how stressful I found the whole process. When I look back with the wisdom of years, the high rate of failure in that class was probably appropriate given that the people who did fail the class were probably very unprepared for the rigors of being a therapist, but this did not foster a sense of safety—nor was it intended to. I was then on to my internship, where I got to work with real clients and be supervised by a different professor, who was also the professor who taught the child and adolescent course. In his class that I had taken the semester before, he had taught that a therapist working with kids needed to make the kids feel safe and the parents feel assured, because parents who bring their kids to therapy are usually feeling pretty discouraged. And that's also how he ran our supervision class: he made it safe. I waited for the censure to come, and it didn't. Instead, he encouraged me to see the children I treated as injured innocents paying for the crimes of others rather than interesting cases where I was trying to perform properly to get the right degree. Soon I found myself showing clips where I thought I had done poorly as a therapist in order to get help, being honest and vulnerable with what I was struggling with, and actively looking forward to class to see what I would learn that week through feedback with my classmates. It was extraordinary being part of a group of therapists where we were all being honest about our struggles and were there to support each other. What a difference some safety makes.

What is true for a bunch of budding therapists about to graduate is true for traumatized children in a therapist's office as well as their parents. Safety makes all the difference. A therapist that works with children should do a lot of work around making children feel safe. A therapist can do this by using humor, games, toys, art, and a generally friendly and welcoming manner. Behavior problems should be met with empathy, tools, and strategies, not shame. I find it a great honor when children trust me with their story, and any vulnerability and honesty shown in my office is amazing. But I've also worked with many children that aren't able to tell their story in my office, but the tools I give them in my office and the attachment work we do helps them open up to their parents at home. This makes me equally happy, because as long as vulnerability is happening, that's all I care about; and if parents are able to handle it well, it can really help toward attachment. I also feel very honored when parents are able to be vulnerable as well; admitting their failures, showing me their "bad tapes" to get feedback on the parts they feel like they are failing in order to get help rather than just trying to perform.

I can't believe that I actually have to say this, but due to experiences some of my clients have had and stories they have told me, I feel like I have to say that therapists should never be punitive, punishing, or threatening. I have heard stories of therapists who would make kids wash dishes or pull weeds if they don't speak in therapy, recommending punitive "respite" homes for kids who misbehave, where they sleep on the floor and do manual labor, and discussing behavior in front of children in a shaming way. If your child doesn't like therapy or like the therapist, it's time to ask serious questions.

The First Pitfall: Focusing on Behavior Rather Than Emotion

Behavior is a means of communication, and sometimes it's the best form of communication that we have for kids that don't have the emotional maturity to tell us what they're feeling. If you view behavior as something to correct and suppress, you are going to become very frustrated parenting a child with trauma. But if you can look at the behaviors and try to figure out the emotions behind the behaviors, you have a lot better chance of actually reducing the problematic behaviors.

A social worker warned me that this ten-year-old girl she wanted me to begin seeing had taken to saying nothing to her previous therapist except the word "cheeseburger." The therapist was getting frustrated, the foster parents were feeling like they were going nowhere, and the social worker knew I was ending with another of her clients, so she knew I had an opening coming up. This is a social worker I greatly respect, and I take her warnings seriously.

"This child does have a lot of behavioral issues," the social worker warned me. "And a terrible trauma history. And she flatly refuses to talk about anything."

"I'm not worried," I assured her. "Kids always talk eventually." I know this from experience; in my internship I once met with a kid in total silence for three months before she started talking to me.

"She doesn't like therapists," she told me. "The foster parents aren't sure they can get her there."

"I recommend bribery," I told her honestly. "A lot of families go out for tacos or milk shakes or something after therapy. If they can get her there, my job is to help her like it."

Of course this young girl, whom I will call Patty,[1] hated therapy. She had had a highly traumatic history and was deeply ambivalent about her relationship with her bio-mom, which made it very confusing and difficult to attach well to her current caregivers. She had had a string of foster homes, some abusive, as well as many professionals involved. And this trauma and unfolding issues were, understandably, causing difficult behavioral and relational issues. But the last therapist had focused on behavior rather than emotion—something often called behavioral therapy. The result is that Patty ended up feeling ashamed, like a failure, and completely misunderstood. So she defended herself as best she could—by hating the therapist and refusing to answer any questions; hence "cheeseburger."

Patty showed up in my office, selectively mute and smirking at me about it. I had met with the foster parents the week before, and they had given me a background and warned me that she was very hard on therapists. I told them about my philosophy of therapy, explained that we would be doing therapy all together, and that the work they would be doing was actually much harder than the work I would be doing. They were eager to help the child they loved very much and were eager to adopt, and so I told them how the first session was going to go so that they were prepared. I also told them to associate something really fun for the child with coming to therapy—and I pointed out the local hamburger and shake joint up the road if they needed a suggestion, as well as a very tasty taco truck.

The next week when I met Patty I smiled kindly, introduced myself, and surprised the child by offering her a lollipop. She took one with trepidation— wasn't that supposed to be a reward for cooperation? She hadn't cooperated! She was suspicious, but, well, it's hard to refuse sugar. I then showed her around my office, not noticing how she refused to answer. Her parents and I chatted pleasantly, and I led them to a large table.

To Patty's surprise, I then took down a plastic bin and addressed her directly, "Do you know how to play *Jenga*?"

"Yes," she answered me, surprising everyone that she answered a question.

"Betcha I can beat you," I told her in a playful manner, dumping out the blocks and starting to stack them up.

Patty smiled, laughed that I would say something so outrageous, and soon we were off. She did beat me the first game, and the second game we included her parents, and we had everyone say something about themselves (favorite flavor of ice cream, name of your dog, etc.) with every block they pulled out of the *Jenga* block. She did say "cheeseburger" a few times; I smiled and just moved on from that.

As the months went on, Patty actually liked coming to therapy, and as we did activities to talk about attachment, safety, communication, and regulation, Patty started being able to talk about her traumatic history. We built a safety plan addressing her more troubling behaviors, talked about grief and her relationship with her bio-mother, and dealt with attachment issues. None of this would have been possible focusing on behavior, and none of this would have been possible if Patty hadn't felt safe.

The Second Pitfall: Parent Shopping

I was working with a fourteen-year-old boy I'll call John[2] who had been adopted at age seven from the foster care system after a horror of abuse, neglect, and rotating foster homes. The adoptive mom adopted two other children previously from much younger ages, and they had fewer problems. But the third child had

had problems from the moment that he came home. He had all the typical issues that traumatized children had—emotional dysregulation, rages, controlling behavior—but he also had something more. He had what we call indiscriminate attachment, which manifests to what we nickname "parent shopping." Basically this behavior happens when kids have a deep, subconscious belief that no home is permanent for them, and so they are always cultivating their next set of parents—hence the name. Kids that do this are often very charming to outsiders and difficult at home, and teachers and other adults in their lives usually love them.

Everyone at John's school loved him, and the fact that he was small for his age and that he had a visible handicap also endeared him to others as well. He had a way of allying himself with sympathetic adults. First it was the school nurse, and then it was one of his teachers. He would first ingratiate himself, show dependency, and then that relationship would shift to an alliance against his adoptive parent. It didn't help that his adoptive mother often came across to the school as somewhat abrasive. Her innate personality was just incredibly forthright. So when John started making untrue accusations against his parent, they were easily believed. These accusations were actually fairly fantastical and easily disproved when Child Protective Services (CPS) investigated, but the entire situation left the teacher feeling betrayed, the mom feeling hurt, and the child ended up in counseling.

Unfortunately, the child ended up in counseling in a community mental health setting with a therapist who was very kind and empathetic but not experienced in working with children with attachment challenges. She did the traditional therapy model, where the child was dropped off for an hour with the therapist, and she did some play therapy and empathetic listening with him, which is very standard therapy modality. The problem was that the therapist didn't understand the dynamic of indiscriminate attachment and parent shopping, and John did the same thing he had done with his teacher with his therapist. Let me be clear that this is not John's fault; this is the result of a deep subconscious belief that he's not safe and that he needs to find a safe home to go to when (not if, in his head) his current mom tired of him. Almost inevitably, the therapist and John were in an alliance against the parent, which never ends well. This blew up in a massive way, with the child running away from home, making accusations against his mom again, telling the therapist that he wanted to live with her, and threatening suicide if he wasn't able to do so. The therapist realized that things were going south at this point, and started distancing herself, causing more alarm for the client. The parent, very alarmed, made an appointment with me.

Hopefully you can see by now why it is critically important for parents to be involved with therapy. I don't meet alone with any client that has attachment issues unless I am sure that the benefit outweighs the cost, and I am always very careful about alliances in the therapeutic process. I am well aware that a therapist is a very tempting target for parent shopping, and the last thing I want to do is be a distraction in any way to a primary bond with a caregiver. You can have a very good therapist that does meet alone with clients without their parents as long as they are aware of this dynamic, but parents should be aware of this dynamic as well. When I do play therapy, I do a type of play therapy called filial play therapy; which involves the parent doing the playing (cue attachment) while I observe and afterward help the parent interpret themes of play. I realize that I may be a bit extreme on this topic, but I have run into enough stories such as John that have made me very wary about these dynamics.

Signs of a Good Therapist

- They make you feel comfortable and heard; they listen to you.

- They greet the child kindly and engage them in a friendly way.

- Everything they do with the child should be about increasing felt safety and reducing shame.

- After the initial apprehension, the child should like going to therapy. Or, in the case of teenagers, at least put up with it without too much complaining.

- The therapist should craft a course of treatment specific to the child and based on their development level and areas of interest.

- They have an office that is interesting and comfortable for kids— including toys, fidgets, games, and appropriate furniture.

- The therapist should speak the child's language and understand them in a kind, compassionate way. The therapist should help you interpret behaviors and actions of your child to help you understand them better.

- A good therapist understands that treating a child is really about treating a whole family, and will engage with the parents as well as the child.

- A therapist should be able to converse with you about issues with school, and give recommendations for other professionals that would be helpful given certain problems that might crop up.

- A therapist should be able to tell you their therapeutic orientation (what they believe) and where they get their theories of practice. Common people for adoption and trauma therapists to be familiar with are Deborah Gray, Daniel Siegel, Karyn Purvis *(The Connected Child)*, the ARC model, and Heather Forbes and Bryan Post *(Beyond Consequences)*.

- A therapist should work with you on making therapy affordable. They should provide billing for your insurance, most have a sliding fee scale, and they should always explain everything to you ahead of time.

- A good therapist also understands that not every therapist clicks with every family. I am not offended if a client wants to see someone else after they've met with me; that's completely fine.

- A good therapist doesn't discriminate on the basis of religion, race, sexual orientation, gender identification, or any other protected class on the clients that they see.

Red Flags for a Therapist

- The therapist is an intern. Kids with attachment problems need long-term care, not interns that will change often.

- They haven't worked with adopted or foster kids, but don't think it should be different than other kids they see.

- The therapist makes you or your child uncomfortable, or seems overly timid or confrontational.

- The therapist doesn't listen to you, keeps trying to fit you into a mold, or doesn't respect you or your child. This can be talking over you, being overly bossy, or talking so much you don't feel heard.

- Their theory is based on their own ideas and not backed up by published, reputable research and practitioners.

- They seem uncomfortable with play or with children. Also, their office isn't set up for play; for example, they might have a lack of toys or their office has too many breakable things to allow a child to play.

- They see a child as a person to be dominated and forced to comply and fit a mold rather than a unique, sensitive, and emotional person that needs help.

- They ask you to do things that make you feel uncomfortable ethically. Ask the therapist why they think you should do this thing, and if it's not a good explanation, follow your conscience.

- They have odd billing practices or their rates seem unreasonably high.

10 Questions to Ask a Potential Therapist

1. How do you see healing happen for a child with trauma?

   The answer should involve attachment to caregivers.

2. How much of your current practice is treating children that have been adopted or are in foster care?

   It should be more than 10 percent, ideally more than 30 percent.

3. What books by adoption specialists have you read and respect? What books do you recommend parents read?

   Write them down and research them. Are they the ones you agree with?

4. What treatment modalities do you incorporate into your practice?

   Good: ARC model; Interpersonal; dialectical behavior therapy (DBT); TF-CBT; play therapy, with bonus points for filial play therapy. Medium: cognitive behavioral therapy (CBT); EMDR. Bad: Something I made up with no basis in research or other writers; whatever feels right at the moment. Criminal: Holding therapies; Rebirthing.

5. What do you do if a child is reluctant to come to therapy?

The answer should be compassionate and acknowledge the child's anxiety.

6. How much are parents involved in therapy?

Not everyone has a treatment modality that has parents as involved as I do, but they should be aware of the two classic pitfalls of adoption work and should at least meet with parents regularly.

7. What are your fees? What insurances do you take? Do you have a sliding fee scale? What is your cancellation policy?

Whatever their policies are, they should make you comfortable. Don't be afraid to ask questions.

8. What clinical assessments do you use to help you understand your clients?

Be wary of too many assessments, or if there's zero. I use three all the time, with a few others as occasional ones.

9. What are common referrals that you make to other providers?

For kids with trauma, the answer should be occupational therapy for kids with sensory processing disorder, psychological evaluations for kids that have trouble in school or possible multiple diagnosis, and to a psychiatrist for kids with conditions that might require psychiatric medication. Don't see a therapist who doesn't refer, who isn't educated as to what needs a child with trauma would likely have, and who doesn't "believe" in medications even if you're reluctant to medicate yourself because you need someone to let you know when the threshold has been met for when a medical evaluation would be appropriate. Even if you choose not to medicate, this is information you need to have.

10. If your child has a comorbid condition like ADHD or autism, or you suspect they might, ask if the therapist has worked with kids that have had these diagnoses before. This may not be a deal-breaker if they haven't, but it would be good to know.

Finding a therapist can feel like a daunting task, and finding one with an opening that can possibly work into your schedule and take your insurance can feel impossible. But I will say that it's better to go with a therapist that you have to struggle with the schedule than one that isn't going to do good work with your family but has tons of openings. And it is better not to go to therapy than to go to a bad therapist; if your child has a bad experience with a therapist, it could make it that much harder for them to engage in therapy in the future.

Trust your instincts. Your therapist should feel like a good fit for your family, and they should also just feel like a good person. Though they are fallible, they should be someone that you respect and trust; you are trusting them with the dynamics of your family, and they should be cognizant of that very sacred role.

22

WORKING WITH SCHOOLS

IT IS COMMON that kids with PTSD might need help at school. Not all kids do, but if your kid struggles in school because of PTSD or has another diagnosis, then they are probably going to need some help. These are the symptoms that you can see with a child with PTSD at school:

- emotional dysregulation
- difficulty with concentration
- social and emotional delays
- sensory issues
- increased anxiety
- difficulty with transitions

Part of the problem of writing about working with schools is that my advice might not translate as well to different states and even different countries. So in writing this, I decided to use what we use in my state, and hope that most of it translates into other people's areas as much as possible. I live in Washington State, and some of these involve federal laws, so most of these should be the same elsewhere in the United States. Even if you live in another country, I hope that at least the ideas can translate into your situation.

Know the Right Words

Knowing the right words to say when you're asking for help for your child is really important. The right words can start an evaluation, and not knowing the right words can get things stalled into nothingness. Here's a list of some words you need to be able to use:

Accommodation: A change to the learning environment in line with their disability to make it easier for the child to learn. For instance, a child with vision issues might be given a tablet that can enlarge the type on a handout the teacher gives the students.

Assistive technology: Any tool given to a child to help them with their education, from a tablet in the above example to something more low-tech.

Due process: This is the name for the process of formally disagreeing with the school and their findings.

Functional behavioral assessment: This is an assessment to see if the child has behavioral problems, and usually must be done to do behavioral interventions.

Independent educational evaluation (IEE): This is an educational evaluation done by someone outside of the school. Parents can request that the school pay for it; sometimes the school will, and sometimes it won't. The school has to take the results into consideration.

Least restrictive environment: This is the idea that it is better for children to be in a typical classroom as much as possible, and taught with typical peers as much as possible.

Modification: This is an altering of the curriculum or the expectations of the curriculum due to a child's disability. An example would be to reduce a student's workload while undergoing chemotherapy or to reduce expectations around reading for a child that is struggling with dyslexia.

Parental request: Often an evaluation for an individualized education plan (IEP) is started by parental request, and the school has a limited time to respond after a request is made. If you think that your child needs to be evaluated or needs accommodations, you can contact the school psychologist or counselor and ask about the process of starting an evaluation for an IEP or 504 plan.

Don't Be Too Trusting

This is going to sound cynical, but I want to start by saying that you are the expert on your child, not the school. Some schools are great at getting children the help that they need, and they are staffed with dedicated professionals that are very talented and good at their jobs. Other schools seem to be rationing out help as if the supply was so short that nobody can access it. I've seen kids that clearly have ADHD have the school psychologist say, "They don't have anything wrong with them; they just need to make better choices," and a teen diagnosed with autism, ADHD, and PTSD who was struggling to pass classes have the school psychologist say, "Study skills help is a limited resource; we don't want to provide this resource to this student because we don't think he's trying hard enough to do his homework outside of school." Both these statements, made by different school psychologists, might raise the question that their behavior is part of the diagnosis and that children should not be expected to improve their mental health before accessing services, but logic doesn't always seem to be a part of these decisions. You might get lucky and get a good school psychologist or counselor, but in my experience, even if they seem great at first, always make sure you're checking that your child is getting what they need.

Part of not being too trusting with your child's school is that if they have something going on and the school isn't helping, you will likely need outside diagnosis. Schools tend to respect diagnoses, at least somewhat, but they rarely if ever hand them out. Do not assume for a moment that the school psychologist is going to meet all of your child's needs; think of them more as the gatekeeper for your child getting services than a mental health provider that is curious about your child and hoping to provide help to them.

But also don't be too combative—I've seen parents get completely dismissed if they're viewed as "difficult" or "combative." The approach I've seen work best is parents that are clear and direct, don't back away from their points, document everything, and use other resources. The school cannot be your only professional providers; you will need outside psychologists, therapists, doctors, occupational therapists, and others helping you on this journey.

Individualized Education Plan (IEP) Versus a 504 Plan

If your child does need help at school, it's a good idea to get it in writing either through what's called an IEP or a 504 plan. An IEP is a more serious, legally binding agreement, and a 504 is less formal. An IEP is based on the federal Individuals with Disabilities Education Act (IDEA), and the 504 is from section 504 of the Rehabilitation Act. Here's a chart with some more of the differences:

IEP	504
Blueprint for special education services and accommodations	Plans for disability accommodations
Is legally binding, parents can sue if it's not followed	Isn't legally binding, easier to ignore
To qualify, a child must have a specific, diagnosed disability, and that disability must interfere with learning.	It is easier to qualify, as the definition is broader.
Is far more complicated, listing accommodations, supports, goals, testing, timing of services, etc.	Lists accommodations and supports
Updated yearly through formal process	Less formal process, usually updated yearly or every three years

Accommodations That Work for Kids with PTSD

There are some accommodations that will help kids with PTSD be able to be in the classroom. Part of figuring out what's going to work with a child is very individual and will be based on what they find soothing and helpful. So I'm going to list some different options that some children find helpful to give you some ideas on what might help your child in their class.

PTSD reaction plan: It's good to have a plan for your child if they have a PTSD reaction, particularly if they are a flight or freeze kid. It's helpful to let the teacher know what type of reaction they might be looking for, and how it's best to engage that trigger. This is what a sample email could look like:

Dear Mr. Holgate,

You have my daughter Anne in your class this year. She's a bright and fun student, and she's looking forward to having you. One thing you should be aware of is that she had a lot of trauma in her developmental years, and as a result she has PTSD, which for the most part shouldn't be too much of a problem in school. We have noticed, though, that in years past there are two situations where she really has problems. One is if she gets reprimanded by a teacher, and the other is if she gets hurt on the playground. When she gets triggered, she becomes slow, noncommunicative, and will sometimes act like she's frozen, or she will cry a lot. We had worked out a plan with her teacher last year, Mrs. White, that if this happens, she goes to the nurse, and the nurse has some tools for her to re-regulate. We'd like to have the same arrangement with you. This happened three times during the course of last year.

A good plan is specific, mentions triggers and her reaction, and the plan for how to soothe the triggers. This plan could be written into a 504, or it could be just an agreement with the child's teachers.

Here's a list of accommodations that I've asked for at one time or another for different children. This list isn't meant to be exhaustive, but more to get you thinking. Also, no child needs all these accommodations, but think about which ones will help your kiddo the most.

1. At times of high anxiety, going to the nurse's office to re-regulate

2. Having sensory tools available to them—gum, lollipops, fidgets, etc.

3. Having a calm-down space in the classroom if triggered

4. Social skills group

5. In-school occupational therapy (this is sometimes available)

6. Positive behavioral intervention (works far better than consequences)

7. Plan to make transitions better: warnings, etc.

8. Specific accommodations to allow the child to avoid things they find triggering: fire alarm drills, a specific person, speaking in front of the class, etc.

9. Help with study skills and organization

10. Making certain consequences not part of the disciplinary repertoire: a traumatized child skipping recess really isn't in anybody's best interest

Other Trauma Complications

Just as a side note, children that have early trauma often have other complications that go along with it that many parents and professionals unfamiliar with early trauma don't expect. Here's a list of some of the common complications that I look for with children:

1. Sensory issues: Read the chapter on sensory issues if you haven't already; it's uncommon for a child with early trauma not to have sensory issues. If sensory issues are causing a problem for your child, they should be evaluated by an occupational therapist, but make sure it is one who treats sensory integration disorder. There are also several good books written on the subject.

2. Eyesight issues: This can stem from babies not being held and rocked in the right position with the right eye contact while they are nursed or fed, so if your child had early neglect, this is a possibility. If your child is slow to learn how to read or seems to have a lot of trouble focusing, it is a good idea to have them evaluated by a specialist, not just a typical ophthalmologist. Several children I have worked with couldn't read and were thought to have a learning disorder. When they received vision therapy and were able to get their eyes working properly, they were able to start reading. It wasn't a learning disorder; it was an eye disorder. But these can be hard to diagnose unless you see a specialized ophthalmologist.

3. Difficulty feeling their body properly: Kids with trauma often feel the smallest scratch overly amplified, or can be seriously injured and hardly whimper. And to be even more confusing, the same kid can do both of these things. The mind and body connection has been disrupted, and it can be frustrating to help it connect properly. Two of the things I recommend the most to help the mind and body connect again are

dance and martial arts, as both are really good about feeling the body as well as learning control over the body.

4. Encopresis and enuresis: This is kids pooping and peeing in their pants when they are of an age that they are usually potty-trained. This is especially true for kids that have been the victim of sexual abuse.

23

PTSD AND MEDICAL CARE

GETTING CHILDREN IMMUNIZATIONS or to cooperate with treating an infected mosquito bite can be complicated with a typical child, but with a child with PTSD, you are entering a vastly more complex arena. Early medical experiences for a child, even if they are newborns withdrawing from drugs they were exposed to in utero, can affect how they feel about a doctor stitching up their latest scooter accident. This chapter will look at some of the different effects of PTSD on how children receive medical care, how the medical establishment treats children with PTSD, and some good strategies to help if you have a child that has issues with medical treatment.

My child, normally one of the sweetest and most cooperative, looks up at me with her tear-stained face, utterly refusing to open her mouth to let the dentist even look at her teeth. At the time she was six and had barely cooperated with cleanings. But now, when there was a filling to be done, she was completely uncooperative. This wasn't an angry refusal; she was truly terrified.

"It's not that bad," I promised her, trying to be reassuring. "I've had tons of fillings. I'll take you out for a smoothie afterwards."

"No, Mommy," she whispered, afraid if she spoke too loudly she might open enough to get tools put in her mouth. "I can't do it."

We tried fruitlessly to convince her, me feeling increasingly embarrassed about wasting the dentist's time, and also increasingly surprised that this was the child that wasn't able to do it. Finally, the dentist called it, and referred me to a pediatric dentist that could sedate her to do the filling she needed.

And then the dentist said something that stuck with me in dealing with my child from then on. He said, "We teach kids that we want them to be able to say what happens to their body, so we have to respect that, even when it's inconvenient to us. We know that giving her the filling today is what's best for her teeth, but obviously her brain doesn't know that."

In the story above, that dentist was right that day, and I've had to remind myself of that, as that daughter has been very challenging to engage in medical care. There have been mornings where it has taken her an hour before she's allowed the nurse to give her immunizations, which has made me late to work. And she's always sweetly apologetic afterward—she's not trying to be naughty, she's truly scared.

She came to us at two and a half years old, and though our records of her life before us are very sparse, we do know that there were some significant medical issues and probably some medical care. The first time I took her to the doctor, she knew exactly what the woman with the needles was going to do, and she was ready. She kicked so hard during her first immunization that she bent the needle, and she cried so much that I found out later the medical assistant took her lunch so that she could cry herself and recover from how terrified that sweet little girl was.

There have been many times that I have given talks about trauma and people haven't even considered medical trauma as a category of trauma for a child. But I can guarantee you that if a child has had significant medical interventions either because they were born prematurely, addicted to drugs, or with a birth defect, then they underwent trauma. Even though the caregivers for these young, fragile babies try very hard to make it as comfortable as possible, there are things that have to happen. A premature baby has to have an IV placed every few days, numerous wires and tubes must be hooked up and placed, there are bright lights, and the baby cannot be held. The world in general is not the soft, warm place that the womb is. Think about the smells and feelings of the hospital and what it's like for an adult, let alone a baby. It is overwhelming, confusing, and painful. And if you throw in detoxing from drugs or recovering from surgeries, that further traumatizes tiny babies. And all this for a baby that should still be in the warm protection of a womb.

Medical trauma doesn't end with newborns—it can also be with medical issues in the first few years of life—cancer, diabetes, or any other childhood scourge.[1] Children that have undergone abuse and trauma that have required medical attention also have the added trauma that the doctor may have been the one to call CPS. So how can we help our child get proper medical care when they get triggered by medical things?

First, think about where your child's medical trauma may have been. Was it preverbal? In the hospital? If you have access to a full and complete medical file, then this question will be a bit easier. Otherwise, you may have to do some guessing or conjecture based on behaviors and reactions. Second, assess their reactions and see what the problems are. I worked with one child that had a bad reaction to the smell of rubbing alcohol, but did fine when the doctor used something else to sterilize their arm for shots. Where do their reactions interfere with medical care? Are there good workarounds?

Here are the rules that I work with regarding kids and getting medical care:

1. Always tell a child what's going to happen to them before it happens, and if they're old enough, tell them why. I've had clients have full panic attacks during routine exams just because a doctor touches them without telling them. Let the child have as much power as possible, and make sure your child's regular provider is good at establishing trust with your child.

2. Do not hold a kid down unless it's an emergency, and especially after a child is old enough to reason. This can be hard because sometimes medical providers do hold kids down, but I would really caution

against this approach. For kids with PTSD, holding them down will probably deeply trigger them, and it will make whatever is happening so much worse. You can ask, "Can I hold your arm to make sure it stays still?" but do not do it without their permission. Now, obviously you might have to hold a two-year-old's leg, but explain what you're doing and why. It's okay if it takes a half hour to give a kid a shot; that's much better than the child feeling like you're not a safe adult because you held them down. Obviously there are very dangerous situations where a child needs to be held down for medical care, but make sure it's about an emergency and not convenience.

3. Give your kids tools. Tools can look like gum, lollipops, a promise of a treat afterward, or a cartoon to watch. This is not bribery; these are tools. Here is the difference: bribery is "If you let them give you a shot, you can have gum." A tool is "I see you need some gum to help you regulate. Here's some gum so you can keep calm enough to get a shot," or "It can really help sometimes when you have something not fun to have something to look forward to, so a tool we're going to use is that you and I are going out for ice cream after we do this so you have something fun to think about." Sensory stuff is particularly helpful: gum, lollipops, and so on. I know one mom who swears by having the child cough right before the shot.

4. Practice. If your child is freaked out about the doctor or dentist, get a doctor's kit and add some real Band-Aids, alcohol wipes, exam gloves, and syringes (without needles, of course) and practice giving each other mock exams. Kids feel mastery in play, and it will make the whole thing feel less scary.

5. Celebrate small victories. Progress will often look small; celebrate it. Even if a child has a long way to go, celebrate the parts they're doing well.

6. For older children, make them part of the plan. For an older child, you can present the problem and help them be part of the solution. For example, you have a child with medical phobias that has an infection in their arm that the doctor wants to drain. You can present the problem, explain why the doctor wants to drain it, and ask the child for

what they think they will need to be able to do it. If a child feels that they have some control over the plan, the plan will work a lot better.

7. Advocate with the doctor. If the doctor or dentist knows the child has PTSD, they might be able to accommodate some medical care differently than they would otherwise. Don't be afraid to ask.

When the Diagnosis of PTSD Works Against You

I would not have thought this chapter necessary in my early years as a therapist, but I have experienced this problem myself as a mom and in my practice with several clients. Sometimes symptoms or concerns of people with a traumatic background can be dismissed by medical professionals as having to do with PTSD and will not warrant further investigation even though clearly the person needs more medical care.

It was New Year's Eve, and we were enjoying a small gathering of friends to watch the fireworks at the Space Needle in downtown Seattle from a dock a short distance away. We had spent the last several months confused and worried about one of our daughters, who had displayed an array of confusing and erratic symptoms, and we found ourselves just hoping she'd get better and we wouldn't have to worry about it. There had been a wide array of tests with no answers, so the doctors had said that it must be due to her PTSD. As we watched the fireworks, she fainted again—a reality that was becoming all too common for us. But this time at the gathering we had a friend of ours who works as a nurse at the local children's hospital.

"You should take her in," he urged. "Her heartbeat is irregular."

"Every time we take her in, they don't find anything," I tell him. "They just say it's her trauma."

"Do you think it's her trauma?" he asked me.

"No," I answered firmly. "I don't."

> "Then you should take her in."
>
> So my husband and I arranged for a friend to stay with our other kids, and we took our daughter in yet again to the ER on that early frosty morning. This time we got a different doctor—one that believed me when I told him that this wasn't her trauma, that there was really something wrong with her. They admitted her for a different round of tests, and sometime in the early hours that New Year's Day, we were lucky enough that her body actually did its dysfunction while being hooked up to the right monitors, and we actually got the proper diagnosis. Those nine months of limbo felt awful until we later found out that most people with her condition often go years before they are properly diagnosed.

Though the story above is just one story, I have heard a similar story echoed by many of my clients. I have seen children not screened for autism or learning disorders because of their PTSD, unexplained body pains not taken seriously because of their trauma background, and parents having to convince doctors to take their child's symptoms seriously.

There are many reasons why this is the case. One reason is simply that doctors and other medical professionals are human, and when a child has symptoms that are not easily explained, it is easy to jump to conclusions—and there is a bias in our society that people who have had trauma are more apt to make things up and overexaggerate. And part of the problem is also that people with a trauma background sometimes don't communicate and express pain in the same way.

For example, there was a case in a city near to Seattle where a young woman who had grown up in foster care and had experienced a great deal of trauma experienced a sexual assault and reported it to the police. Because her reactions seemed different than that of a typical victim, she wasn't believed by the police and by those around her, and she ended up being coerced into falsely confessing that she had made it up, and was charged with lying to the police. Later, proof was found that she had indeed been telling the truth, shocking the police and her foster parents.[2] If that police officer had been familiar with early childhood trauma, he would have seen her reactions as someone who used disassociation for survival, and would not have jumped to the conclusion that he did.

Doctors have the same problem; if they aren't familiar with early childhood trauma, the child who dissociates with pain may be seen as not having pain, and the child who reacts to even the smallest pain as if they were losing their leg as being melodramatic and unreliable. People with PTSD often have different reactions to pain, to traumatic things like shots, procedures, and exams. These reactions can be confusing to medical providers and can affect proper diagnosis.

SIBLINGS

SIBLING RELATIONSHIPS CAN be very complicated to navigate. On the one hand, you want kids to be able to negotiate and work out their problems together. On the other hand, there is usually a power differential between ages and sizes, and you don't want kids to get abused. When you throw foster and adopted kids into the mix, things become even more complicated. Here are some ideas and concepts to think about when you decide how to parent siblings:

Kids that come from dysfunctional families have dysfunctional sibling relationships. In families that are suffering the effects of domestic violence, drug and alcohol addiction, child abuse, neglect, and sexual abuse, kids learn how to survive. Oftentimes this survival means that they engaged in behaviors that were adaptive for their dysfunctional family but that are not adaptive in their new home. For instance, many older kids in dysfunctional families end up parenting their younger siblings. They care for them and discipline them, but a ten-year-old does not have the maturity to parent. Discipline can look like bullying, and the older sibling has to grow up too fast. In an ideal foster or adoptive home, the older child is freed to once again be a child, but giving up the parenting role can be challenging. This also means that in families where there is domestic violence and sexual abuse, abuse can happen between siblings as well. Sibling abuse is one of the most underrecognized forms of abuse and trauma. Siblings staying together in care is usually a positive thing, but for kids coming from highly dysfunctional families, it can actually be detrimental to their safety.

Foster and adoptive parents are always worried about how having foster and adoptive kids affects their biological children. Having foster and adoptive kids will affect your bio-kids—for good and bad. Before you decide to foster or adopt, take an inventory of your children: their personalities and strengths. You do not need your child's permission to foster or adopt, but the more they can participate in the process, the better it is for everyone.

You cannot prevent every bad thing from happening. Even the most watchful parent needs to use the bathroom, cook dinner, or mow the lawn on occasion. You are not going to prevent every slap or mean word; how you handle it is key.

So, in thinking of these principles, here are some ideas to consider:

- **Set clear boundaries within your family.** You should make clear expectations for safety and enforce them consistently. Good boundaries include rules such as kids are not allowed in each other's bedrooms without permission or after bedtime; nobody hits anybody for any reason; children do not wear each other's clothes or borrow toys without permission, and so on. For a lot of kids with traumatic backgrounds, this could be their first experience in having healthy boundaries, and their foster or adoptive siblings could be teaching them a lot about social norms.

- **Be as fair as possible, but recognize that kids have different needs.** If you had a child in a wheelchair, you wouldn't have the same expectations from them as for a child who was not in a wheelchair. There are accommodations you need to make for kids with trauma that you do not need to make for your bio-kids. Bio-kids can understand this as well, especially when they see that they are treated well.

- **Do not try to make everything even all of the time.** You will drive yourself crazy if every time you buy one kid something every kid has to have something of equal value. Practice celebrating others and what they need. For example, one kid needs soccer cleats this week; another child gets a sleepover the next week. Obviously, don't play favorites—if one child is getting more things and treats than the other overall, try to balance it out a bit.

- **Try to help your children work things out, but don't allow abuse.** It is always better for children to be able to speak for themselves and work out differences without parents interfering. As much as possible, up until the point of abuse, try to let the kids negotiate and complain to each other. Try reading *Siblings without Rivalry* by Adele Faber and Elaine Mazlish. Keep in mind, this is a book about typical siblings and does not take into account traumatized children, so modify it as needed. But having some good answers ready for tattling, like "Wow, it sounds like that was pretty mean of Bobby to say to you. What do you think you should do about it?" can help, and also get your child thinking about social issues.

- **Restorative discipline is especially effective with siblings.** If one sibling hurts another, she has to do something nice to make it up to him, like do his chores for the day or vacuum his room.

When you're parenting children, it's good to think about two strategies that you have in parenting—one is as a coach and one is a referee. A referee in a game keeps everything fair and everything safe, and they can call a time-out if needed. If a referee sees something dangerous happening, they stop in and make sure that both sides follow the rules. The other parenting strategy is the coach, and that's the part where you're helping the siblings get along through social guidance.

If two children are getting into an argument, you could intervene to help with an overall statement of getting along, such as "Hmm, things are getting heated here. Let's be thinking of using kind words here." (This is coaching.) Then things might start getting heated, and you say, "Whoa, this is pretty heated. Everyone take a break now, take a break, and we'll talk in a sec." (Being a referee.) Then you can go from coaching and refereeing from there. But just as with their soccer team, kids do better with more coaching and less refereeing. But the referee is important to keep everyone safe.

To Learn More about Siblings

Adele Faber and Elaine Mazlish, *Siblings without Rivalry: How to Help Your Children Live Together So You Can Live Too* (New York: W. W. Norton, 2012).
Caveat: This is a great book about sibling rivalry, but it is about typical children and not traumatized children. If you choose to read it, there needs to be
some translation into a situation with trauma.

25

LYING AND STEALING

LYING IS ONE of the most common and often most troubling behaviors that children with trauma histories engage in. Typical children engage in lying as well, but kids with trauma do it much more frequently and with much more desperation. Parents panic when their child lies, assuming that they will not be able to grow up to be functional and normal adults unless they are severely reprimanded. Unfortunately, the reprimands tend to trigger traumatized children, setting up a vicious cycle. Lying also makes us uncomfortable because we remember times that people have lied to us, and it hits our own trauma buttons of betrayal. Parents worry that their children will grow up to be criminals and psychopaths due to the ease with which they lie, and fret that they will never be able to trust their child. Parents do not have to view lying this way. Post and Forbes write,

> Research in the field of neuroscience has shown that children who have experienced trauma react to stress out of a state of fear, from an unconscious level, as deep as the state memory. The fear receptor in the brain becomes overly triggered and, in this stress state, the traumatized child's perception of the situation at hand becomes distorted and exceptionally fearful. Children with

trauma histories are living out of a primal state of survival. They literally lie from a place of life or death. Their survival is dependent on convincing you that they are telling the truth. In this distortion of their mind, the state level of memory drives them with the conviction that they must persist with this lie at all costs in order to survive.[1]

This trauma reaction can happen with very simple things in their day and can happen even if you have just witnessed whatever they are lying about. This type of lying is very difficult for teachers and parents and causes a stress reaction in our own brains. In that reactive state, we tend to parent from fear and punishment rather than love and concern. If your reaction is so strong that you can't see past it, oftentimes this indicates the areas in which you have been lied to in your own life. In order to be able to handle a child's lying, the parent needs to be able to stay calm and avoid the stress reaction, so they can stay in their own thinking brain. Your desire for justice and your fear for what happens if you don't address the lying will not help your child tell the truth.

In order for the child to tell the truth, the parent needs to help them calm down enough to be in their thinking brain, where a conversation could actually be helpful. If we treat lying as a triggered reaction just like other triggered reactions, suddenly it becomes a lot easier to deal with.

Steps to Take When Your Child Lies

1. **Ignore the lying; engage the child.** The goal is to help the child regulate by them being able to "borrow your brain" (regulation skills). You do not need to defend why what they said is a lie and you are not tacitly agreeing with the lie if you decide to address it later. Recognize the lie as the child acting out of stress. It takes positive and reassuring interactions with the parent in order to calm the child enough to talk about the lie.

2. **Control your own fear and stress reaction.** Take deep breaths, tell yourself that this is not about you, and do whatever you need to do to stay in your thinking brain.

3. **Take steps to calm the child.** Recognize that they are having a stress reaction and offer assurance.

4. **When things are calmer, make a statement about how it hurts you when they lie, and how they don't have to do it.** Do not be punitive about it, but state that they don't have to lie because you are safe and that it hurts you when they lie. Then, look for other opportunities to talk about lying in a more neutral setting. For example, when a friend lies to them at school, you can talk about how lying is hard because then they can't trust their friend and it makes it hard to have a relationship with them. Put lying in the context of relational skills rather than moral failing.

"I didn't do it!" your six-year-old traumatized child yells at you, her eyes flashing with anger. "It wasn't me!" In her mind, she's thinking, "I'm bad! If I'm bad, they'll get rid of me! I need to be good to stay here and be safe. They might hurt me if they knew I hurt my brother. I must survive!"

You had just seen her hit her brother, so what do you do? It is tempting to yell back, "Of course you did! I saw it! Time-out, now!" but that's not going to be helpful. Instead, try calming yourself, taking her by the hand and placing her beside you or maybe on your lap. You can even say, "I can tell you're scared right now. Let's sit together until you feel better. You're okay; nothing is going to hurt you. I love you." Then, when she's calmer, you say, "I understand why you lied. Sometimes when people get scared they lie to try and keep themselves safe. You don't have to lie to me. I'm safe. It hurts me when you lie to me. I love you and you are not going anywhere. You can always tell me the truth, honey."

Top strategies for helping a child that lies:

1. Don't back them into a corner where they feel like they don't have a choice but to lie. Do not ever ask questions like "Did you do that?" or "Who did that?" because these will invoke that fear reaction that will automatically lead to lying. Do not give them a chance to protest their innocence or to tell stories, and instead go through other channels for information that you need rather than from the child. Instead say, "So I see that happened . . ."

2. If a child tells you the truth even when it is to their disadvantage, celebrate!

3. Work at making the environment as safe as possible to help the child tell the truth. Speak to their fear, and try to make it as safe as possible for them.

4. Getting them to tell the truth is the important thing—a good policy is to tell them that if they tell the truth, there are no further consequences.

5. Give kids a second chance—when they lie about something, say, "I think you didn't mean what you just said. I'm going to give you a second to think about it and see if that's what you really wanted to say." This can especially help with the knee-jerk kind of lying that happens without kids even really realizing it.

Stealing

Stealing is very similar to lying in a lot of ways, in that it is a reaction to stress. The difference is that it is often related to impulse control and also hoarding. Pay attention to what your child is stealing—is it food? Toys they are jealous about? Things of yours? What they're stealing makes a difference on how you address it.

First, think about whether it's really stealing. Sometimes kids really want to have something of yours, or it is more an issue of food hoarding. Think about their motivations, when it happens, and why it happens as well as what they are stealing. Are they defensive? Do they know it's wrong? Are they hiding it?

If the stealing really is stealing, such as stealing things from other children at school, then you want to have a conversation with the child much like you would with a child who lies—be an ally, not an adversary. No punishment is going to change this behavior; instead you want to convey worry that they're going to impact friendships and how other people view them, and how stealing loses people's trust. Remind them of how hard it would be on them if someone stole something from them as well. Try to limit their opportunities to steal as well—it can be a really effective boundary that you search a child's backpack every day when they come home, and keep money somewhere inaccessible.

Kids won't stop stealing or lying until they decide for themselves that they want to be people that other people trust that don't steal or lie. You can't punish them to get them to that place faster. What they need is enough attachment and regulation to have what other people think matters to them. While they are getting to that place, limit the amount they can do and focus on creating felt safety so they are able to work on telling the truth.

There had been a candy theft while on vacation, and given the circumstances, it was very clear which two children had participated in the theft of Dad's Tic Tacs. In our family it was a policy that if you tell the truth about things like this, you didn't get further consequences, and so the nontraumatized kid fessed up pretty quickly. For the traumatized one, it was much harder, however. I gave her some time, and we went down to the hotel pool to swim. Letting her have some sensory time to re-regulate, I talked to her about the candy again.

"Hey honey, we need to talk about the candy again."

"It wasn't me! I didn't do it!"

"I hear what you're saying, sweetie, and I know you're scared," I tell her softly. "I know that when you do something wrong, you get scared. It's okay."

"Mom, I didn't do it!"

"Look, honey, we both know you did, and I'm not mad. You're safe. I know when I was your age and I did something wrong, I was always really scared. But I'm worried about you, because when we tell lies, it hurts our hearts."

"I'm scared."

"I know, I get it. And I'm worried that if you don't tell me the truth, your heart is going to be hurt by it, and it makes me sad because it hurts my feelings too. I want both of us not to be hurt, and the only way that works is if you can tell me the truth."

Because she is a freeze kid, this conversation takes a lot more time than represented here, but in general it was a long, slow, soft conversation that eventually resulted in the child feeling safe enough to finally admit to what happened and my telling her how proud I was of her that she was able to tell me the truth. This is intentional and slow parenting, but the fact that she got to that place of truth-telling was a turning point in her being able to tell the truth in the future.

More Help with Difficult Behavior

Heather T. Forbes and B. Bryan Post, *Beyond Consequences, Logic, and Control: A Love-Based Approach to Helping Attachment-Challenged Children with Severe Behaviors* (Boulder, CO: Beyond Consequences Institute, 2009).

WHEN IT'S MORE
THAN PTSD
ADHD, FASD, Autism

ONE OF THE THINGS that is incredibly hard to figure out without the help of a professional is whether or not your child has something other than PTSD going on. The big three—attention deficit hyperactivity disorder (ADHD), autism, and fetal alcohol spectrum disorder (FASD)—occur at a higher rate among adoptees than in the general population. It's beyond the scope of this book to deal with any of these diagnoses comprehensively, and if you have a child with one of these diagnoses, please do a lot more research than what I have here. But I thought it would be useful to discuss briefly how trauma affects each of these conditions and what to look for with kids with trauma who might potentially have these other conditions.

But how can you tell if your child's behavior is trauma-related or might be related to another condition? There's not a blood test for these conditions, but there are some indicators if there is something going on other than just trauma:

You've been doing attachment work, and your child is feeling more attached to you, and the behavior isn't decreasing. With increased attachment should come decreased troubling behavior, and if this doesn't happen, it's time to ask questions.

The behavior is consistent in many different situations. Behavior related to trauma and attachment problems is usually worse at home and less severe or even nonexistent at school or with extended family. Kids with attachment problems usually seem charming and cooperative to other people than to their parents, much to the exasperation of their parents. It's not unusual for a child with attachment problems to be raging at home and to win a citizenship award at school. But a child with PTSD as well as a condition like ADHD, autism, or FASD will have problems at school as well.

The behavior is severe and pervasive, and doesn't respond to interventions designed to help with trauma. This is especially true if your child reacts in a very strongly negative way to interventions designed to help.

The child has a history that puts them at a higher risk for another diagnosis. For instance, if you know of a family history of autism or ADHD, or if you know of prebirth exposure to substances, then those should be thoughts in your mind.

Attention Deficit Hyperactivity Disorder

ADHD is one of the most common yet one of the most misunderstood diagnoses I run into in my practice. Thinking about ADHD had changed a lot over the past thirty years, as well as how it is diagnosed and treated. Research is finding that many of the assumptions people have had for years, such as "Oh, he'll grow out of it," are patently untrue. And advances in brain science are giving us a better look into this very common brain disorder.

When we are discussing ADHD, first of all, you need to know your terms. With the release of the new *DSM-5,* the manual by which psychologists diagnose all mental disorders, ADHD has gotten a makeover. Gone is the term *attention-deficit disorder (ADD);* we now have three types of ADHD: ADHD

Inattentive type (what we used to call ADD), ADHD Hyperactive and Impulsive type, and ADHD Combined type (where you have both the other types).

ADHD is usually diagnosed using a form called the Vanderbilt Assessment Scale, and it is usually diagnosed by a medical doctor or psychiatrist, or a psych ARNP (advanced registered nurse practitioner). A psychologist can diagnose it, and if the diagnosis is positive, refer the client to a prescriber for medication. To diagnose, one Vanderbilt form is filled out by one or both parents, and then a form is filled out by the child's teacher. Then the practitioner making the diagnosis looks at the data and makes the diagnosis. Because school is so important in making the diagnosis, it can make it hard at times like summer break and even early fall to diagnose your child. Diagnosis usually happens no earlier than age six, though it sometimes happens at five for children who are more severe. Only a licensed, trained provider can diagnose ADHD, but knowing some symptoms can give you an idea if your child needs to be screened for it. According to the *DSM-5,* here are the basic symptoms of ADHD:

Inattentive type (used to be called ADD):

- makes careless mistakes in schoolwork
- has trouble holding attention in tasks or play activities; is easily distracted
- doesn't seem to listen when spoken to directly
- has trouble organizing tasks and activities; loses necessary things
- avoids and dislikes talks that require mental effort over a long period of time
- is often forgetful and easily distracted

Hyperactive and Impulsive type:

- Symptoms must be disruptive and inappropriate to the person's developmental level.
- often leaves when sitting is expected
- fidgets, taps, makes noises, squirms
- runs around, climbs, seems "on the go" all the time
- unable to do quiet activities (except video games)

- has trouble waiting their turn
- talks excessively, interrupts others[1]

One of the problems with diagnosing ADHD is that many of the symptoms can look a lot like PTSD in children. ADHD Inattentive can look a lot like when hypervigilance distracts kids, or with kids who are freeze kids who dissociate. ADHD Hyperactive type can look a lot like kids that qualify as sensory-seeking on the Sensory Processing Disorder evaluation, as they are often seeking sensory input. They can often be oppositional as well, which is similar to kids with attachment challenges. It is very important to have an experienced clinician helping make these diagnoses and to determine if a child has both ADHD and PTSD.

ADHD is often treated with medication, and for many families with children affected by ADHD, medication completely changes the dynamic. I am not a prescriber or a doctor, so please always consult with one of them about medical issues. But, that disclaimer given, I have noticed one complication with children with PTSD with the medications that are used to treat ADHD. The stimulants that are used quite successfully to treat ADHD can sometimes trigger PTSD symptoms. Several parents notice that although

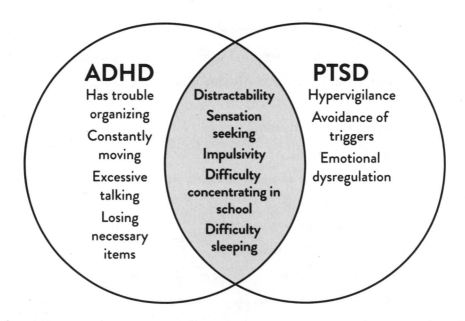

the ADHD symptoms decrease, the PTSD symptoms can go through the roof. I always warn clients to watch for this, and if this happens to your child, there are a few options. One is to try a nonstimulant like guanfacine; but for a lot of people these medications don't provide as good a treatment for ADHD as the stimulant. Most of the kids I work with seem to do best with a combination of taking a stimulant in the morning and guanfacine in the afternoon. Again, this is something to discuss with your doctor, but it is a wise and educated parent who knows what to look for and that there are other options.

The decision to medicate can be a tricky one, and I was faced with it myself when one of my children was diagnosed with ADHD. He had been having trouble in school with behavior, but the decision to start him on medication gave me pause. I had all the questions that I believe most parents have—is it necessary? What about side effects?

Around this time I had an intake with a client, and one of the questions I always ask parents during intake is about their own childhood trauma. I do this because parents' trauma can radically affect how they parent, so it's very helpful for me to know the nature of the trauma they experienced. The family had the very typical response and demurred, saying that they hadn't had a lot of trauma.

"So if I asked what was the worst thing about your childhood, or the worst thing that happened during your childhood, how would you answer?" I asked.

The answer to this question often gets varying results. The parent that tells me the worst thing that happened to them was getting pantsed on the playground in second grade leads me to believe that there wasn't a lot of trauma for them. But I've had answers to this question range from a sibling dying to previously undisclosed sexual abuse to witnessing domestic violence. But this time the dad in the family caught me off guard.

"Untreated ADHD," the dad answered without hesitation. "I had ADHD, but nobody recognized it, and I didn't get diagnosed and treated until I was an adult. I grew up thinking I was stupid and weird and bad. I was miserable."

I was stunned. It was one of those moments where I saw this man and the pain he had grown up with, and I recognized that my son could grow up with the same pain. I realized then that the decision not to medicate his ADHD would be as much a decision with consequences as the decision to treat it—and I had to decide which story I wanted my son to have.

Fetal Alcohol Syndrome and Other Drug Exposure

FASD and other drug exposure are unfortunately very common among adoptees, and scientists are now estimating Americans affected by FASD to be between 2 and 5 percent of the general population. It is the current leading cause of brain damage in the world.[2] Trauma also causes its own type of brain damage, and researchers have found that when children with FASD are exposed to trauma, this brain damage compounds and creates much more intense and difficult behaviors and cognitive impairment.[3]

It is ironic that alcohol seems to do more damage than what we consider more serious drugs, and often the damage is done early on in pregnancy, before the mother even knows she's pregnant. The bad news is that drug effects are extremely difficult to treat and can often be a lifelong disability. The good news is that treatment of intrauterine drug effects is a cutting-edge field, and new therapies are being tried and proving successful. In the Seattle area, where I live, there is an exciting new clinic opening called Hope Rising that is solely dedicated to working with kids with prebirth exposures.

When you have a child that has both trauma and substance exposure, it is still very important to treat their trauma. The parts of their behavior and attachment that have been caused by trauma can be healed and can get better, so it's important to address that. Using trauma-informed parenting strategies will give your child's brain the best shot at healing, and will also give you a better idea of what is trauma and what is substance exposure.

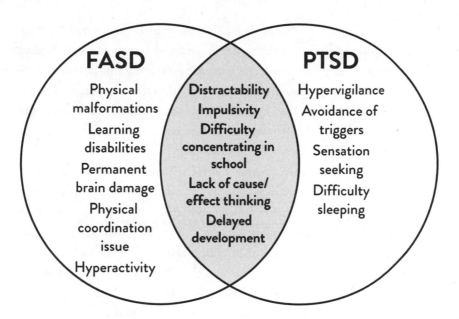

It's also important to get your child assessed and diagnosed if you believe your child has had in utero exposure to drugs, especially alcohol. It is a very difficult diagnosis to get; the clinic in Seattle has a waiting list of over a year. However, if your child does have FASD, then they will probably need some sort of help and support the rest of their lives, and they are going to be a vulnerable adult. With a diagnosis, they will qualify for services designed to help them. As more and more treatments are becoming available, hopefully there will be something to treat them soon.

Autism Spectrum Disorder

Autism spectrum disorder (ASD) is rarer than either ADHD or FASD, but it does still crop up for adoptees. Children with autism are in fact 2.4 times more likely to enter foster care than children without autism.[4] There is debate as to why children with autism are so overrepresented in foster care, but the fact is that they are there. One study found children with an ACE (adverse childhood experience) score of 4 or higher have double the risk of being diagnosed with autism.[5] Another study suggests that because of some of the limitations of autism, some childhood experiences might be more traumatic on the child.[6]

For example, children with ASD are more likely to be victimized by their peers, are more vulnerable to victimization, and have less coping skills to deal with it. To make matters more complicated, people with autism that experience trauma can have different symptomatology than their neurotypical peers. One researcher writes, "When a person with autism experiences trauma, the symptoms can look quite different from others experiencing trauma. Current research on what PTSD looks like in people with autism is scant."[7]

Children with attachment trauma and PTSD with autism definitely need to be in the care of an experienced therapist. How a person on the spectrum experiences traumatic stress can be very different than a typical person, and how that stress manifests can be different as well.[8] Even how they take traumatic stress evaluations can be different than typical children, so they need an experienced therapist to help them navigate how their trauma and autism intersect.

Added to the difficulty of the intersection of trauma and autism is the fact that they can be very difficult to tell apart in young children. Many of the symptoms are the same, but they are caused by different things. For instance, both children with PTSD and ASD often have anger outbursts, but for children with ASD it comes from the anxiety created from their inflexible routines, and from children with PTSD, it comes from the emotional volatility that comes from PTSD. Both groups will have repetitive play, but for ASD children, it is their repetitive use of objects, and for children with PTSD, it is an acting out of intrusive memories or flashbacks that keep coming back from the trauma. Sleep is an issue for both groups—but for PTSD children it is usually because of nightmares, whereas for ASD kids it's not.[9]

To get a diagnosis of autism is usually a long process involving at least an expert or two, sometimes a whole team. I've also experienced several clients in my practice who have had to be evaluated several times before they received a diagnosis of autism, and I think it's because doctors just want to be really careful when handing out this diagnosis. And for high-functioning people with autism, what was called Asperger's syndrome before the *DSM-5* came out, it can be much more challenging. Here is a paraphrased version of the symptoms in the *DSM-5:*

- deficits in social-emotional reciprocity
- deficits in nonverbal communication, i.e., not good at eye contact or body language

- deficits in peer relationships, either in making and keeping friends or a lack of interest in them

- repetitive motor movements (lining up cars, saying things over again, etc.)

- rigid and inflexible routines

- obsessive fixation on something (trains, a superhero, etc.)

- sensory disturbance, either unaware of sensory input or very sensitive[10]

A child doesn't have to have all these symptoms to be diagnosed, just some of them. And they have to be disruptive to their lives to be diagnosed as well. If your child is inflexible and rigid, has trouble making and keeping friends, and seems to have communication issues, then it's probably time they were screened.

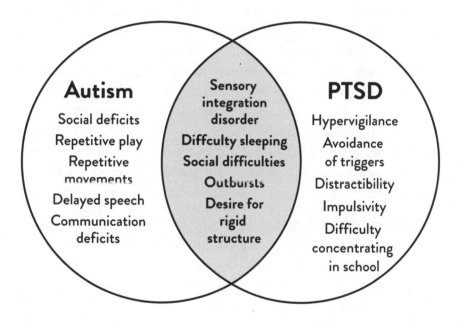

Diagnosis in General

Those are the big three, but there are other diagnoses that families deal with in my practice: generalized anxiety disorder, encopresis, trichotillomania, phobias, panic disorder, nonverbal learning disorder, Tourette's syndrome, oppositional defiant disorder, obsessive compulsive disorder, bipolar disorder, depression, and eating disorders. Sometimes a diagnosis can come as a shock, and parents have to work through a lot of feelings and grief when they receive it. Sometimes a diagnosis can actually come as a bit of a relief—parents have known something was wrong for a long time, and now that they have a name for it, it feels like something they can treat and have some hope about. Sometimes it just feels good to have a name for something so that it feels less crazy. I worked with one parent who was shocked and scared when her child started pulling their hair out, convinced they were the only person this had ever happened to. It was a relief to be diagnosed with trichotillomania, and be referred to a psychiatric ARNP (advanced registered nurse practitioner) for anxiety medications to help treat the condition.

Wherever you are on this journey, it is perfectly fine to be grieving. It is also perfectly fine to be relieved that there's a plan in place. It's okay to be both and go back and forth. But I will definitely say that if you're seeing behaviors and symptoms that are getting to be more than you can handle and seem along the lines of what I've described, then it might be time to call in some of the experts and see if there's a diagnosis waiting to help you out. But I would also say, never be afraid of calling a condition what it actually is, and getting some help for it. If your child does have autism, not labeling it doesn't really help anybody, and might deprive them of help that they will need along the way.

But there also needs to be some caution in mislabeling children who actually have PTSD as having something else. Van der Kolk writes,

> *Eighty-two percent of the traumatized children seen in the National Child Traumatic Stress Network do not meet diagnostic criteria for PTSD. Because they often are shut down, suspicious, or aggressive they now receive pseudoscientific diagnoses such as "oppositional defiant disorder," meaning "This kid hates my guts and won't do anything I tell him to do," or "disruptive mood dysregulation disorder," meaning he has temper tantrums. Having as many problems as they do, these kids accumulate numerous diagnoses over time. Before they reach their twenties, many patients have been given four, five, six, or more of these impressive but meaningless labels. If they receive treatment at all, they get whatever is being promulgated as the method of management du jour: medications, behavioral modification, or exposure therapy. These rarely work and often cause more damage.[11]*

Van der Kolk is a bit fiery in this passage, and I echo his frustration in sometimes seeing children in my practice with multiple diagnoses that really just boil down to PTSD. I agree that oppositional defiant disorder (ODD) is almost meaningless as a diagnosis—it should really be a diagnosable symptom. If your child is being oppositional, don't just label it; you need to figure out why. Is it PTSD? Autism? ADHD? Depression? While I do think that medication can be really helpful for children to help them get a handle on uncontrollable behaviors and begin to work on better skills, they are never the only solution. For a child with depression or massive anxiety, medication can be a good first step to calming things down long enough to learn some better skills. Medication cannot ever be the only answer. The exception for this, I believe, is ADHD, which seems like it might be a lifelong condition that often seems best treated by medication.

27

WHILE YOU ARE WAITING AND THE FIRST FEW MONTHS

OH, THAT EXPECTANT TIME of waiting, when you just can't wait to see the child! What will the child be like? Or, if you're playing foster care bingo, will you get a sibling set? A baby or a grade schooler? Often in the flurry of getting licensed, it seems like the hardest part of becoming a foster or an adoptive parent is making sure that your blind cords are properly shortened or you have the right fire extinguisher. Sometimes it feels like you just can't wait to get started, until there are small bodies filling those beds you have so carefully procured. But there are some excellent things you can do while you're waiting, and also how to structure your first few months to get your foster parenting or adoptive journey off to a good start. For each age of the child, I have listed what you can do to prepare and good books to read in preparation as well as what to expect the first few months.

Infants

To prepare: First, read chapter 3, about infant trauma, if you haven't already, and read at least a book or two in preparation. It's a lot harder to read once the baby comes! Set up as much as you can in advance, which can be hard to do if you don't know the age of the child you might be getting. Many a new foster or adoptive parent has stopped at Target on the way to pick up the child to get a car seat. If you have friends who are getting rid of baby clothes, or if you are a garage-sale shopper, it might not be a bad idea to have a few outfits in different sizes just to have something when the child comes home to get you through a few days until friends and family can show up with the instant baby shower.

A close friend of mine wanted to adopt, and said she would take any child up to three years old. Reasonably, she expected a toddler, so she had a toddler bed and a few things ready. When she was placed with a six-day-old baby that she needed to pick up within a few hours, she called me from Target asking which car seat and bottles to buy. Another friend and I sorted through our old baby clothes, along with my son's old swaddling blankets, made a few new purchases, washed them, and had them at her house within a few hours. Luckily I still had the crib that my son had just outgrown, as well as a few other things, and another friend showed up with a large pack of diapers. She was fully set up within a few days, mostly due to her close-knit Japanese-American community rising to the challenge. It can be done to set you up completely within a few days, especially if you have a good community around you, but if you have less help or want a quieter beginning with your child, some planning ahead might be helpful.

When you take custody: Enjoy the moment; be present. The memories you are making during this time, you will remember forever. But also take pictures: this will be information your child will want later. Take pictures of the hospital, the nurses, and any bio-family that is around. Whatever the situation where you take custody, take pictures. If there are hospital clothes or bracelets, keep them. If you know the identity of the birth parents, Facebook stalk them and download pictures as soon as you can, within the first few days if you are able. Facebook pages change and disappear; do not rely on them being around later for you to use.

For the first few months: Expect the child to be grieving. Babies grieve differently than we do. The baby has spent the last several months attaching to the mom who was carrying them, getting used to her sound and her smell, and suddenly that mom isn't there. Their brain can't tell the difference between a loving decision made in their best interest and the mother's death. For some babies, they might also be dealing with withdrawal from drugs they have been exposed to in utero or high cortisol (the stress hormone) levels, which also can wreak havoc on an infant's brain. If there were drugs involved, be in close contact with your doctor and make sure that your child is being monitored, but know that children do recover from this. The child will need lots of comfort and time with you, contact, and quiet. Be as responsive and reassuring as you can be, employ calming techniques if the child becomes upset. Dr. Harvey Karp talks about the five S's of soothing a crying newborn that can be very helpful to a new parent: swaddle, side or stomach position, shush (making the *shush* noise), swing, and suck.[1] I highly recommend reading his website (www.happiestbaby.com) or his book to learn about soothing a crying baby.

Take as much time off work as you can and delay sending your child to day care as long as you can. Time with you is the best thing for them in the beginning. Try to cocoon as much as possible, try to fend off happy friends and relatives as much as possible, and keep the child's world as quiet and as small as you can. If people want to help, give them specific things to help with—bring you dinner, bring a pack of diapers, give you a break to take a nap and a shower.

A word on postpartum depression: There is a myth out there that only women who give birth get postpartum depression, and many women who come into my office are surprised that I ask them about it. In reality, about 10 to 15 percent of adoptive mothers get it, which is about the same rate as biological mothers.[2] If you're feeling overwhelmed, are depressed, are having odd thoughts, or have any other symptoms that are worrying you, get help. Postpartum depression is common, and very treatable; the earlier the better. You can see your family doctor, your ob-gyn, a psych ARNP (advanced registered nurse practitioner), or even an urgent care facility if you need help right now and can't get to your family doctor.

Toddler and Preschool Age

In preparation for a child of this age, definitely get their room ready and make sure you have a lot of sensory options available to them. Kids this age are sensory anyway, but a child with trauma has sensory issues gone wild. Here are some good things to include as you set up their room (just a few; you don't have to get them all):

- large stuffed animal (human-size)

- bean bag

- sand or rice tray (this can be as easy as some rice or sand in a large Tupperware container with a lid, or a bucket with a lid)

- Orbeez

- mini trampoline (or larger if you have the room)

- yoga ball

- bubbles

- swing

- climbing wall (for the more adventurous parent)

Make sure before they come home that your fridge is stocked with kid-appropriate food. Depending on whether they are coming straight from their bio-family or from another foster family, you may be shocked at what they are familiar with eating. This is not the time to insist they eat quinoa and basil salad—get fish crackers, cheese sticks, grapes, yogurt, chicken nuggets, pizza, cereal, and basic childhood staples. The children will be frightened, and familiar food will make them feel more at home. You can work on their palate at a later date. Most kids coming into foster care are most familiar with cereal and fast food—usually chicken nuggets and pizza. Be ready to serve those for a while until kids feel safe enough to try some new options.

Also, be prepared for children not to come with a lot of clothes. Sometimes they do, sometimes they don't—you may be making a shopping trip during the first few days. Make sure you also have some basics at your house at all times: a kid's toothbrush with children's toothpaste (kids hate adult toothpaste; it's too intense for them), a stuffed animal waiting for the child, and basic bedding. A few pairs of pajamas in different sizes, even from garage sales or a thrift store, aren't a bad idea either.

When you take custody: Just as with an infant, take pictures. You will likely have less "picture" type moments, but it's good to have at least a few moments of them on their first day with you. Offer them a snack almost as soon as you meet them—something easy and fun, like applesauce served in a pouch or a cookie and juice. They will likely be scared, and receiving something like a snack from you will help lower that fear for them. Try to make the first few days as low-key as you can. Have the basic routine you plan to have as much as you can, but expect disruptions to sleep and eating habits. If you can get hints from their last caregiver on what helps them sleep, great. If not, start a good sleep routine with a nice bath (or skip it if it's triggering for them; the bath can be pretty triggering for victims of sexual abuse), tooth-brushing, a bedtime story, and soft music. Make sure you have a soft toy waiting for them that's theirs to keep, and stay with them for a bit to help them fall asleep if it seems to help.

First few months: Try to keep the routine as basic as possible. If you are able not to start them in preschool or day care right away, and have some time at home with them, that is definitely better. Grieving at this age can look like sadness, with the child saying, "I miss Mama!" or it can look like rage, anger, and acting out. They will also likely regress in things like toilet training and bottle feeding—it's very common for kids who have had a trauma to suddenly want to act younger than their age. Follow their lead; if they feel the need to act younger, then let them do it. Your job is to be calm and loving, and help them ride it out. If they come from a background of abuse, you will likely see them scared of you at times as well, especially if you raise your voice or if they do something to "get in trouble." You will have to spend some time reassuring them that you don't hurt kids and that kids are safe in your home. Expect it to take some time for them to believe you, though—I'm talking years.

School-Age Children

To prepare: The setup for school-age children is very similar to that of preschoolers: make sure you have kid-appropriate foods, some sensory activities, and some ways to watch some kid-appropriate screen time. Most kids coming into care have had a great deal of screen time, and they will find it comforting to watch a movie as a family with you. Be prepared for them not to have a lot of clothes. If you know in advance who's coming, it's not a bad idea to have some things picked out for them, just to get them started. You should have a kid's toothbrush and kid's toothpaste waiting, along with a stuffed animal for the child you're waiting for. It's really good to be able to hand a scared child a stuffed animal they can cuddle.

Taking custody: Take pictures, but likely there will be less to document. Still, a few snaps for their lifebook are helpful. This is definitely the age not to expect them to be excited at all about this—they are probably going to be pretty sad, mad, or scared, or all three at once. Make taking custody as easy as possible. Plan a low-key first day, like a simple dinner and a movie night with a treat. Do whatever bedtime routine you are hoping to establish, but be flexible and kind about it—the child is likely very scared. Most children are compliant in the first few days, at least of a placement; they are usually shell-shocked and scared. Check with your social worker if the child is in foster care as to what your state requirements are, but if you're allowed to sleep on a mattress in their bedroom, it might make them feel a lot better. If it's not allowed, then sit in there for a while to let them fall asleep, and make sure they know they can wake you if they need you during the night.

The first few months: Resist the urge to sign them up for soccer, choir, karate, and the school musical. If there's one activity they really want to do, go ahead—but for the most part, try to keep their world small and give yourselves plenty of time to bond. There will be time after this initial bonding time to become the parent chauffeur extraordinaire. The more time together, the better. Play games, talk, do crafts, and just get to know each other in general. Here are some good games to play with children:

Jenga

Sorry

Catan Junior

Connect 4

Mancala

KerPlunk

Guess Who?

Sleeping Queens

Uno

Work on learning your child's ways and understanding them on a deep level, and enjoy spending time with them. Attachment will follow.

Teens

To prepare: Teens are a particular group in placement, and one of the rarest. But more and more teens are getting placed and adopted, which is great! Teens need good homes too; eighteen is way too young to be without a family if you age out of the system. Preparation for teens isn't too hard, and it is very individual for the kid, so it's hard to make suggestions here. Except, if you haven't fed a teenager before, they will likely surprise you with how much they eat. Make sure you have some card games and board games on hand; you would be surprised how many games of *Jenga* and *Sorry* I've played with teens in my office.

The first few months: With teens, grief can look like moodiness and lashing out, or it can look like depression. The good news is that they're old enough to talk about these things. Have a conversation about the grief cycle, share about grief you've gone through, and work on connection. The tricky thing about accepting the placement of a teenager is that they're trying to differentiate at the time they're trying to attach, so that's difficult to navigate. The good part is that often they are verbal enough to process what's going on, and that can be a real benefit. As with younger kids, work on attunement and enjoyment. They are going to test your boundaries, so make sure that you are clear on what they are, but that you are kind and solutions-oriented when they are broken.

28

FOSTER CARE
Licensed to Parent

THERE ARE MANY adoptive parents in this country who take a child into their home and form a legal and emotional bond with them that will (hopefully!) last a lifetime. Then there are the parents who offer a temporary safe space to a child, a space that perhaps allows a biological parent to get their life in order, a suitable relative to be located, or maybe to allow for some other long-term placement to be found. Foster parents are a needed part of the system, and having caring, compassionate care for kids during some of the scariest times in their lives is extremely important. However, I have often heard of a cultural stereotype about foster parents being "in it for the money" or some such nonsense, with Miss Hannigan from the 2014 remake of the film *Annie* being the template. With as little as foster parents are compensated, it is very hard to believe that is true, but still this idea persists. I'm not saying that there aren't bad foster parents out there; I'm just saying that if you want to make money and abuse kids, there are a lot easier ways to go about it.

When I watched the 2019 movie *Shazam!*, I knew it was about a boy in foster care and was bracing for the standard depiction of abusive and uncaring foster parents. I was so surprised when it showed caring people as foster parents that I realized it was one of the first times I'd seen a nonrelative foster care provider being shown in a positive light in a film of this kind.[1] It takes a special type of person to welcome scared, abused kids into their home and love them and care for them, not knowing how long they are going to be there. Foster parents do a really tough job and open themselves up for heartbreak, while enduring suspicion and stereotypes, and get very little recognition nor compensation.

My parents were foster parents when I was very small. They had no intention of adopting; they just wanted to help foster kids. My first foster brother was Bryan,[2] and we were very close to the same age. He came into care fighting and biting, and I was the one who was mostly on the receiving end of those sharp two-year-old teeth. But he calmed down, stopped biting me so much, and we became inseparable friends. I cried for days when he went home to his mother. Then we had the twins, who were older than both me and my older sister. They were mean to us and had a lot of behavioral problems, but my parents tried very hard to work with them. They ended up going back to their mother too, and when they did, we all breathed a sigh of relief, and my parents decided to hang up their foster license. Working with them and their bio-mom had just been too difficult, and the death threat that my mom had gotten for getting the girls' hair trimmed was the last straw. Then the local social worker (I come from a small town) called my parents and asked if she could place this sweet young toddler with us just for a few days. The social worker was right—she was absolutely adorable, with red curls and big blue eyes. The social worker was also wrong in that it wasn't a few days—that little girl became my younger sister. And my parents did hang up their foster license after that, though they did dust it off for a few years when I was in high school and I had a friend run away from her home due to abuse.

If there's one thing I can say about foster care, it's that it is unpredictable—and people that go into it really never know what they're going to get. Some people foster because they want to adopt; some people foster with the express purpose of never wanting to adopt, and sometimes they fall in love with a child. That's what happened to my parents—they didn't intend to adopt, but once that sweet little girl was in their home, it was impossible not to fall in love with her.

These are some myths and truths about foster care, but I also want to recognize that the foster care experience can vary widely state to state, area to area, and country to country. But here are the myths that I have come across.

Myth 1: The State Covers Most of the Expenses for the Child

Truth: I live in Seattle, which has some of the highest rents in the country, so I would make more money renting out the room. The money that the state gives you helps, but it is likely that you will spend more on your foster child than the state gives you. Most foster kids come with limited if any clothes and toiletries, leaving the foster parents to pick up the tab. There are often organizations to help with this, and experienced foster parents figure out how to access resources. As of the writing of this book, the current pay for respite care to care for a foster child for one day is only a few dollars above an hour's work on minimum wage, and to be a respite care provider, you must undergo a background check, be cardiopulmonary resuscitation (CPR) and first-aid certified, and provide care in a home that has passed a home inspection. This is not exactly a moneymaking proposition, nor should it be. But it's good to know going into it that there will be at least some start-up costs.

Myth 2: Foster Kids Are Always Problem Children

Truth: There are as many types of foster kids as there are kids. There are ones that are sweet, shy, aggressive, smart, slow, friendly, withdrawn, and everything in between. The only thing that they have in common is that they have all had some form of trauma, but how they deal with that is very different. Some kids barely miss a step and bond easily to new parents; some take years to learn to trust. Classifying all foster kids as being problem children isn't helpful, but neither is expecting that the trauma they endured would have no effects. The best thing is to treat all children as individuals, and to be curious as to how the trauma has affected them.

Myth 3: I Have to Be an Expert Parent to Be a Foster Parent

Truth: Some skills are helpful, and not every foster parent can parent every kid—but if you love kids, and are willing to learn, then you can be a foster parent. Kids need to feel safe, they need to feel loved, and they need a safe, consistent home. If that's something you can provide, then you can be a foster parent.

Myth 4: My House, Cooking, Whatever Has to Be Better to Be a Foster Parent

Truth: You should look into your local requirements, but many people get too worried about making their home perfect to be a foster parent, or that they aren't providing dinners with organic quinoa or something. You need to provide a clean, functional space that is adequate for a child's needs, but it doesn't need to be in the latest style or anything like that. In fact, a social worker responsible for licensing foster homes once confided in me that she actually got nervous if a potential foster home was too perfect—would a perfect cream-colored carpet in the dining room really be ready for a five-year-old?

Myth 5: You Have to Be a Traditional Family to Be a Foster Family

Truth: In most areas the state welcomes all sorts of families to be foster families: single adults, same-sex couples, older adults, people who rent their homes, and so on. I've worked with people who have been as young as twenty-five when they became foster parents, and others who are grandparents. Check your local regulations if you are a nontraditional family; you may be surprised that there are fewer restrictions than you might think. Total equality doesn't exist yet for everybody, however. Though LGBTQ people have a long history of fostering and adopting kids that are harder to place, and though scientific studies show again and again that kids do well when adopted and fostered by LGBTQ parents, discrimination does still exist.[3]

Myth 6: I Can Protect Myself from Sadness as a Foster Parent by Just Not Bonding with My Foster Child

Truth: If you do it well, foster parenting involves pain. Kids need you to care about them, and if you don't, then you're being a babysitter, not a foster parent. Wherever the child goes next—whether they're reunified with parents, placed with relatives, placed in a longer-term home, or staying with you—having a loving, intimate, and safe experience with a foster parent is the best thing that can happen for them. For a lot of kids, the time they spend in foster care is the only time in their childhood that they get a good model of a healthy family.

So What Does Make a Good Foster Parent?

By talking about myths, by no means do I want to say that being a foster parent is easy, or even that everyone can be a foster parent. For example, people with extensive trauma should do work on themselves and work through their trauma before trying to parent a traumatized child. After they've done their work, however, a parent that has firsthand experience with trauma can be an especially sympathetic advocate for a traumatized child. Here are the traits that I see foster parents have that are the most successful:

Flexibility: Successful foster parents learn to be flexible because things are so uncertain in the realm of foster care. Successful foster parents are flexible enough to try different approaches with different kids, and they are able to try to provide what the child needs. Rigid parents are rarely successful with traumatized children—if a parent says, "It's my way or the highway," well, most traumatized children won't feel safe unless they've tested to see if you mean it.

Warmth: Successful foster parents are able to disarm foster kids with warmth and genuine concern for their well-being. Kids respond to genuineness and warmth, and if the foster parents are able to convey this, they will get a lot farther.

Attunement: Successful foster parents are able to look at things from the child's perspective, and try to understand their emotions.

Good communication: A good foster parent has good two-way communication—they are able to listen and to communicate effectively. They are able to have good communication with the child in their care and also with the myriad of other professionals involved in their care.

A sense of humor: There are many times that a sense of humor can defuse a tense situation, and being able to laugh can be a great asset as a foster parent.

Good self-care: Being a foster parent is a tough job, and you will burn out if you are not able to take care of yourself.

Objectivity: Part of being a foster parent is to realize that the child is a temporary part of your home, and your ability to stay objective and to keep in mind what is best for the child is paramount. Part of this is an ability to work with caseworkers and birth family, as well as helping the child access school or other services they might need. And all of this is for a child that you parent in a loving way that you know will not be staying in your home.

Perseverance without getting jaded: This one is a little harder to quantify, but a good foster parent is able to weather the tough things that happen with foster care and is still emotionally available to their foster children without getting hardened from it. I have seen people for whom this becomes too much to do; working with the system and the courts and the social workers just becomes too much. Sometimes it is the child's behaviors that are the difficulties to weather, but for the most part, what I see burning people out is frustration with the system—Court Appointed Special Advocates (CASAs) that are difficult, endless changes in social workers, nonsensical orders from judges, and children returned to bio-parents in dangerous circumstances. Foster parenting is hard work, and the system is difficult to navigate; successful foster parents need to be able to navigate it.

Proper motivation: Research shows that the motivations that are associated with successful foster and adoptive parenting are the desire to parent a child when a person is unable to conceive a child, identification with deprived children as a result of an unhappy childhood, and parents who act from motives of social concern.[4]

The Real Truth about Foster Parenting

The real truth about foster parenting is that it is hard, and it is hard in ways that are very difficult to prepare people for. When I was going into foster parenting, I assumed that it would be difficult—I had seen my parents do it, and I thought I knew what to expect. But the truth is that you never really know what to expect, because every child is an individual and every situation is different. Almost all foster parents say that they are not prepared for how hard it ultimately was on them, but most foster parents I know are glad that they did it.

The goal of foster parenting is to give the child in your care the best experience they can have of safety, attachment, and family. The message that you are sending is that they are safe now, and that hopefully you can give them a safe and sane place to regroup and find peace and calm.

And as crazy as the foster care system is on the foster family, it is even more so on the child. If you are a foster parent, your self-care has to be incredibly robust for you to survive burnout. Make sure that you have regular times and ways to recharge, connect with people you love, and rest. Sometimes well-meaning foster parents can easily take on too much, thinking that they can save the world—when really, their job is just the child in front of them, or even the break in front of them, in order to rest up for the next child.

29

WHEN THINGS ARE
REALLY HARD

SOMETIMES THINGS ARE really hard, especially if the child has had a lot of trauma and has a complicating diagnosis of ADHD, FASD, or autism. Sometimes families come to my office on the brink of falling apart, and are desperate for anything that can help. This chapter is for families in that place, so they can know their options. And again, if your family is in this place, please get professionals involved. But here are my best recommendations if you should find yourself in this place.

Psychiatric Evaluation

If your child is having trouble to the point of significant dysfunction at home or school, it is a good idea for them to have a psychiatric evaluation. If the child has underlying depression, anxiety, ADHD, or other treatable conditions, that is the first place to start. There have been several families that I have worked with where treating an underlying disorder has made a massive difference in the child's ability to cope in the rest of their life.

Safety Plans

A safety plan is especially a good idea if there's been aggression, suicidal ideation, cutting, abuse, or anything of this nature. Safety plans are really helpful because they have clear expectations: everybody knows what to expect, and everyone has input ahead of time before emotions are going too high. In the heat of the moment is not the time to try to come up with a safety plan or to try to decide what to do. It is a good idea to have a therapist help you make a safety plan, especially if the plan involves anything around suicide. But I also wanted to include this so that you can get an idea of what one could look like and have a template for a safety plan and how they work.

The theory behind a safety plan is very important, because they are different than a behavioral plan. A behavioral plan, like a child might have at school, has rewards and consequences for behaviors such as showing respect, paying attention, and exercising good citizenship. Safety plans only deal with behaviors that have to do with safety, so they should be short and only cover the things that are the most important. It's also important to make an agreement about what happens with certain behaviors that everyone agrees on, and what steps will be taken, and in what order. Here's an example of what one might look like:

Safety Plan Agreement between Ralph and Mom and Dad

Ralph and Mom and Dad agree that they want everyone in the house to feel safe.

These are the things in our house that make people feel unsafe:

1. Yelling

2. Hitting

3. Threatening

4. Self-harming

Ralph, Mom, and Dad all agree that if they're feeling unsafe, they will say, "I'm feeling unsafe," and then everyone will go to their own room until people calm down and feel safe again. This time can be as long as people need but not less than twenty minutes. When people are in their room, they will do their calm-down activities until they're feeling better. Mom's calm-down activities are reading, deep breathing, yoga, playing little games on her phone, and calling her friend Lisa. Dad's calm down activities are watching funny YouTube videos, calling his friend Jim, and doing push-ups. Ralph's calm-down activities are watching YouTube videos, meditating, drawing, doing stretches, and calling Grandma.

If anybody is unable to go to their own room, then the other people will go to their room until things are calmer.

If the unsafe behavior continues, then Mom or Dad will call the Mental Health Crisis Line; the number is 206-461-3222.

If the situation becomes very unsafe and the parents are afraid that people will get hurt, they will call 911.

How to Write the Plan

This is a very simple plan, but clear and hopefully not shaming. When parents write this plan, they should do it at a time the child is calm, and get their input. It should be a discussion, starting with, "When does everyone feel unsafe at home? What types of things make people feel unsafe?" In this scenario, Ralph also gets to say what makes him feel unsafe, and it's good to respect it if he says that he feels unsafe when Mom yells at him. Encourage him to use the "safe phrase" that everyone agrees to if he's feeling unsafe, and respect it. Safety plans work best if Ralph feels buy-in as well. If Ralph feels that "Ralph is bad and this is a plan to fix him," it won't work as well.

Also built into the plan is caring for yourself when you're triggered—for everyone. This is really good modeling, as well as good non-shaming language. It acknowledges that everyone gets triggered and everyone needs self-care, and it teaches how to set boundaries in relationships for safety.

When I was a new foster parent to a very explosive child, I hadn't had any training on safety plans. I was two months' pregnant when she came, and as my belly grew, I knew that I needed some way to contain her rages for when the little one came. So we began to work on the basic agreement that she would go to her room when we asked her to go, and we would ask her to go if things felt unsafe. We didn't care how she went—she could go stomping and yelling—but I knew when I was nursing a baby, we needed to have some basic safety agreements in place. She wasn't in trouble, but it was simply to make sure everyone was safe. As the months passed and the baby was coming, I became so worried that she wasn't going to be able to do it, and I was worried about what it was going to look like once the baby came. But with patience and consistency, about a month before the arrival of my son, she was actually starting to comply with our safety plan most of the time, at least enough of the time that we were no longer worried about the baby.

Family Preservation Services

These services can be called different things in different areas and states, but many states offer some sort of family preservation services to desperate families. I advise parents to call their local Child Protective Services and explain that they're having trouble and see what services are available. Children that are in danger of disrupting from their adoptive homes can be given things such as respite care (going to a foster care placement on weekends), parent coaching, counseling, drug treatment for the child, school coaching, and other services that might be helpful to preserve the adoptive family unit. If it scares you to call child services, you can always call anonymously and ask for information on services they can provide before giving them your information. People often think of Child Protective Services as just the state taking children away from their parents, but actually they exist to help children, and they usually like to keep children with their families as much as they can.

Residential Care or Boarding School

Sometimes kids get to the point where it's not safe for them to stay at home, either for them or for the rest of the family. Making the choice for them to go somewhere like a therapeutic boarding school is a very difficult one for many parents, and it's an especially heartbreaking one. And of course it's not ideal for a child with attachment problems, as it's hard to repair attachment problems when the child isn't with their parents. But there are times that things have become so toxic at home that it's healthier for everyone to have a break than it is for things to continue how they are going. This is especially true if there are major psychiatric issues or drug dependency issues. I have worked with several families that did better after a break with residential treatment than they had been doing before. And it is far better for a family to have a break and come back together than to have an adoption dissolve. Studies have shown that children that have had residential treatment have less risk of disruption of adoption.[1]

If this is something you are considering for your family, first please take some time to work through your own feelings. Many parents have a lot of feelings of guilt and failure by the time they get to this place, and it is with a great deal of shame that they approach these options. If you don't already have a therapist or someone sympathetic to discuss these feelings with, please take the time to do so.

When choosing a residential facility, make sure you choose one that focuses on trauma and treatment, not on behavior. Residential treatment that focuses on trauma, such as proven programs like the ARC model, have been shown to be effective in reducing PTSD symptoms.[2] Also, make sure they are aware of the dynamics of attachment and that they encourage that as much as possible within the residential structure. There should also be a clear treatment plan for the child's return home.

Adoption Dissolution

Dissolution is the term used when an adoption is legally ended, similar to when divorce ends a marriage. The rate of dissolution of adoptions that happened through foster care is somewhere between 6 to 25 percent, depending on several different factors, with adoptions happening at birth having the lowest rate.[3] There are a lot of legal implications for what happens for a dissolution of an adoption, and I am not a lawyer, so do not rely on what I say for legal advice. I have only worked in a few cases where there has been dissolution, and it is heartbreaking for all involved. But in those few cases where dissolution happened in cases I was involved with, the child's PTSD was triggering the parents' PTSD, and there just didn't seem to be any hope for improvement. Dissolution is something that usually comes at the end of a great many tries at many other things and after a great deal of heartache, and it is something to be approached soberly and with trepidation. Quite simply, it is the option of last resort.

Scientists have studied and attempted to predict what makes some adoptions dissolve. Age at adoption is one of the most reliable predictors of dissolution, with researchers finding the chance of dissolution increasing by a factor of 1.4 with each year of age at the time of adoption.[4] Other factors that increase the chance of dissolution are the existence of preadoption sexual, physical, or emotional abuse, the child having witnessed drug use by the original bio-parents, the child having spent more time in the foster system with multiple placements, adoption by a relative, and the child having more physical, behavioral, or emotional needs. Strangely enough, another factor associated with increased dissolutions is an increased level of education in the adoptive mother.[5]

When adoptions dissolve, the child most often enters the foster system again in hopes of finding another adoptive home. There are also adoption agencies that specialize in finding secondary adoptive homes for children that have disrupted from their first adoptive homes; this is often called second-chance adoptions. Families that decide to work with one of these agencies should make sure that these agencies are accredited and have a good reputation, and that there are social workers and lawyers involved. In recent years there have been investigations about the practice of "rehoming" adopted children without any governmental oversight, including an explosive series of articles done by Reuters. The unregulated practice of putting unwanted adopted children into a stranger's home with no government oversight is really akin to trafficking, and it is not in the child's best interest.[6] More and more states are outlawing the practice, because without oversight and involvement by social workers and courts, people who are unsuitable to be parents (such as sex offenders and people with a history of child abuse) can get access to children with very little protection for the children.

For families that are facing the heartbreaking reality of a really tough situation, the best thing they can do is to reach out for help. Whether that is through safety planning, family preservation services in their state, residential treatment, or assistance with decisions about dissolution, the decisions that they have to make aren't easy ones, and they're going to need help.

30

LEAVING HOME

I WAS AT A CONFERENCE for parents of adopted and foster kids, and nursing a pretty sad heart. One of my kids had just left home, and left home badly. I had been grieving for her, and had tried to find my belief in love and attachment enough to go on and continue to parent my other children at home. Was I destined for heartbreak as my kids left home?

The problem that happens in adolescence is that kids need to differentiate from their parents as they grow and mature, and when children are well attached, this process can still be fraught with emotion and difficulty. But when a child has attachment challenges as well as emotional regulation challenges, this process is far more complicated and rocky.

And when it comes to leaving home, even typical children can face a huge amount of anxiety, attachment worries, and uncertainty about the future. For children with PTSD, this pushes buttons of abandonment as well, and this can make the process of leaving home very difficult for young adults. Some kids stick around home for long periods of time and fail to "launch." Some leave and just don't answer texts much—acting as if there was never any attachment at all. Others leave badly, sometimes even violently—almost as if they have to shove away as hard as they can in order to launch.

So while I was at this conference giving a talk about how to parent a child with trauma, I felt so discouraged myself about the future. At the break, I wandered around and spoke to many others—speakers, presenters, foster parents, social workers. But then I talked to someone who was the person I needed to talk to: a woman who had fostered over twenty traumatized children. I found myself telling her about my own heartbreak, of my worries and fear and grief. I had spoken to my therapist, to friends, and to my husband, but for some reason this woman felt more like she understood than anyone I had spoken to before.

"I feel so hurt," I told her. "I really did give her my whole heart. I love her so much, and now I don't even know if she's ever going to talk to me again."

"They always leave badly," she told me, patting my hand with comfort. "All twenty-six kids I've had, they all have left badly. But, if you stay open, they will come back."

And so, with her wise words spoken over me like a benediction, my husband and I set forth on the journey of finding out what it meant to "stay open" and to parent an adult child with trauma. It turns out that staying open means doing a lot of the same things that you do when the child is in your home, except that it means a lot more patience and perseverance. In your home, if your child doesn't talk to you for a few days, you can intervene with some ice cream and start up a conversation. When your adult child doesn't talk to you for a month, there's not a lot you can do but be patient and open.

Truths we have learned about parenting adult children:

1. Eighteen-year-old kids still need parents. There is not some magic thing that happens on your eighteenth birthday that makes you completely independent. And if you know someone in their thirties or forties that has lost their parents, they feel that loss not just in relationship but also as a mentor.

2. You need to think about differentiation. It's very important to give your child space to be a young adult—and to make decisions that you don't necessarily agree with. It's a hard transition to make from active parenting to being cool with your child's new tattoo, but the alternative isn't great either. Which brings me to the next point.

3. Your role has changed. Trying to crack down won't get you what you want; it will just build resentment. So now is the time to sit back and trust the parenting that you have done up to this point. You are still the parent, but your role has changed—you are now becoming more of a mentor.

4. They will need help with the milestones—graduation, jobs, marriage, babies—these are areas that adult children need extra support. And if there are bio-relatives or other people in the mix who are less stable, you can be the stable, helpful ones that make things work.

5. Boundaries—if your child should make some truly bad decisions, such as drugs, then you need to figure out what sort of boundaries you want to have in having a relationship with your adult child. For instance, a good boundary might be that you don't give the child cash, but you're happy to give your son or daughter food or clothes. But even if your child is making good decisions, it is still good to think about where your boundaries are and what you feel comfortable with. Good boundaries make good neighbors.

6. Look for opportunities to connect. It can be much harder when they don't live in your home. Holidays, routines, and rituals that you set up as the child grew up with you will play a huge part here.

7. The human brain isn't fully developed until the mid-twenties, so neurologically speaking, young adults are still adolescents until that time.[1] The last part of the brain to develop is cause-effect thinking, which explains why young adults can be so impulsive.

My daughter didn't speak to me for a year when she left home, and the year was excruciating, I think, for everyone involved. At Christmas, three months into our estrangement, I sent her a set of pajamas and socks, as I always gave all the children for the holidays, and took it on faith that she received them. I had to find peace in myself to trust that she would be all right, and I had to find peace that someday I would be able to connect with her again. The story from that point on was tangled and long, but trust was rebuilt, and I can truly say now that our relationship is stronger and better than it had ever been before.

Preparing Your Child

The other part of thinking about when a child leaves home is the lead-up until that time. It may seem like it is miles away when your child is thirteen, but in reality those last years fly past in a flurry of soccer games and school concerts. Let's do a frightening thought experiment, shall we? Think about how many years your child has until they're eighteen. Now, think about where you were that many years ago. If you currently have a two-year-old, you're probably not freaking out. If you have a fourteen-year-old, you probably are. Because that fourteen-year-old that currently can't remember to put on deodorant reliably will, in a few short years, be needing to know how to drive a car, manage a bank account, pay taxes, and navigate how to get a job. And whatever time you have with your child between now and then is the time you have to prepare them for doing those tasks.

Kids with trauma tend to be delayed developmentally with social and emotional tasks, and these can very much be the developmental tasks that they need for living on their own. Also, there is a higher likelihood with traumatized kids that they will go through a time of estrangement from you when they leave home and will be less likely to ask you questions, so it's good to make sure they know as many of these things as possible. Here is a list of a few of the major developmental tasks that kids with trauma tend to have difficulty with when living on their own.

Financial issues: Many people without trauma have issues dealing with financial issues, but kids with trauma have extra challenges in this area. It's a good idea to address this early—start your child with a debit card by fifteen with a monthly allowance in which they are responsible for a certain part of their budget—either saving for their clothes, entertainment, or other regular expenses. You can sit down together, build a budget, and then deposit a certain amount per month for them to spend. Then, as they approach adulthood, you can teach them all sorts of financial ideas—debt, savings, budgeting, and what happens if you overspend. If you start this at fifteen, this can work its way up naturally until your child is an adult and can take over for themselves. A few tips: make sure that the bank you use stops the debit card if there's not enough money in the account, so you're not responsible for overages. Also, make sure your child knows to keep financial information private. Before a child leaves your home, make sure you have a conversation about how to buy a car and how to manage a credit card, because those are issues that can pop up right away, and predatory lenders are looking for naive young adults.

Relational boundaries: It is a very good idea to make sure you have a good conversation with your child about relational boundaries. Explicitly talk about red flags for domestic violence and manipulation in relationships, and look up helpful websites if you need guidance on explaining them. Young adults with trauma are especially susceptible to predators, and it's very important that you educate them on how to recognize predatory behaviors. Teach them to listen to their bodies and instincts, watch for controlling behavior, make sure that their friends and family like their partner, and that a loving partner shouldn't pressure them to do something they don't want to do.

Relational boundaries also include how people should be treated in employment situations by bosses and coworkers, and where to go for help when you need it. It is not uncommon for young teens and adults to be subject to unethical and even predatory managers in early job situations, so make sure that they are aware of their rights and how to handle situations should they arise. Before a first job, it's a good idea to have a discussion about sexual harassment, unfair pressure for things like overtime, and to go over your local laws about overtime, breaks, and minimum wage. An educated worker is much less likely to be taken advantage of.

Basic life skills: It always surprises me how many kids leave home without being able to cook a simple meal, do laundry, sew on a button, make a dentist appointment, use basic household tools, or clean a toilet. To think about all the things that an adult needs to be able to do for themselves, make a list of all of the things you have done for yourself in the last few weeks. Which of those things does your child still have to learn? Which are important to your family values? Some families put great stock in everyone being able to change a tire and fix your own brake pads, while others are much more worried about a child learning proper rock-climbing techniques. What is important to you that your child learn? What are you grateful that your parents taught you?

TROUBLESHOOTING
The Q and A Section

I LOVE GIVING talks to different groups, and I do it as much as I can. When I do it, I often try to have a question-and-answer time at the end of the talk. There are several questions that I have gotten more than once but that weren't big enough to devote a whole chapter to answer. This chapter addresses some of those questions.

HOW DO I CALM A RAGING CHILD?
First, recognize that they're triggered, and that words and logic won't work. Here are your best options:

1. First off, you stay calm. If you can stay calm, you will hopefully help trigger their mirror neurons in their brain. I often do some deep breathing for myself, and keep my voice barely above a whisper to emphasize that I am calm.

2. Reflective listening: Reread chapter 12 to get the details, but basically tell them back calmly what they're saying to you. Kids are less likely to keep yelling at you if they hear that you hear them.

3. Sensory intervention: especially something like gum or a lollipop. The best way to do this for a highly oppositional child is to have one yourself and then offer them one, or even just hand it to them. Other good sensory things are scented lotion, a weighted blanket, a trampoline, music, and so on.

4. If you have one of the 3 percent of kids who will actually do deep breathing or meditation with you, great! I find that most of the time the suggestion of deep breathing just irritates kids. Some kids can be tricked into it by blowing bubbles or blowing up a balloon. But just because kids won't do it doesn't mean that *you* can't. I find that if I'm doing things like taking deep breaths, counting to ten, and talking about going to my happy place in my head, kids will begin to model that behavior.

MY CHILD STAYS PRETTY REGULATED DURING THE WEEK BUT GOES BAT CRAZY ON SATURDAY. ANY IDEAS?

This is actually really common, and it's because kids do better with structure and predictable routine. Parents sometimes don't like the solution to this, but the answer really is to make your Saturday as routine as you can. Draw up a schedule, and make it so your child can read it. It doesn't have to be "at 9:15 we eat breakfast" but here's an example of a sample schedule:

- Early morning: Kids get up and watch TV while parents sleep.
- Mid-morning: Parents get up and make pancakes.
- Late morning: Family chore time
- Around noon: Lunch time together
- Early afternoon: Rest time or quiet activity
- Afternoon: Fun family time
- Early evening: Dinner
- Evening: Movie and popcorn

Having traditions and routines that you do is important, but they can change. Notice that this schedule is very flexible; "chore" time could mean grocery shopping or raking leaves, and "fun family time" could mean riding bikes or going to the library. This schedule is probably what you were doing already, but writing it down and letting the child know what to expect help a lot to help their brains regulate. And having a tradition like pancakes or movies and popcorn helps the child mark the week and have something to look forward to, whatever that tradition is for your family. If you're not the pancake types, maybe you have homemade granola or go out for doughnuts. It doesn't matter what it is that you do, but the routine of what you are doing.

VACATIONS ARE SUPPOSED TO BE FUN, BUT THEY'VE TURNED INTO A VERY STRESSFUL TIME OF YEAR FOR MY KIDS. ANY ADVICE?

This is super common, and there's a lot you can do to help this. First, are you choosing a vacation that works for your child? A road trip may not be great for a really active kid, and a theme park might be hard for a child who gets easily overwhelmed with noise and other stimulation. With traumatized kids, my advice is always to give yourself lots of extra time and space that you don't think you'll need, because kids are unpredictable. Don't try to do Disneyland in a day; plan for several. And your sensory sensitive kid is going to hate the roller coasters, so plan for that.

If you can get the child to help plan the vacation, that can actually help a lot. The more involved they are, the more likely they are to enjoy it. Also, just like the Saturday advice, having something of a schedule will help a lot with helping the child feel regulated. Making some sort of tangible, age-appropriate schedule that the child can look at can really help.

Also, make sure you plan ahead. Vacations with inadequate planning can tend toward late meals, inadequate entertainment, and frayed nerves. Always make sure you have enough snacks, emergency entertainment, sensory interventions, and a sense of humor.

I FEEL TERRIBLE ABOUT THIS, BUT I DON'T FEEL AS ATTACHED TO MY ADOPTED CHILD AS I DO TO MY BIRTH CHILDREN. AM I A BAD PERSON?

No, you're not. Try to believe me when I say this, because that guilt and shame that you carry with you about this can actually make it worse. Reread (or read, if you skipped it the first time) chapter 6, "Attachment," and accept that attachment is a process, and forgive who you are in the process. Just because you aren't where you want to be right now, that doesn't mean you aren't the right person for your child to attach to. Keep working on attunement and enjoyment, and be patient with yourself as well. Parents often experience feeling a difference in attachment with children they've given birth to because of a variety of factors—birth trauma, the personality of the child, and factors for the mother such as postpartum depression. It's okay for attachment levels to be different; however, it is good to continue to work toward making it better.

Sometimes, though, this difficulty of attaching to your child might actually be the result of your child's trauma interacting with some of your trauma. If that's the case, see a therapist so you can work on some of those issues. It's incredibly hard to attach if your trauma reactions are being triggered.

I'VE TRIED PARENTING IN THE WAY THAT YOU ADVOCATE, AND THE REST OF MY FAMILY DOESN'T UNDERSTAND AND THINKS I'M CRAZY. HOW DO I CONVINCE THEM?

It would be great if they had genuine curiosity and would read this book, but I'm assuming that they're not willing to do so. I usually try to explain to people that if your child was in a wheelchair, people would have no problems making accommodations for them. This is the same thing; the wheelchair is just in their brain, and the accommodations look a little bit different. We had this issue with my parents once when they were watching the children for a few days. I made up a folder of information about each child—what triggered them, what to do if they got triggered, and so on. For one child I told them that she got triggered when she got into trouble, so if she did something wrong, not to put her in a time-out, but instead I walked them through what a time-in looked like. They were very confused, but I gave them concrete examples of what would happen if they tried to put her into a time-out, what we did instead, and why. They did understand, and we got to a better level of understanding in the end. And they did great with her.

I HAD NO IDEA PARENTING A TRAUMATIZED CHILD WOULD BE THIS HARD ON MY MARRIAGE. HELP!

Any cracks in a marriage will become chasms under the stress of parenting a traumatized child. Some therapists that work with traumatized children recommend therapy for parents just as a matter of course because all marriages can use marital therapy when parenting a difficult child. Please find a therapist as soon as you can. It's helpful if you can find one that knows anything about trauma. If you don't know where to look, you can start by looking for therapists that work with the Gottman Institute; they are well respected and research-based.

Other than therapy, make sure that you're doing good marriage care outside of your parenting duties. Bringing a child into a marriage can be one of the hardest things you can do to a marriage, so the marriage will need extra care to stay strong. Plan dates and times to connect, even if it means just turning off the television and drinking a glass of wine together on the couch after the kids go to bed. If you have a respite option, take nights away when you can. Try to be kind and loving to your partner—after all, this person will be with you for the long haul, long after the child has grown up and started a family of their own.

I'M WORRIED THAT ADOPTING A CHILD WILL DO DAMAGE TO MY BIO-CHILD.

I hear a version of this question a lot, and the problem is that there is no guarantee one way or the other. For the most part, and for most families that I work with, having an adopted sibling is a cost benefit sort of a thing. Of course there are costs; there always are when you add a sibling, but what benefits are there? Here is a list of some costs and benefits to get you thinking:

COSTS	BENEFITS
• less one-on-one parental time	• increased empathy with a sibling with different needs
• potentially less family money	
• possible upset with sibling emotional dysregulation	• someone to play with
	• increased social interactions with people of a different race or culture
• potential for abuse	
• less traditional-looking family	• expanded sense of family and hospitality
• potential for sadness, especially in foster care if sibling is reunified with bio-family	• increased awareness of social justice issues

I would also like to say that many things on the costs lists happen with any siblings, but you should think carefully about going into foster care or adoption with bio-kids in the family and thinking about how it will impact them.

Our family had increased from two to six rapidly, and my first child (a bio-kid) was now a bubbly four-year-old. I had a few people that week ask me specifically how she was doing with all of the new siblings, and if I was worried about how adding children was going to affect her. Sometimes I worried about her being lost in the shuffle with so many new siblings, but I wasn't really sure how to talk to her about it. I finally decided that I had to do it, and I pulled her aside to ask her one day.

"It's sure busy being a family with six kids," I told her.

"It is," she agreed.

"How would you feel if our family was smaller?" I asked her. "If it was just you and your brother?" (He was the other bio-kid.)

"That would be terrible," she told me. "Who would I play with?"

"Good point," I agreed. "But is it hard for you when some of the older girls have problems and cry and yell sometimes?"

"Sometimes," she shrugged. "But I know you and Daddy are there."

"Thanks," I told her, near tears.

I wouldn't say it's always been easy for my bio-kids, but at no point in the history of our family has one of my bio-kids had the other bio-kid as their family bestie.

CAN YOU ADOPT KIDS OUT OF BIRTH ORDER?

Yep, sure can. Full disclosure: I am a second-born and my husband is a third-born, so we think the people more into preserving the birth order stuff are usually firstborns.

Sorry for being flippant; it's my second-child nature. The only time adopting kids out of birth order is really a problem is if you put a lot of stock into older children having a lot of power over younger children, which isn't a great idea with traumatized children anyway. You also might want to think about privileges being tied to age as well—they're much better tied to responsibilities and demonstrated maturity.

You also might want to be careful about the kids that you bring into your home if they have a lot of expectations on what an older child does as well—make sure you communicate that they don't have power over a younger sibling. Always be safe with boundaries with younger and older siblings.

MY CHILD SEEMS REALLY TRIGGERED AROUND DOING CHORES. IS THIS NORMAL?

Some of my colleagues and I have noticed this, and we have a pet theory about this—especially if the child was placed at an older age. I think that it's because often older children can be really suspicious about why parents adopt children, and when you ask them to do chores—even extremely reasonable, barely anything sort of chores—this can trigger a fear for them that the only reason you wanted them is because you wanted a servant. If your child reacts like this, a great way to overcome this is to do chores together—not only is this good modeling and attachment time, but this eliminates this fear.

I WANT TO ADOPT AND HAVE BIO-KIDS. ARE THERE ANY COMBINATIONS THAT I SHOULD BE CAREFUL TO AVOID?

There are two combinations that I've seen cause problems with placements and would be good to avoid. First, something called "twinning," which is accepting a placement of a child that is the same age and gender as your bio-child. This can be problematic because it can make your bio-child feel territorial and have a lot of overlap with friends and such. A placement should be at least a year or two older or at least six months younger, providing the younger would be in a different grade. The reason the younger child can be closer is that usually a child with trauma is delayed and will likely be younger emotionally. Differently gendered children seem not to trip this issue as much, but that leads us to the next problematic placement of differently gendered adolescents. It's easy to believe that taking an adolescent immediately makes people feel like siblings, but that isn't always the case. I have worked in enough situations where this has gone badly that I would caution against this placement. As a traumatized child starts feeling attachment and affection for their new family, this can easily get confused with romantic feelings when there's an adolescent teenager handy that is attractive to them. When accepting a placement of an older child, either do the same gender as your bio-child if they're an adolescent or stick to preadolescent children.

I AM WONDERING—AT WHAT POINT DO I GET A NEUROPSYCH EVALUATION DONE ON MY CHILD? I'M WORRIED ABOUT HIM, BUT I DON'T KNOW WHAT THE THRESHOLD IS.

I would say the first step is to get the child into therapy with a competent therapist, and see what the therapist says. If you feel like the therapist thinks there are no problems, then I would wonder why that is. My usual rule of thumb as a therapist for getting another professional involved, either a neuropsych or a psychiatrist for medication, is if the child's quality of life is being substantially impaired. Is he having trouble with his friends? Is he miserable at home? Is he able to function with his family? If whatever you're sensing is wrong with him is substantially impairing his normal tasks of daily life, which for a child is play, school, and family life, then it's time to probably get another professional involved. When I work with a family, I usually give it a few months to see if the interventions I do help enough, but if I don't see significant improvement, then I refer for other treatment, usually in addition to what I do.

I FEEL LIKE THE RULES OF FOSTER CARE ARE INTERFERING WITH MY ABILITY TO BOND WITH MY FOSTER CHILD. HELP?

These rules are tedious, I get it. I wish that the rules of foster care were simply love your child and treat them well, but unfortunately the rules have to be more explicit. It is sobering when you read the rules: you know that for every rule, there is a story for how an abusive foster parent was mistreating a child. Why else would they have to specify that you give a child a bath that's warm but not too warm, or that you are required to provide three meals a day separated by a specified number of hours? But you also don't want to break the rules and lose your license, so work around them the best you can. If a scared child comes into your room at night with a nightmare, you can cuddle on the couch or take them back to their room and sing to them rather than pulling them into your bed as you might with your bio-child. Just focus on the idea that you are not much good to your child without a license, and do the best you can.

HOW DO I KNOW IF MY CHILD IS GETTING BETTER?

Progress can be hard to tell, so the first thing I recommend is keeping a journal. Just a sentence or two or even a number for how the day went from 1 to 10 can be invaluable information when tracking how a child is improving. Progress for a child looks like increased attachment to caregivers, fewer instances of dysregulation, longer periods between dysregulation, and faster recoveries after periods of dysregulation.

DO YOU HAVE ANY ADVICE ON A PRIVATE VERSUS A PUBLIC ADOPTION AGENCY?

I usually recommend going with a private foster or adoption agency if you are able to, as you get more attention and care from the agency social worker. There are pros and cons for each, however.

PRIVATE FOSTER OR ADOPTION AGENCY?

Pros: More individual attention, fewer random calls, less social worker turnover, more selective placements, can match your religion or ideology.

Cons: Can be more financially costly, can be harder to find for more rural communities, can involve religious or ideological mismatch, some are small and don't have a good track record.

Tips for working with private agencies: First, make sure the agency has a good reputation in the adoption and foster care world. There are a few agencies out there that aren't great, and you can save yourself some heartbreak by avoiding them. Second, make sure that your ethics line up with that of the agency that you are working with. For example, I have worked with parents that, after starting with an agency, became disturbed to learn that they didn't place children with same-sex couples.

PUBLIC FOSTER OR ADOPTION SOCIAL WORKER?

Pros: Can be less expensive, is easily available.

Cons: Less individual attention from the social worker, you might get a lot of random calls, social worker is more interested in placing kids in beds than finding good long-term matches.

Tips for working with a public social worker: Be clear on what children you think you can handle in your family and try not to be swayed by desperate calls should you get one. Also, realize that your social worker may not have a lot of time, so be efficient in your emails and phone calls and patient in your responses. However, if you feel that you are not getting answered at all and it is starting to become a problem, you can loop in a supervisor as a last resort.

MY CHILD IS AN OLDER INTERNATIONAL ADOPTEE. DO YOU HAVE ANY TIPS?

Yes! First, do whatever you can to speak your child's language, and that will likely be food, clothes, and community. Food and culture are very important to a lot of older international kids, so do as much as you can to support them in this. Look online for recipes, and find nearby (or as near as you can) grocery stores and cultural events. When we have been placed with older international children, we try to connect them with their culture as soon as we can, and we try to provide as much as we can to help them integrate into their new home. Some tastes and sights from their home country will probably be incredibly comforting. Find clothes and hygiene products familiar to the child as much as you can; there are good online stores for many different ethnic communities. And, as much as possible for your area, try to get them in relationship with the community of immigrants from their community of origin. Communities of faith and secular community centers are usually great options for finding ethnic groups.

MY TEENAGER WANTS TO READ THEIR ADOPTION FILE.
IS THIS A GOOD IDEA?

The rule of thumb in the adoption world is that children should know the skeleton of their story by the age of eleven or twelve. This means basic facts such as how many foster homes they were in, why they were removed from their bio-family's care, and incidents of major abuse. If there are any major secrets, like birth-mom was a prostitute or the child is the product of rape, they need to know by age twelve. The adoption file can be quite a different situation, however, as it contains names, dates, and often horrible descriptions of what happened. My advice, however, is that if a teenager is asking to see it, it is a good idea for them to see it. Don't just plunk it down in front of them, however. Have them go through it thoughtfully, a chunk at a time, with a sympathetic therapist to help make sense of the hardest parts. Some parents worry that seeing their file might make kids dysregulate further, and feel that they are barely surviving as it is. If you are feeling this resistant, think of it this way—in most states kids can access their records at age eighteen. Wouldn't you rather they be living at home and have access to a therapist when they work through this? There is also hope—I have seen kids be able to emotionally regulate better after they are able to work through the issues that are brought up by their file.

MY FRIENDS ALL SAY THAT MY FOUR-YEAR-OLD IS JUST BEING NORMAL, BUT I'M SURE THIS ISN'T NORMAL. HOW DO I SEPARATE NORMAL DEVELOPMENT FROM TRAUMA?

Traumatized kids do many of the things that typical kids do, but it's at a much more elevated level. Most kids lie at some point, but traumatized kids will lie as a knee-jerk reaction with the conviction as if their life depends on it—because it is their trauma response to believe that it does. Give yourself room to believe that trauma has affected your child and that their behavior is not just typical. And if you're not sure if some behavior is typical or trauma, err on the side of thinking about trauma first. If it ends up that it is a typical development sort of issue, you'll figure it out eventually! But for kids with trauma, almost every behavior is at least affected somewhat by their trauma—if for no other reason than feeling like they're in trouble is a major trigger for children.

WHY ARE SO MANY THINGS IN THIS BOOK AND IN COUNSELING TALKING ABOUT ME WHEN IT'S MY KID THAT HAS THE PROBLEM?

This is often said in a much kinder way, often along the lines of "Well, if my child is the one who has suffered trauma, why should I be involved in therapy?" or "Shouldn't my child be able to heal, and I can parent him more like a typical kid?" To answer this question, we are going to do a little thought experiment and pretend your child has been in a terrible accident that has damaged their nervous system. The child will need to be in a wheelchair for now, but with gentle, persistent physical therapy, it's possible that they might be able to regain some use of their limbs. How would you react as a parent? Of course you would install wheelchair ramps, order the disabled bus to pick up the child, and perhaps change their after-school activity from soccer to swimming. Maybe you plan for a family vacation somewhere wheelchair accessible, and you change family life to care for the child because they always have to have a caregiver with them. Our family knows this reality intimately, as some health problems forced one of our daughters to spend time in and out of a wheelchair for the past several years. Nobody questioned the accommodations we made for her, and in fact we would have been seen as bad parents had we said that it was her problem and not made those accommodations for her. Can you imagine a parent that would expect a child in a wheelchair to navigate a typical bus? Or go on a hiking trip for vacation? Yet sometimes parents view the child's trauma issues as their problem and do not make accommodations for them. Asking a child in a wheelchair to hike up a mountain can be equivalent to asking a traumatized child to stay regulated at Grandma's house or not to lie when caught doing something wrong. A wheelchair is easier to see and sympathize with, but a child with trauma needs just as much care and accommodation. The skills that work with typical kids won't work with traumatized kids either: you have to change the way that you parent if you're going to be successful.

The other reason that books and counseling often talk to the parent is that all you can change is yourself. If you are parenting a raging teenager, you are not going to get them to sit down and read a book and come to some realization that they are doing something wrong and change their lives. Adoption and trauma counselors realize that to change the child, they have to work with both the parents and the child. It doesn't do much good to just work with one.

WHAT IF I DON'T LIKE MY KID?

I get this one sometimes from exhausted and fed-up parents, and for the most part, my heart really goes out to the parents that are asking it. Usually there is a lot of shame and hurt behind those words, as people who sign up to be adoptive parents usually do it because they love children and want to attach to them. Not clicking with their child isn't what they wanted. If this is you, first I would say, give yourself a break. Deep breaths for a few minutes, and listen to the prescription: self-care and enjoyable activities. First, if you're burned out, it means you need better self-care. Read chapter 5, on self-care, and figure out where you need to bump it up. Get into counseling, schedule more time with friends, give yourself time to paint, start taking guitar lessons, buy a bicycle, something. Self-care is critical. Second, find some enjoyable activities to do with your child. It should be stuff you enjoy as well as your child. If you can't think of anything else, you can go out for ice cream. If you can build shared memories of good times together, this will help get past feeling burned out and unattached.

Book List

IN MAKING RECOMMENDATIONS for books, I want to acknowledge that there are many books that should be on this list that aren't. There are three reasons for this—first, I don't want to overwhelm people with a hundred recommendations. Second, I don't want to recommend any book I haven't thoroughly read. And third, I don't want to recommend anything that is at all iffy, so books that I only mostly agree with didn't make the list. I've also put recommendations throughout this book in the appropriate sections, but here they are all together in one place.

Adoption Issues in Fiction

Anne of Green Gables by L. M. Montgomery
The Harry Potter series J. K. Rowling
Jane Eyre by Charlotte Brontë
Matilda by Roald Dahl
A Series of Unfortunate Events by Lemony Snicket
Oliver Twist by Charles Dickens
The Secret Garden by Frances Hodgson Burnett
The Book Thief by Markus Zusak
Cinder by Marissa Meyer

Young Children's Books

ABC, Adoption & Me by Gayle H. Swift and Casey A. Swift
Tell Me Again About the Night I Was Born by Jamie Lee Curtis
Maybe Days: A Book for Children in Foster Care by Jennifer Wilgocki and Marcia Kahn Wright

Not Quite Narwhal by Jessie Sima
The Invisible String by Patrice Karst
Quackers by Liz Wong
The Goose Egg by Liz Wong

Nonfiction

Bessel van der Kolk, *The Body Keeps the Score: Brain, Mind, and Body in the Healing of Trauma* (New York: Penguin, 2015).

Nancy Newton Verrier, *The Primal Wound: Understanding the Adopted Child* (London: BAAF, 2009).

Deborah D. Gray, *Nurturing Adoptions: Creating Resilience after Neglect and Trauma* (London: Jessica Kingsley, 2012).

Daniel J. Siegel and Tina Payne Bryson, *No-Drama Discipline: The Whole-Brain Way to Calm the Chaos and Nurture Your Child's Developing Mind* (New York: Bantam, 2014).

Karyn B. Purvis, David R. Cross, and Wendy Lyons Sunshine, *The Connected Child: Bring Hope and Healing to Your Adoptive Family* (New York: McGraw-Hill, 2007).

Heather T. Forbes and B. Bryan Post, *Beyond Consequences, Logic, and Control: A Love-Based Approach to Helping Attachment-Challenged Children with Severe Behaviors* (Boulder, CO: Beyond Consequences Institute, 2009).

Lindsey Biel and Nancy Peske, *Raising a Sensory Smart Child: The Definitive Handbook for Helping Your Child with Sensory Processing Issues* (New York: Penguin, 2005).

Carol Kranowitz and Lucy Jane Miller, *The Out-of-Sync Child: Recognizing and Coping with Sensory Processing Disorder* (New York: Tarcher Perigee, 2005).

Adele Faber and Elaine Mazlish, *Siblings without Rivalry: How to Help Your Children Live Together So You Can Live Too* (New York: W. W. Norton, 2012). Caveat: This is a great book about sibling rivalry, but it is about typical children and not traumatized children. If you choose to read it, there needs to be some translation into a situation with trauma.

Movie List

MOVIES CAN SOMETIMES be a great way to talk about adoption, trauma, and different issues around PTSD that are hard to bring up in other ways. Here is a list of movies that deal with these issues (warning: there are spoilers for the plots):

Anne with an E (2017): This Netflix series is grittier and more realistic than the earlier miniseries done based on the books by L. M. Montgomery, and delves more into the realities of Anne being an orphan during that era. The show does depict some violence, so it's definitely for older children.

Annie (2014): A complicated and difficult movie for many foster parents, Annie has a drug-addicted foster mother and returns to the place where her bio-mother abandoned her many years before. It's heart-wrenching, but it can also be the catalyst for many conversations. Use at your own risk.

Closure (2013): Full disclosure: the filmmaker is someone I know personally; we used to work together. This documentary was made by a woman who was transracially adopted and then made contact with her birth family as an adult. It is currently available on Amazon Prime Video. It is at moments funny, poignant, entertaining, and deeply personal, and engaging for kids from adolescents and up.

The *Despicable Me* trilogy: This trio of movies is unexpectedly adoption-positive, as the father, Gru, initially takes in three children for selfish reasons. They eventually grow into a loving family, however, and are even joined by a mother in the third movie.

Elf (2003): About a human child raised as an elf at the North Pole who sets out to find his birth family. It deals with a lot of the complicated emotions that come with birth parent meetings surprisingly well for a holiday movie starring Will Ferrell, while maintaining his connection to his adoptive parents as well.

Good Hair (2009): This is a must-see for anybody raising a girl of African American descent, as it deals with over a century of hair politics. It is highly educational and very well done.

Guardians of the Galaxy Vol. 2 (2017): The main plot of this movie is in the main character, Peter, finding his birth father, Ego. After some initial fun with him, it quickly becomes clear that Ego is actually evil and wants to use Peter to conquer the entire galaxy. In the end, Peter recognizes that Yondu, a very imperfect father figure who mostly raised him, was actually his "daddy." This movie is very adoption-friendly and can be a good movie to spark discussion when dealing with difficult birth family.

The Harry Potter movies (any of them): The Harry Potter series of movies and books are a great way to talk about PTSD. Harry has all the classic signs of PTSD—emotional volatility, flashbacks, bad dreams, avoidance of triggers, and difficulty with trust. He also has bad foster parents (his aunt and uncle) and suffers by not knowing enough about his adoption story. This is a good story to talk about why it's important for kids to know their story. This story also has a great deal of talk about grief (a person who wants to become his adoptive father dies), depression (there are physical representations of depression, called Dementors, starting in the third book), and Harry's difficulty controlling his anger.

Hunt for the Wilderpeople (2016): This funny movie, based in New Zealand, sees a troubled teen in foster care placed in a remote foster home and who responds well to a loving foster parent. After her death, he ends up running away with her partner, a man with whom he previously had a prickly relationship, and they become the target of a manhunt. This shows a troubled foster child in a positive light, making good connections with people.

Ice Age (2002): Basically a bunch of nutty animals act like foster parents to a small child who is lost, and they hope to return her to her people. They grow attached to her, and want the best for her. A great movie explaining temporary foster care.

Inside Out (2015): Not adoption-specific, really, but an excellent movie talking to kids about their emotions and helping them identify them, which is something that's really hard for many adopted kids.

Instant Family (2018): An extremely realistic and well-done picture of one family's journey through the foster care system toward adoption. It is about a white childless couple who adopts a sibling set of three Latino children. This movie talks about transracial issues, behavioral issues, how the system works, and so on. It might be a little intense for younger viewers, and it has a little adult language. Because it is so realistic, it also might trigger issues with kids; be prepared for a conversation afterward.

The Jungle Book (2016): This movie does a great job talking about the conflict that the main character has between being a human and being a wolf, as he was raised. It does have one scene in which a snake, one of the bad guys in the story, tells an anti-adoption story about a cuckoo in a different bird's nest that ultimately causes the death of the other juvenile birds, and this might be a little hard for some kids. Otherwise, this was a good adoption-positive movie.

Juno (2007): A great movie for teens that talks about the issues around teen pregnancy and the choice to place a child for adoption. It's complicated and compelling, probably best for older teens, as it has an R rating, unless you can catch a more kid-friendly version on television.

Kung Fu Panda 2 (2011): An excellent movie with real integrity and sensitivity in dealing with the issues around adoption. The adoptive parent and the birth parents are treated fairly, and the issues that come up in our human world are well represented.

Leap! (2016): A pair of ambitious orphans escaping an actually decently run orphanage try their luck at life in Paris—with the main character trying to become a ballet dancer. She forms a significant relationship with a woman there, who becomes like a foster parent, and eventually is able to enter school.

The LEGO Batman Movie (2017): While silly and goofy, this movie also explores Batman's relationship with Alfred, who raised him, and with Dick Grayson, a teen he accidentally adopts. It is unrealistic in many ways, but it does deal with Batman's fear of intimacy, which could be a good conversation starter with kids.

Lilo and Stitch (2002): This is an excellent movie to talk about kids with behavioral problems still being safe in a family. Stitch has behavioral problems, but the theme of the movie is that "family" means nobody is left behind. There are social workers in the movie that the characters are worried about, because it is a situation where the parents are dead and the adult sister is caring for the younger sister.

Martian Child (2007): This is more an adult movie, or perhaps for older teenagers. It is about a science fiction writer who fosters a very unusual child—one who believes he is a Martian. This movie has a lot of heart and is a tear-jerker.

Matilda (1996): This movie has neglectful bio-parents, a crazily abusive headmistress, and then the main character finds a teacher who is sympathetic, and the teacher ends up adopting her. This movie can be intense for some children; if you have young or sensitive kids, it might be better to watch it yourself before you have the children watch it.

Meet the Robinsons (2007): The main character is a child who is adopted into a family, and the villain is a boy that wasn't adopted. It is a little trite in places, but good to talk about belonging and fears.

Secondhand Lions (2003): A young boy has a chronically irresponsible mother, who we come to find out has lied to her son many times and has had a string of problems. She drops him off with his great-uncles for what is supposed to be the summer but ends up being much longer. The mom pops back up with an abusive boyfriend at one point, and the main character realizes that she's not going to change, and chooses the stability of living with his great-uncles. This is a very positive movie about relative care (though there are no official social workers in this situation), and the child has a deep and loving relationship with his great-uncles. There is also an issue throughout the film where the boy has to decide whether he believes his uncles' stories about being adventurers or his mom's belief that they were bank robbers, and whether he is going to be cynical or believe his uncles. This is a powerful picture of what it looks like to build trust with a foster parent.

Shazam! (2019): This is a rare movie in which the main character is a foster child and most people around him are good people who want to connect with him. The foster parents show good skills, and the foster siblings are realistic. They talk about forming family together.

A Wrinkle in Time (2018): The story centers around a family with an older bio-child and a younger adopted child. There are some dynamics around the adopted child that are challenging (he is possessed by an evil entity at one point), but overall the movie is very adoption-positive.

For a more complete list of adoption-friendly movies and good ways to structure conversations around them, I recommend:

Addison Cooper, *Adoption at the Movies: A Year of Adoption-Friendly Movie Nights to Get Your Family Talking* (Philadelphia: Jessica Kingsley, 2017).

Glossary

504 plan. A plan at a child's school that is less formal than an IEP (individualized education plan) that helps accommodate for a child's special needs.

accommodation. Something that meets a need for a person with a disability in order for them to participate fully in the community.

adoptee. A person who has been adopted. Some people prefer the terms *adopted person* or *adopted child.*

adoption. The radically life-altering process of making a person who isn't biologically your child legally and emotionally your child. When this process is done legally, the law recognizes no difference between an adopted child and one born biologically to a family.

adoption, closed. *See* closed adoption.

adoption file. This is the file that the adoptive family receives, generally speaking prior to adoption, when they are adopting a foster child. This file contains heavily redacted reports and other paperwork that documents the child's involvement with Child Protective Services.

adoption, open. *See* open adoption.

adoption plan. The plan that the birth family makes in order to place that child for adoption in the home they select. This plan can include how long the hospital stay should be, how they choose the adoptive family, and the open adoption agreement.

adoption triad. The three major parties in an adoption—the birth family, the adoptive family, and the adopted child.

adverse childhood experiences (ACE) score. A score between 0 and 10, with 10 being the worst, that gives a measurement to the types of trauma experienced in childhood.

ARC model. A model of treatment for children with trauma based on focusing on the child's attachments, regulation, and competencies.

attachment. The trust and bond that builds between people over time. Attachment is based on biological processes, including the hormone oxytocin, and on emotional realities as well.

attachment style. The category a person can be classified into for their type of attachment. The attachment styles are *secure, ambivalent, disorganized,* and *avoidant.*

attention deficit hyperactivity disorder (ADHD). A disorder marked by three different subgroups (attention deficit, hyperactive impulse control, or mixed) that has to do with a person's ability to maintain focus or to control their impulses.

attunement. The process of recognizing and understanding another person in a deep and sympathetic way. This is the precursor to attachment.

autism. A broad range of conditions marked by challenges in reading social cues, repetitive behavior, and communication difficulties.

birth family. Also called *bio-family* or *first family.* An adopted child's original biological parents that gave birth to them.

boarding school, therapeutic. An out-of-home residential option for a child or adolescent who is having extreme behaviors, including substance abuse and violence, to get help.

case worker. A person employed by an adoption or social services agency to monitor the welfare of a child or to assist in foster care or adoption. This person may or may not have a master's degree and a license.

Child Protective Services. A governmental agency that might be called different things in different states, but is generally there to make sure that kids aren't being abused. If there is a report about child abuse, CPS investigates. This agency can also be a resource if a family is having trouble.

closed adoption. An adoption where the record is sealed and confidential, and there is no contact between the birth family and the adopted child. Typically in a closed adoption, an adoptee can find information once they have turned eighteen, but in some circumstances even then information remains confidential. Closed adoptions used to be typical, but they are becoming rarer and are usually only used now in certain circumstances, such as safety concerns with the biological parents.

cognitive behavioral therapy (CBT). A type of therapy that focuses on changing unhelpful cognitive distortions and behaviors and improving emotional regulation through the use of coping strategies.

cortisol. Also called the stress hormone, it regulates the body's fight, flight, or freeze response. It is present in higher concentrations in the blood during times of stress, and can take a while to return to a normal level after a stressful episode. For chronic stress, it remains at an elevated level.

developmental trauma. A term used to describe the complex trauma symptoms experienced by people who have suffered from physical, sexual, or emotional abuse during their early years of development.

dialectical behavioral therapy (DBT). A type of CBT that uses traditional methods as well as skills such as mindfulness, acceptance, and distress tolerance. DBT was developed to treat people with borderline personality disorder (BPD), but it can treat other conditions as well. DBT usually has a group component.

differentiation. The psychological process of recognizing another person as a separate and distinct entity apart from yourself, with their own opinions and power.

disruption. When a child in foster care leaves their current foster home and is placed in another foster home.

dissolution. The legal end to an adoption, the equivalent to a divorce ending a marriage.

DSM. The *Diagnostic and Statistical Manual of Mental Disorders.* It is how everybody in the psychological world diagnoses people. The current version is the *DSM-5,* which made changes from the *DSM-IV,* such as discontinuing the diagnosis of Asperger's disorder in favor of the more comprehensive autism spectrum disorder.

dysregulation. The emotional state of a person being outside the zone of regulation or where a person feels that they are functionally operating and experiencing emotions at a manageable level. When a person is dysregulated, they are often triggered, which can look different for different people. For a freeze person, this could look like being unable to speak, heart pounding, and being frozen. For a fight person, they are usually yelling, angry, and sometimes crying. For a flight person, this will often be trying to get away, scared, and desperate.

encopresis. A person soiling their underwear with stool after they are past the age of potty training, and also over four years of age. This condition sometimes happens for children who have experienced sexual abuse.

felt safety. The goal of having an environment for your child that not only is in reality safe for them, but that they will also perceive to be truly safe for them.

fetal alcohol spectrum disorder (FASD). An umbrella term for the myriad of effects that a child can have from the mother consuming alcohol during pregnancy.

foster parents. State-licensed providers who courageously open their homes to invest in and love children who need a temporary home. Sometimes foster parents go on to adopt the children in their care, and sometimes foster parents simply provide a safe place for children to be while a safe place is found with a relative or a permanent adoptive home, or they are able to return home safely.

grief. Grief is the emotional process that a person goes through to adjust to the reality of loss.

home study. The process by which a social worker educates and evaluates a prospective foster or adoptive home to evaluate their suitability to be an adoptive or foster placement.

hypervigilance. The subconscious need for people to always be aware and alert to everything around them, constantly scanning for danger and assessing what's going on.

individualized education plan (IEP). A plan agreed upon by the parents and the school to best meet the needs of the child. This is a formal, legal document covered under the Americans with Disabilities Act, and is meant to make school accessible for children with disabilities.

lifebook. A book commonly made for foster and adopted children that includes photos and a story of their life. It can include where they were born, where they lived, biological relatives, and their story written in a way that makes sense to them.

mandated reporter. Someone that is a social worker, foster parent, teacher, counselor, or medical provider that must report child abuse or neglect if they have reasonable suspicion that it has occurred.

open adoption. A more common adoption option in which some information is passed between the bio-family and the adoptive family. How much information and how it is communicated are usually agreed before the adoption through an open adoption agreement (OAA). Open adoption agreements can range from a letter and pictures sent to an adoption agency once a year to monthly in-person visits.

oppositional defiant disorder (ODD). A psychological disorder marked by a person (usually a child) having difficulty complying with authority, who is often angry and blames others. One of the problems with this diagnosis is that it often has an underlying cause—PTSD, ADHD, autism, or anxiety. It is difficult to treat ODD without treating the underlying cause for the condition if there's an underlying condition.

parent shopping. The state that kids are in when they subconsciously believe that their home is not permanent and they are continually cultivating relationships of suitable adults to be their next caregivers.

placement. The point at which a child begins to live with a new family.

post-traumatic stress disorder (PTSD). A chronic psychological condition that is a reaction to a severe trauma or a culmination of a series of traumatic events. PTSD symptoms generally include avoidance, intrusive memories, emotional dysregulation, negative thinking, and physical reactions.

power struggle. A conflict between two forces in which both are trying hard to win. When this happens between parent and child, the best way to win is to not engage with it.

psychiatric evaluation. This is an evaluation, usually done by a PhD level psychologist, that can help with diagnosing if there is something else going on with a child other than just trauma. There are different types of psychiatric evaluations—some focus on diagnosing ADHD or autism, and some focus on seeing if the child might have a learning disability.

RAD. Reactive attachment disorder, a rare attachment disorder that is a result of serious early childhood trauma. It is characterized by a person who is unable to make significant attachments to people, and that the feelings of attachment themselves can trigger PTSD symptoms. People with RAD can often seem charming, they have easily replaced relationships, and any real attachment and connection can lead to severe dysregulation.

reenactment. The situation in which victims of trauma recreate a traumatic situation in their normal life. This happens when a child who has experienced physical abuse tries to provoke a foster or adoptive parent to violence. This is not done consciously but is part of an unconscious processing of the trauma.

regression. When a person experiences a state of being emotionally younger than their chronological age. When this happens to a child with attachment trauma, it can be a chance to reparent them at younger ages. Regression should always be under the child's control and should be enjoyable and comfortable for them.

rehoming. The practice of finding adopted kids a new adoptive family with no governmental oversight, home studies, or social workers involved. This seemingly innocuous term refers to what can amount to human trafficking with adopted kids, and it is becoming illegal in more and more states.

relinquishment. This is the voluntary termination of parental rights. The more adoption-friendly term is *making an adoption plan.*

residential care. Care for a person who is out of the home; the person lives at the facility at which they are being treated. Examples of residential care are therapeutic boarding schools, inpatient psychiatric care, and inpatient drug rehab centers, among others.

safety plan. A plan made by a family in order to help everyone feel safe. It usually includes what behaviors make people feel unsafe, how to cope with those behaviors, and what actions parents will take if those behaviors get dangerous.

second-chance adoption. The situation when a child has been adopted but the adoption, for whatever reason, hasn't worked well, and an agency is seeking a new adoptive home for the child.

self-care. The practice of taking an active role in protecting and enhancing your own well-being, especially during times of stress.

sensory diet. A plan that you make to meet the daily sensory needs of your child. This can consist of activities, strategies, and planning around daily activities.

sensory processing disorder. When a person has significant dysfunction with the information their senses perceive and how their body processes and organizes that information. This is not a diagnosis under the *DSM-5,* and there is controversy as to whether or not it is its own disorder or just symptomatic of other disorders.

social worker. A masters-level professional that usually works for the state or an adoption or foster agency in order to protect the rights of the child, license foster and adoptive parents, and monitor children in foster care.

termination of parental rights (TPR). An action brought by the state in which the rights of the biological parents are terminated and the child becomes a permanent ward of the courts, or becomes legally free to be adopted. This is different from when a parent voluntarily gives up their rights, either through making an adoption plan (typically at birth, though not always) or by signing an agreement (called relinquishment) when the state brings charges and begins the process of termination.

transracial adoption. Adopting from a race, ethnicity, or culture to which you personally do not belong.

trauma. Trauma is any event or situation that causes a person to feel terror and horror to the point of feeling like your life and safety are in serious jeopardy. Trauma is inflicted when a person either experiences or witnesses such an event; in fact, there is little difference to the amount of trauma between experiencing or witnessing.

trigger. Something that reminds a person with PTSD enough of their trauma that it causes a flashback or for them to reexperience their trauma in some way. A trigger is something that is otherwise harmless and can include things such as a smell, a sound, a time of year, or being told "no."

white privilege. The unearned favor and privileges that people of white ancestry enjoy in certain Western countries because of prevailing systemic racism.

Notes

1. ORIGINS

1. Dan Allender, "Marriage and Family Class," lecture, Seattle School of Theology and Psychology, 2008.
2. A. H. Maslow, "A Theory of Human Motivation," *Psychological Review* 50 (1943): 370–96. https://tinyurl.com/236kc.
3. Praveen Shrestha, "Maslow Hierarchy of Needs," *Psychestudy,* June 16, 2019. https://tinyurl.com/ycddecb8.
4. Kristine M. Kinniburgh and Margaret E. Blaustein, "ARC Model," National Child Traumatic Stress Network, 2008.
5. Joshua Arvidson, Kristine Kinniburgh, Kristin Howard, Joseph Spinazzola, Helen Strothers, Mary Evans, Barry Andres, Chantal Cohen, and Margaret E. Blaustein, "Treatment of Complex Trauma in Young Children: Developmental and Cultural Considerations in Application of the ARC Intervention Model," *Journal of Child & Adolescent Trauma* 4:1 (2011), 34–51. doi:10.1080/19361521.2011.545046.

2. TRAUMA

1. Joseph Spinazzola, Bessel van der Kolk, and Julian D. Ford, "When Nowhere Is Safe: Interpersonal Trauma and Attachment Adversity as Antecedents of Post-Traumatic Stress Disorder and Developmental Trauma Disorder," *Journal of Traumatic Stress* 31:5 (2018), 631–42. doi:10.1002/jts.22320.
2. Bruce D. Perry, "Stress, Trauma and Post-Traumatic Stress Disorders in Children," The Child Trauma Academy, 2007, p. 5. https://tinyurl.com/rxh5tdr.
3. Perry, "Stress, Trauma and Post-Traumatic Stress Disorders," 6.
4. Candace N. Plotkin, "Study Finds Foster Kids Suffer PTSD," *Harvard Crimson,* April 11, 2005. https://tinyurl.com/s6jamyx.
5. Spinazzola et al., "When Nowhere Is Safe."

6. R. F. Anda and V. J. Felitti, "Origins and Essence of the Study," *ACE Reporter* 1 (April 2003), 1–4.

7. Vincent J. Felitti, R. F. Anda, D. Nordenberg, D. F. Williamson, A. M. Spitz, V. Edwards, M. P. Koss, and J. S. Marks, "Relationship of Childhood Abuse and Household Dysfunction to Many of the Leading Causes of Death in Adults: The Adverse Childhood Experiences (ACE) Study," *American Journal of Preventive Medicine* 56:6 (2019). doi:10.1016/j.amepre.2019.04.001.

8. Terrie E. Moffitt, "Childhood Exposure to Violence and Lifelong Health: Clinical Intervention Science and Stress-Biology Research Join Forces," *Development and Psychopathology* 25:4 pt. 2 (2013): 1619–34. doi:10.1017/s0954579413000801.

9. Bessel van der Kolk, *The Body Keeps the Score: Brain, Mind, and Body in the Healing of Trauma* (New York: Penguin, 2015).

10. Ally Jamieson, "Biology of Trauma: How Trauma Impacts the Developing Mind," pamphlet, Portland State University Center for Improvement of Child and Family Services. https://tinyurl.com/sjxcyga.

11. Sara B. Johnson, Robert W. Blum, and Jay N. Giedd, "Adolescent Maturity and the Brain: The Promise and Pitfalls of Neuroscience Research in Adolescent Health Policy," *Journal of Adolescent Health* 45:3 (2009), 216–21. doi:10.1016/j.jadohealth.2009.05.016.

12. Harvard Health Publishing, "Understanding the Stress Response," Harvard Health, March 2011. https://tinyurl.com/y6w9dnam.

13. Shanta R. Dube, Vincent J. Felitti, Maxia Dong, Daniel P. Chapman, Wayne H. Giles, and Robert F. Anda, "Childhood Abuse, Neglect, and Household Dysfunction and the Risk of Illicit Drug Use: The Adverse Childhood Experiences Study," *Pediatrics* 111:3 (2003). doi:10.1542/peds.111.3.564.

14. Nicholas T. Van Dam, K. Rando, M. N. Potenza, K. Tuit, and R. Sinha, "Childhood Maltreatment, Altered Limbic Neurobiology, and Substance Use Relapse Severity via Trauma-Specific Reductions in Limbic Gray Matter Volume," *JAMA Psychiatry* 71:8 (2014). doi:10.1001/jamapsychiatry.2014.680.

15. Dan Allender, "Marriage and Family Class," lecture, Seattle School of Theology and Psychology, 2008.

16. Spinazzola et al., "When Nowhere Is Safe."

3. INFANT TRAUMA

1. K. Z. Lewinn, L. R. Stroud, B. E. Molnar, J. H. Ware, K. C. Koenen, and S. L. Buka, "Elevated Maternal Cortisol Levels during Pregnancy Are Associated

with Reduced Childhood IQ," *International Journal of Epidemiology* 38:6 (July 2009), 1700–10. doi:10.1093/ije/dyp200.

2. Margaret A. Keyes, Anu Sharma, Irene J. Elkins, William G. Iacono, and Matt McGue, "The Mental Health of U.S. Adolescents Adopted in Infancy," *Archives of Pediatrics & Adolescent Medicine* 162:5 (January 2008), 419. doi:10.1001 /archpedi.162.5.419.

3. Nicholas Zill, "The Paradox of Adoption," Institute for Family Studies, October 7, 2015. https://tinyurl.com/rk3hwmt.

4. Nancy Ma Verrier, "The Primal Wound: A Preliminary Investigation into the Effects of Separation from the Birth Mother on Adopted Children," *Pre- and Peri-Natal Psychology Journal* 2:2 (1987), 75–87. https://tinyurl.com/yxy7b2hf.

5. Robert Winston and Rebecca Chicot, "The Importance of Early Bonding on the Long-Term Mental Health and Resilience of Children," *London Journal of Primary Care* 8:1 (February 24, 2016), 12–14. doi:10.1080/17571472.2015.1133012.

6. Barbara Waterman, "Mourning the Loss Builds the Bond: Primal Communication between Foster, Adoptive, or Stepmother and Child," *Journal of Loss and Trauma* 6:4 (2001), 277–300. doi:10.1080/108114401317087806.

7. John Medina, *Brain Rules for Baby: How to Raise a Smart and Happy Child from Zero to Five* (Seattle: Pear Press, 2010).

4. PTSD AND FIGHT, FLIGHT, AND FREEZE

1. Peter J. Pecora, Peter S. Jensen, Lisa Hunter Romanelli, Lovie J. Jackson, and Abel Ortiz, "Mental Health Services for Children Placed in Foster Care: An Overview of Current Challenges," *Child Welfare* 88:1 (2009), 5–26. https:// tinyurl.com/ulhuko8.

2. Bessel van der Kolk, *The Body Keeps the Score: Brain, Mind, and Body in the Healing of Trauma* (New York: Penguin, 2015).

3. Vanessa LoBue, "People Aren't Born Afraid of Spiders and Snakes: Fear Is Quickly Learned During Infancy," Association for Psychological Science, January 24, 2011. https://tinyurl.com/w7e559e.

5. OLYMPIC-LEVEL SELF-CARE

1. Shauna Niequist, *Bread & Wine: A Love Letter to Life around the Table, with Recipes* (Grand Rapids, MI: Zondervan, 2017).

2. Kirsten Weir, "The Exercise Effect," *Monitor on Psychology* 42:11 (December 2011). https://tinyurl.com/yyrpkofy.

6. ATTACHMENT

1. Gerard McCarthy and Alan Taylor, "Avoidant/Ambivalent Attachment Style as a Mediator between Abusive Childhood Experiences and Adult Relationship Difficulties," *Journal of Child Psychology and Psychiatry* 40:3 (1999), 465–77. doi:10.1017/s0021963098003734.

2. Christa Nelson, "What Is Healthy Attachment?" Attachment and Trauma Network, May 18, 2014. https://tinyurl.com/rqmpbn8.

3. Saul McLeod, "Mary Ainsworth: The Strange Situation," Simply Psychology, 2018. https://tinyurl.com/y9l4fpz3.

4. John Bowlby, *Attachment and Loss, Volume III: Loss, Sadness and Depression* (New York: Basic Books, 1980), 242.

5. Diane Benoit, "Infant-Parent Attachment: Definition, Types, Antecedents, Measurement and Outcome," *Paediatrics & Child Health* 9:8 (2004), 541–45. doi:10.1093/pch/9.8.541.

6. McLeod, "Mary Ainsworth."

7. Benoit, "Infant-Parent Attachment."

8. Benoit.

9. G. Spangler and K. E. Grossmann, "Biobehavioral Organization in Securely and Insecurely Attached Infants," *Child Development* 64:5 (1993), 1439. doi:10.2307/1131544.

10. Georgia A. DeGangi, *The Dysregulated Adult: Integrated Treatment Approaches* (Amsterdam: Elsevier Academic Press, 2012).

11. David J. Wallin, *Attachment in Psychotherapy* (New York: Guilford Press, 2007), 22.

12. Karlen Lyons-Ruth, Elisa Bronfman, and Gwendolyn Atwood, "A Relational Diathesis Model of Hostile-Helpless States of Mind: Expressions in Mother-Infant Interactions," *Attachment Disorganization* 1999, 33–70. https://tinyurl.com/yx5zo22q.

13. Benoit, "Infant-Parent Attachment."

14. Molly S. Castelloe, "Disorganized Attachment: Fears That Go Unanswered—the Long Reach of Interactions between Caregiver and Infant," *Psychology Today,* April 12, 2017. https://tinyurl.com/sv84y5y.

15. Pehr L. Granqvist, Alan Sroufe, Mary Dozier, Erik Hesse, Miriam Steele, Marinus van Ijzendoorn, Judith Solomon, et al., "Disorganized Attachment in Infancy: A Review of the Phenomenon and Its Implications for Clinicians and Policy-Makers," Experts@Minnesota, University of Minnesota Institute of Child Development, November 2, 2017. https://tinyurl.com/uqnep6z.

16. Benoit, "Infant-Parent Attachment."

17. Elizabeth E. Ellis and Abdolreza Saadabadi, "Reactive Attachment Disorder," StatPearls, January 2019, https://tinyurl.com/wean9g6.

18. American Psychiatric Association, *Diagnostic and Statistical Manual of Mental Disorders, Fifth Edition (DSM-5)* (Arlington, VA: American Psychiatric Association, 2017).

7. HEALING ATTACHMENT DAMAGE

1. David J. Wallin, *Attachment in Psychotherapy* (New York: Guilford Press, 2007), 73, 78–79.

2. Mark Chaffin, Rochelle Hanson, Benjamin E. Saunders, Todd Nichols, Douglas Barnett, Charles Zeanah, Lucy Berliner, et al., "Report of the APSAC Task Force on Attachment Therapy, Reactive Attachment Disorder, and Attachment Problems," *Child Maltreatment* 11:1 (2006), 76–89. doi:10.1177/1077559505283699.

3. Bruce Duncan Perry and Maia Szalavitz, *The Boy Who Was Raised as a Dog and Other Stories from a Child Psychiatrist's Notebook: What Traumatized Children Can Teach Us about Loss, Love, and Healing* (New York: Basic Books, 2017), 160–69.

4. Arthur Becker-Weidman, "Treatment for Children with Trauma-Attachment Disorders: Dyadic Developmental Psychotherapy," *Child and Adolescent Social Work Journal* 23:2 (March 2006), 147–71. doi:10.1007/s10560-005-0039-0.

8. GOOD DISCIPLINE STRATEGIES

1. Brenna Hicks, "Parenting Tip: 30 Second Burst of Attention," The Kid Counselor, December 7, 2018. https://tinyurl.com/ydpvl5a4.

2. Karyn B. Purvis, David R. Cross, and Wendy Lyons Sunshine, *The Connected Child: Bring Hope and Healing to Your Adoptive Family* (New York: McGraw-Hill, 2007), 97–98.

3. Bessel van der Kolk, *The Body Keeps the Score: Brain, Mind, and Body in the Healing of Trauma* (New York: Penguin, 2015).

9. ROUTINES AND RITUALS

1. Joshua Arvidson, Kristine Kinniburgh, Kristin Howard, Joseph Spinazzola, Helen Strothers, Mary Evans, Barry Andres, Chantal Cohen, and Margaret E. Blaustein, "Treatment of Complex Trauma in Young Children: Developmental and Cultural Considerations in Application of the ARC Intervention Model," *Journal of Child & Adolescent Trauma* 4:1 (2011), 34–51.

11. ATTUNEMENT AND MANIPULATION

1. *Merriam-Webster*, s.v. "manipulate," www.merriam-webster.com.

13. SENSORY SUCCESS

1. Kerry Fraser, Diane Mackenzie, and Joan Versnel, "Complex Trauma in Children and Youth: A Scoping Review of Sensory-Based Interventions," *Occupational Therapy in Mental Health* 33:3 (2017). doi:10.1080/0164212x.2016.1265475.

2. Erika M. Kaiser, Craig S. Gillette, and Joseph Spinazzola, "A Controlled Pilot-Outcome Study of Sensory Integration (SI) in the Treatment of Complex Adaptation to Traumatic Stress," *Journal of Aggression, Maltreatment & Trauma* 19:7 (2010); 699–720. doi:10.1080/10926771.2010.515162.

3. Elizabeth Warner, Jane Koomar, Bryan Lary, and Alexandra Cook, "Can the Body Change the Score? Application of Sensory Modulation Principles in the Treatment of Traumatized Adolescents in Residential Settings," *Journal of Family Violence* 28:7 (October 2013), 729–38. doi:10.1007/s10896-013-9535-8.

4. Lindsey Biel, *Sensory Processing Challenges: Effective Clinical Work with Kids & Teens* (New York: W. W. Norton, 2014), 119.

5. Batya Engel-Yeger, Dafna Palgy-Levin, and Rachel Lev-Wiesel, "Predicting Fears of Intimacy among Individuals with Post-Traumatic Stress Symptoms by Their Sensory Profile," *British Journal of Occupational Therapy* 78:1 (2015). doi:10.1177/0308022614557628.

6. Batya Engel-Yeger and Winnie Dunn, "The Relationship between Sensory Processing Difficulties and Anxiety Level of Healthy Adults," *British Journal of Occupational Therapy* 74:5 (2011), 210–16. doi:10.4276/030802211x13046730116407.

14. TRANSRACIAL AND TRANSETHNIC ADOPTION

1. Nicholas Zill, "The Changing Face of Adoption in the United States," Institute for Family Studies, August 8, 2017. https://tinyurl.com/t7kzkj5.

2. Karen Valby, "The Realities of Raising a Kid of a Different Race," *Time*. n.d. https://tinyurl.com/yyah5uzk.

3. National Association of Black Social Workers, "Transracial Adoption Statement, 1972," NABSW Position Statements, 1972. https://tinyurl.com/wy857oy.

4. NAACP, "NAACP Policy Handbook: Resolutions Approved by the National Board of Directors 1976–2006." www.naacp.org.

5. Rebecca Compton, "Is Transracial Adoption Harmful to Kids?" *Psychology Today,* May 11, 2016. https://tinyurl.com/r65j7ug.

6. Emma Hamilton, Diana R. Samek, Margaret Keyes, Matthew K. McGue, and William G. Iacono, "Identity Development in a Transracial Environment:

Racial/Ethnic Minority Adoptees in Minnesota," *Adoption Quarterly* 18:3 (2015), 217–33. doi:10.1080/10926755.2015.1013593.

7. Rosa Rosnati and Laura Ferrari, "Parental Cultural Socialization and Perception of Discrimination as Antecedents for Transracial Adoptees' Ethnic Identity," *Procedia—Social and Behavioral Sciences* 140 (2014), 103–108. doi:10.1016/j.sbspro.2014.04.393.

8. Claudia Manzi, Laura Ferrari, Rosa Rosnati, and Veronica Benet-Martinez, "Bicultural Identity Integration of Transracial Adolescent Adoptees," *Journal of Cross-Cultural Psychology* 45:6 (2014), 888–904. doi:10.1177/0022022114530495.

9. William Feigelman, "Adjustments of Transracially and Inracially Adopted Young Adults," *Child and Adolescent Social Work Journal* 17:3 (June 2000), 165–83. doi:10.1023/A:1007531829378.

10. Valby, " Realities of Raising a Kid of a Different Race."

11. Peggy McIntosh, "'White Privilege: Unpacking the Invisible Knapsack' and 'Some Notes for Facilitators,'" National SEED Project, 1989. https://tinyurl.com/y7u82cmg.

12. NPR, "Six Words: 'Black Babies Cost Less to Adopt.'" NPR, June 27, 2013. https://tinyurl.com/t4fs4uw.

13. Glenn Morey, "Adult Adoptee Voices Are Changing Adoption Narrative," *Psychology Today,* November 19, 2018. https://tinyurl.com/quxdjpt.

14. Nirej Sekhon, "Blue on Black: An Empirical Assessment of Police Shootings," *SSRN Electronic Journal* 2016. doi:10.2139/ssrn.2700724.

15. Ryan Gabrielson, Eric Sagara, and Ryann Grochowski Jones, "Deadly Force, in Black and White," ProPublica, March 9, 2019. https://tinyurl.com/mfw73kb.

15. OLDER CHILD ADOPTION

1. Katharine Brind, "An Exploration of Adopters Views Regarding Children's Ages at the Time of Placement," *Child & Family Social Work* 13:3 (2008), 319–28. doi:10.1111/j.1365-2206.2008.00556.x.

2. Richard P. Barth, Marianne Berry, Rogers Yoshikami, Regina K. Goodfield, and Mary Lou Carson, "Predicting Adoption Disruption," *Social Work* 33:3 (January 1988), 227–33. doi:10.1093/sw/33.3.227.

3. Lisa Hutton, "The Effects of Older Child Adoption on the Family," *Undergraduate Research Journal Blog,* 2010. https://tinyurl.com/rwsyw3j.

16. WORKING WITH BIRTH FAMILY

1. Mandi MacDonald and Dominic McSherry, "Open Adoption: Adoptive Parents' Experiences of Birth Family Contact and Talking to Their Child about Adoption," *Adoption & Fostering* 35:3 (2011), 4–16. doi:10.1177/030857591103500302.

19. THE CHILD YOU HAVE

1. Caitlin Ryan, Russell B. Toomey, Rafael M. Diaz, and Stephen T. Russell, "Parent-Initiated Sexual Orientation Change Efforts with LGBT Adolescents: Implications for Young Adult Mental Health and Adjustment," *Journal of Homosexuality,* 2018. doi:10.1080/00918369.2018.1538407.

2. Laura Baams, Bianca D. M. Wilson, and Stephen T. Russell, "LGBTQ Youth in Unstable Housing and Foster Care," *Pediatrics* 143:3 (November 2019). doi:10.1542/peds.2017-4211.

3. Soon Kyu Choi, Bianca D. M. Wilson, Jama Shelton, and Gary J. Gates, "Serving Our Youth 2015: The Needs and Experiences of Lesbian, Gay, Bisexual, Transgender, and Questioning Youth Experiencing Homelessness." eScholarship, University of California, August 6, 2015. https://escholarship.org/uc/item/1pd9886n.

4. Adam McCormick, Kathryn Schmidt, and Samuel Terrazas, "LGBTQ Youth in the Child Welfare System: An Overview of Research, Practice, and Policy," *Journal of Public Child Welfare* 11:1 (November 2016), 27–39. doi:10.1080/1554 8732.2016.1221368.

5. Rob Woronoff, Rudy Estrada, and Susan Sommer, "Out of the Margins," Lambda Legal, July 31, 2014. https://tinyurl.com/slfun3m.

6. Woronoff, Estrada, and Sommer, "Out of the Margins."

7. Adam McCormick, Kathryn Schmidt, and Samuel Terrazas, "Foster Family Acceptance: Understanding the Role of Foster Family Acceptance in the Lives of LGBTQ Youth," *Children and Youth Services Review* 61 (2016): 69–74. doi:10.1016/j.childyouth.2015.12.005.

8. Michael E. Newcomb, Michael C. Lasala, Alida Bouris, Brian Mustanski, Guillermo Prado, Sheree M. Schrager, and David M. Huebner, "The Influence of Families on LGBTQ Youth Health: A Call to Action for Innovation in Research and Intervention Development," *LGBT Health* 6:4 (2019), 139–45. doi:10.1089/lgbt.2018.0157.

9. Liz Owen, "Parents: Quick Tips for Supporting Your LGBTQ Kids—and Yourself—During the Coming-Out Process," PFLAG, June 21, 2017. https://tinyurl.com/qldayy6.

10. Barbara Turnage and Justin Bucchio, "Be Ready to Support LGBTQ Youth," Adoptive Families Association of BC, August 20, 2018. https://tinyurl.com/utahese.

11. Laura Selby, "Caring for Transgender Children: A Physician's Advice," The DO, February 3, 2017. https://tinyurl.com/snrh2qj.

12. Anna I. R. Van Der Miesen, Hannah Hurley, and Annelou L. C. De Vries, "Gender Dysphoria and Autism Spectrum Disorder: A Narrative Review," *International Review of Psychiatry* 28:1 (February 2016), 70–80. doi:10.3109/0 9540261.2015.1111199; Steven D. Stagg and Jaime Vincent, "Autistic Traits in Individuals Self-Defining as Transgender or Nonbinary," *European Psychiatry* 61 (2019), 17–22. doi:10.1016/j.eurpsy.2019.06.003.

13. Amaya Perez-Brumer, Jack K. Day, Stephen T. Russell, and Mark L. Hatzenbuehler, "Prevalence and Correlates of Suicidal Ideation Among Transgender Youth in California: Findings from a Representative, Population-Based Sample of High School Students," *Journal of the American Academy of Child & Adolescent Psychiatry* 56:9 (2017), 739–46. doi:10.1016/j.jaac.2017.06.010.

20. SLEEP AND FOOD STRATEGIES

1. Joshua Arvidson, Kristine Kinniburgh, Kristin Howard, Joseph Spinazzola, Helen Strothers, Mary Evans, Barry Andres, Chantal Cohen, and Margaret E. Blaustein, "Treatment of Complex Trauma in Young Children: Developmental and Cultural Considerations in Application of the ARC Intervention Model," *Journal of Child & Adolescent Trauma* 4:1 (2011), 34–51.

2. Tracey Peter, "Exploring Taboos," *Journal of Interpersonal Violence* 24:7 (2008), 1111–28. doi:10.1177/0886260508322194.

21. HOW TO CHOOSE THE RIGHT THERAPIST

1. Client's name and certain identifying information have been changed to protect their privacy.

2. Client's name and certain identifying information have been changed to protect their privacy.

23. PTSD AND MEDICAL CARE

1. Mary T. Rourke, Wendy L. Hobbie, Lisa Schwartz, and Anne E. Kazak, "Post-Traumatic Stress Disorder (PTSD) in Young Adult Survivors of Childhood Cancer," *Pediatric Blood & Cancer* 49:2 (2007), 177–82. doi:10.1002/pbc.20942.

2. T. Christian Miller and Ken Armstrong, "An Unbelievable Story of Rape," ProPublica, September 16, 2019. https://tinyurl.com/q7on4mr.

25. LYING AND STEALING

1. Heather T. Forbes and B. Bryan Post, *Beyond Consequences, Logic, and Control: A Love-Based Approach to Helping Children with Severe Behaviors* (Boulder, CO: Beyond Consequences Institute, 2009), 47.

26. WHEN IT'S MORE THAN PTSD

1. American Psychiatric Association, *Diagnostic and Statistical Manual of Mental Disorders,* Fifth Edition (DSM-5) (Arlington, VA: American Psychiatric Association, 2017).

2. Deborah Rutman, "Article Commentary: Becoming FASD Informed: Strengthening Practice and Programs Working with Women with FASD," *Substance Abuse: Research and Treatment* 10: suppl. 1 (2016). doi:10.4137/sart.s34543.

3. Alan Price, Penny A. Cook, Sarah Norgate, and Raja Mukherjee, "Prenatal Alcohol Exposure and Traumatic Childhood Experiences: A Systematic Review," *Neuroscience & Biobehavioral Reviews* 80 (2017), 89–98. doi:10.1016/j.neubiorev.2017.05.018.

4. David Mandell, "Why Too Many Children with Autism End up in Foster Care," *Spectrum,* January 8, 2018. https://tinyurl.com/yx242tjl.

5. Kristin L. Berg, Cheng-Shi Shiu, Kruti Acharya, Bradley C. Stolbach, and Michael E. Msall, "Disparities in Adversity among Children with Autism Spectrum Disorder: A Population-Based Study," *Developmental Medicine & Child Neurology* 58:11 (February 2016), 1124–31. doi:10.1111/dmcn.13161.

6. Samantha Fuld, "Autism Spectrum Disorder: The Impact of Stressful and Traumatic Life Events and Implications for Clinical Practice," *Clinical Social Work Journal* 46:3 (2018), 210–19. doi:10.1007/s10615-018-0649-6.

7. Bushraa Khatib, "An In-Depth Look into How People with Autism Experience Trauma," Drexel University Life Course Outcomes, December 2016. https://tinyurl.com/tvvddcd.

8. Lauren Gravitz, "At the Intersection of Autism and Trauma," *Spectrum,* May 30, 2019. https://tinyurl.com/yy33qnvq.

9. Katherine Stavropoulos, "Autism and PTSD: Similarities and Differences," *Psychology Today,* October 1, 2018. https://tinyurl.com/v8guuqy.

10. American Psychiatric Association, *DSM-5.*

11. Bessel van der Kolk, *The Body Keeps the Score: Brain, Mind, and Body in the Healing of Trauma* (New York: Penguin, 2015).

27. WHILE YOU ARE WAITING AND THE FIRST FEW MONTHS

1. Harvey Karp, "The 5 S's for Soothing Babies," Happiest Baby, October 12, 2018. https://tinyurl.com/qlskjj9. See www.happiestbaby.com.

2. Yehuda Senecky, Hanoch Agassi, Dov Inbar, Netta Horesh, Gary Diamond, Yoav S. Bergman, and Alan Apter, "Post-Adoption Depression among Adoptive Mothers," *Journal of Affective Disorders* 115:1–2 (2009), 62–68. doi:10.1016/j.jad.2008.09.002.

28. FOSTER CARE

1. *Shazam!,* movie, Newline Cinemas, DC Films, 2019.

2. Name changed to protect privacy.

3. Julie Moreau, "LGBTQ Parents Face 'State-Sanctioned Discrimination,' American Bar Association Says," NBC News, February 6, 2019. https://tinyurl.com /ya76kqcg.

4. Isabel Dando and Brian Minty, "What Makes Good Foster Parents?," *British Journal of Social Work* 17:4 (August 1987), 383–99. doi:10.1093/oxfordjournals .bjsw.a055354.

29. WHEN THINGS ARE REALLY HARD

1. Child Welfare Information Gateway, *Adoption Disruption and Dissolution* (Washington, DC: U.S. Department of Health and Human Services, Children's Bureau, 2012).

2. H. B. Hodgdon, K. Kinniburgh, D. Gabowitz, Margaret E. Blaustein, and Joseph Spinazzola, "Development and Implementation of Trauma-Informed Programming in Youth Residential Treatment Centers Using the ARC Framework," *Journal of Family Violence* 28 (2013), 679. doi:10.1007/s10896-013-9531-z.

3. Child Welfare Information Gateway, *Adoption Disruption.*

4. Jennifer Foulkes Coakley, *Finalized Adoption Disruption: A Family Perspective* (Berkeley, CA: University of California, 2005).

5. Elinam Dellor and Bridget Freisthler, "Predicting Adoption Dissolutions for Children Involved in the Child Welfare System," *Journal of Child Custody* 15:2 (April 30, 2018), 136–46, doi:10.1080/15379418.2018.1460001.

6. Megan Twohey, "The Child Exchange: Inside America's Underground Market for Adopted Children," Reuters Investigates, September 9, 2013. https:// tinyurl.com/y8plaasr.

30. LEAVING HOME

1. Sara B. Johnson, Robert W. Blum, and Jay N. Giedd, "Adolescent Maturity and the Brain: The Promise and Pitfalls of Neuroscience Research in Adolescent Health Policy," *Journal of Adolescent Health* 45:3 (2009), 216–21.

Bibliography

Allender, Dan. "Marriage and Family Class." Lecture. Seattle School of Theology and Psychology. 2008.

American Psychiatric Association. *Diagnostic and Statistical Manual of Mental Disorders, Fifth Edition (DSM-5)*. Arlington, VA: American Psychiatric Association, 2017.

Anda, R. F., and V. J. Felitti. "Origins and Essence of the Study." *ACE Reporter* 1 (April 2003), 1–4.

Arvidson, Joshua, Kristine Kinniburgh, Kristin Howard, Joseph Spinazzola, Helen Strothers, Mary Evans, Barry Andres, Chantal Cohen, and Margaret E. Blaustein. "Treatment of Complex Trauma in Young Children: Developmental and Cultural Considerations in Application of the ARC Intervention Model." *Journal of Child & Adolescent Trauma* 4:1 (2011), 34–51. doi:10.1080/1936152 .2011.545046.

Baams, Laura, Bianca D. M. Wilson, and Stephen T. Russell. "LGBTQ Youth in Unstable Housing and Foster Care." *Pediatrics* 143:3 (November 2019). doi:10.1542/peds.2017-4211.

Barth, Richard P., Marianne Berry, Rogers Yoshikami, Regina K. Goodfield, and Mary Lou Carson. "Predicting Adoption Disruption." *Social Work* 33:3 (January 1988), 227–33. doi:10.1093/sw/33.3.227.

Becker-Weidman, Arthur. "Treatment for Children with Trauma-Attachment Disorders: Dyadic Developmental Psychotherapy." *Child and Adolescent Social Work Journal* 23:2 (March 2006), 147–71. doi:10.1007/s10560-005-0039-0.

Benoit, Diane. "Infant-Parent Attachment: Definition, Types, Antecedents, Measurement and Outcome." *Paediatrics & Child Health* 9:8 (2004), 541–45. doi:10.1093/pch/9.8.541.

Berg, Kristin L., Cheng-Shi Shiu, Kruti Acharya, Bradley C. Stolbach, and Michael E. Msall. "Disparities in Adversity among Children with Autism Spectrum

Disorder: A Population-Based Study." *Developmental Medicine & Child Neurology* 58:11 (February 2016), 1124–31. doi:10.1111/dmcn.13161.

Biel, Lindsey. *Sensory Processing Challenges: Effective Clinical Work with Kids & Teens*. New York: W.W. Norton & Company, 2014.

Biel, Lindsey, and Nancy Peske. *Raising a Sensory Smart Child: The Definitive Handbook for Helping Your Child with Sensory Processing Issues*. New York: Penguin, 2005.

Bowlby, John. *Attachment and Loss: Volume III: Loss, Sadness and Depression*. New York, NY: Basic Books, 1980.

Brind, Katharine. "An Exploration of Adopters Views Regarding Children's Ages at the Time of Placement." *Child & Family Social Work* 13:3 (2008), 319–28. doi:10.1111/j.1365-2206.2008.00556.x.

Castelloe, Molly S. "Disorganized Attachment: Fears That Go Unanswered—the Long Reach of Interactions between Caregiver and Infant." *Psychology Today*. April 12, 2017. https://tinyurl.com/sv84y5y.

Chaffin, Mark, Rochelle Hanson, Benjamin E. Saunders, Todd Nichols, Douglas Barnett, Charles Zeanah, Lucy Berliner, Byron Egeland, Elana Newman, Tom Lyon, et al. "Report of the APSAC Task Force on Attachment Therapy, Reactive Attachment Disorder, and Attachment Problems." *Child Maltreatment* 11:1 (2006), 76–89. doi:10.1177/1077559505283699.

Child Welfare Information Gateway. *Adoption Disruption and Dissolution*. Washington, DC: U.S. Department of Health and Human Services, Children's Bureau, 2012.

Choi, Soon Kyu, Bianca D. M. Wilson, Jama Shelton, and Gary J. Gates. "Serving Our Youth 2015: The Needs and Experiences of Lesbian, Gay, Bisexual, Transgender, and Questioning Youth Experiencing Homelessness." eScholarship, University of California. August 6, 2015. https://escholarship.org/uc/item/1pd9886n.

Coakley, Jennifer Foulkes. *Finalized Adoption Disruption: A Family Perspective*. Berkeley, CA: University of California, 2005.

Compton, Rebecca. "Is Transracial Adoption Harmful to Kids?" *Psychology Today*. May 11, 2016. https://tinyurl.com/r65j7ug.

Cooper, Addison. *Adoption at the Movies: A Year of Adoption-Friendly Movie Nights to Get Your Family Talking*. Philadelphia: Jessica Kingsley, 2017.

Dando, Isabel, and Brian Minty. "What Makes Good Foster Parents?" *The British Journal of Social Work* 17:4 (August 1987), 383–99. doi:10.1093/oxfordjournals.bjsw.a055354.

DeGangi, Georgia A. *The Dysregulated Adult: Integrated Treatment Approaches.* Amsterdam: Elsevier Academic Press, 2012.

Dellor, Elinam, and Bridget Freisthler. "Predicting Adoption Dissolutions for Children Involved in the Child Welfare System." *Journal of Child Custody* 15:2 (April 30, 2018), 136–46, doi:10.1080/15379418.2018.1460001.

Dube, Shanta R., Vincent J. Felitti, Maxia Dong, Daniel P. Chapman, Wayne H. Giles, and Robert F. Anda. "Childhood Abuse, Neglect, and Household Dysfunction and the Risk of Illicit Drug Use: The Adverse Childhood Experiences Study." *Pediatrics* 111:3 (2003). doi:10.1542/peds.111.3.564.

Ellis, Elizabeth E., and Abdolreza Saadabadi. "Reactive Attachment Disorder." StatPearls. January 2019. https://tinyurl.com/wean9g6.

Engel-Yeger, Batya, and Winnie Dunn. "The Relationship between Sensory Processing Difficulties and Anxiety Level of Healthy Adults." *British Journal of Occupational Therapy* 74:5 (2011), 210–16. doi:10.4276/030802211x13046730116407.

Engel-Yeger, Batya, Dafna Palgy-Levin, and Rachel Lev-Wiesel. "Predicting Fears of Intimacy among Individuals with Post-Traumatic Stress Symptoms by Their Sensory Profile." *British Journal of Occupational Therapy* 78:1 (2015). doi:10.1177/0308022614557628.

Ezzo, Gary, and Robert Bucknam. *On Becoming Babywise: Giving Your Infant the Gift of Nighttime Sleep.* Mount Pleasant, SC: Hawksflight, 1990.

Faber, Adele, and Elaine Mazlish. *Siblings without Rivalry: How to Help Your Children Live Together So You Can Live Too.* New York: W. W. Norton, 2012.

Feigelman, William. "Adjustments of Transracially and Inracially Adopted Young Adults." *Child and Adolescent Social Work Journal* 17:3 (June 2000), 165–83. doi:10.1023/A:1007531829378.

Felitti, Vincent J., R. F. Anda, D. Nordenberg, D. F. Williamson, A. M. Spitz, V. Edwards, M. P. Koss, and J. S. Marks. "Relationship of Childhood Abuse and Household Dysfunction to Many of the Leading Causes of Death in Adults: The Adverse Childhood Experiences (ACE) Study." *American Journal of Preventive Medicine* 56:6 (2019). doi:10.1016/j.amepre.2019.04.001.

Ferber, Richard. *Solve Your Child's Sleep Problems.* New York: Touchstone, 1985.

Forbes, Heather T., and B. Bryan Post. *Beyond Consequences, Logic, and Control: A Love-Based Approach to Helping Children with Severe Behaviors.* Boulder, CO: Beyond Consequences Institute, 2009.

Fraser, Kerry, Diane Mackenzie, and Joan Versnel. "Complex Trauma in Children and Youth: A Scoping Review of Sensory-Based Interventions." *Occupational Therapy in Mental Health* 33:3 (2017). doi:10.1080/0164212x.2016.1265475.

Fuld, Samantha. "Autism Spectrum Disorder: The Impact of Stressful and Traumatic Life Events and Implications for Clinical Practice." *Clinical Social Work
Journal* 46:3 (2018), 210–19. doi:10.1007/s10615-018-0649-6.

Gabrielson, Ryan, Eric Sagara, and Ryann Grochowski Jones. "Deadly Force, in
Black and White." ProPublica. March 9, 2019. https://tinyurl.com/mfw73kb.

Granqvist, Pehr L., Alan Sroufe, Mary Dozier, Erik Hesse, Miriam Steele, Mari-
nus van Ijzendoorn, Judith Solomon, Carlo Schuengel, Pasco Fearon, Marian
Bakermans-Kranenburg, et al. "Disorganized Attachment in Infancy: A Review
of the Phenomenon and Its Implications for Clinicians and Policy-Makers."
Experts@Minnesota. University of Minnesota Institute of Child Development.
November 2, 2017. https://tinyurl.com/uqnep6z.

Gravitz, Lauren. "At the Intersection of Autism and Trauma." *Spectrum.* May 30,
2019. https://tinyurl.com/yy33qnvq.

Gray, Deborah D. *Nurturing Adoptions: Creating Resilience after Neglect and
Trauma.* London: Jessica Kingsley, 2012.

Hamilton, Emma, Diana R. Samek, Margaret Keyes, Matthew K. McGue, and
William G. Iacono. "Identity Development in a Transracial Environment:
Racial/Ethnic Minority Adoptees in Minnesota." *Adoption Quarterly* 18:3
(2015), 217–33. doi:10.1080/10926755.2015.1013593.

Harvard Health Publishing. "Understanding the Stress Response." Harvard Health.
March 2011. https://tinyurl.com/y6w9dnam.

Hicks, Brenna. "Parenting Tip: 30 Second Burst of Attention." The Kid Counselor.
December 7, 2018. https://tinyurl.com/ydpvl5a4.

Hodgdon, H. B., K. Kinniburgh, D. Gabowitz, Margaret E. Blaustein, and Joseph
Spinazzola. "Development and Implementation of Trauma-Informed Program-
ming in Youth Residential Treatment Centers Using the ARC Framework."
Journal of Family Violence 28 (2013), 679. doi:10.1007/s10896-013-9531-z.

Hogg, Tracy. *Secrets of the Baby Whisperer: How to Calm, Connect, and Communicate with Your Baby.* New York: Ballantine, 2001.

Hoyt-Oliver, Jane, Hope Haslam Straughan, and Jayne E. Schooler. *Parenting in
Transracial Adoption.* Santa Barbara, CA: ABC-CLIO, 2016.

Hutton, Lisa. "The Effects of Older Child Adoption on the Family." *Undergraduate
Research Journal Blog.* 2010. https://tinyurl.com/rwsyw3j.

Jamieson, Ally. "Biology of Trauma: How Trauma Impacts the Developing Mind."
Pamphlet. Portland State University Center for Improvement of Child and
Family Services. https://tinyurl.com/sjxcyga.

Johnson, Sara B., Robert W. Blum, and Jay N. Giedd. "Adolescent Maturity and the Brain: The Promise and Pitfalls of Neuroscience Research in Adolescent Health Policy." *Journal of Adolescent Health* 45:3 (2009), 216–21. doi:10.1016/j.jadohealth.2009.05.016.

Kaiser, Erika M., Craig S. Gillette, and Joseph Spinazzola. "A Controlled Pilot-Outcome Study of Sensory Integration (SI) in the Treatment of Complex Adaptation to Traumatic Stress." *Journal of Aggression, Maltreatment & Trauma* 19:7 (2010), 699–720. doi:10.1080/10926771.2010.515162.

Karp, Harvey. "The 5 S's for Soothing Babies." Happiest Baby. October 12, 2018. https://tinyurl.com/qlskjj9.

Karp, Harvey. *The Happiest Baby on the Block: Fully Revised and Updated Second Edition: The New Way to Calm Crying and Help Your Newborn Baby Sleep Longer.* New York: Bantam, 2002.

Keyes, Margaret A., Anu Sharma, Irene J. Elkins, William G. Iacono, and Matt McGue. "The Mental Health of U.S. Adolescents Adopted in Infancy." *Archives of Pediatrics & Adolescent Medicine* 162:5 (January 2008), 419. doi:10.1001/archpedi.162.5.419.

Khatib, Bushraa. "An In-Depth Look into How People with Autism Experience Trauma." Drexel University Life Course Outcomes. December 2016. https://tinyurl.com/tvvddcd.

Kinniburgh, Kristine M., and Margaret E. Blaustein. "ARC Model." National Child Traumatic Stress Network. 2008.

Kranowitz, Carol, and Lucy Jane Miller. *The Out-of-Sync Child: Recognizing and Coping with Sensory Processing Disorder.* New York: Tarcher Perigee, 2005.

Lewinn, K. Z., L. R. Stroud, B. E. Molnar, J. H. Ware, K. C. Koenen, and S. L. Buka. "Elevated Maternal Cortisol Levels during Pregnancy Are Associated with Reduced Childhood IQ." *International Journal of Epidemiology* 38:6 (July 2009), 1700–10. doi:10.1093/ije/dyp200.

LoBue, Vanessa. "People Aren't Born Afraid of Spiders and Snakes: Fear Is Quickly Learned During Infancy." Association for Psychological Science. January 24, 2011. https://tinyurl.com/w7e559e.

Lyons-Ruth, Karlen, Elisa Bronfman, and Gwendolyn Atwood. "A Relational Diathesis Model of Hostile-Helpless States of Mind: Expressions in Mother-Infant Interactions." *Attachment Disorganization* 1999, 33–70. https://tinyurl.com/yx5zo22q.

MacDonald, Mandi, and Dominic McSherry. "Open Adoption: Adoptive Parents' Experiences of Birth Family Contact and Talking to Their Child about Adoption." *Adoption & Fostering* 35:3 (2011), 4–16. doi:10.1177/030857591103500302.

Mandell, David. "Why Too Many Children with Autism End up in Foster Care." *Spectrum.* January 8, 2018. https://tinyurl.com/yx242tjl.

Manzi, Claudia, Laura Ferrari, Rosa Rosnati, and Veronica Benet-Martinez. "Bicultural Identity Integration of Transracial Adolescent Adoptees." *Journal of Cross-Cultural Psychology* 45:6 (2014), 888–904. doi:10.1177/0022022114530495.

Maslow, A. H. "A Theory of Human Motivation." *Psychological Review* 50 (1943): 370–96. https://tinyurl.com/236kc.

McCarthy, Gerard, and Alan Taylor. "Avoidant/Ambivalent Attachment Style as a Mediator between Abusive Childhood Experiences and Adult Relationship Difficulties." *Journal of Child Psychology and Psychiatry* 40:3 (1999), 465–77. doi:10.1017/s0021963098003734.

McCormick, Adam, Kathryn Schmidt, and Samuel Terrazas. "Foster Family Acceptance: Understanding the Role of Foster Family Acceptance in the Lives of LGBTQ Youth." *Children and Youth Services Review* 61 (2016): 69–74. doi:10.1016/j.childyouth.2015.12.005.

McCormick, Adam, Kathryn Schmidt, and Samuel Terrazas. "LGBTQ Youth in the Child Welfare System: An Overview of Research, Practice, and Policy." *Journal of Public Child Welfare* 11:1 (November 2016), 27–39. doi:10.1080/1554 8732.2016.1221368.

McIntosh, Peggy. "'White Privilege: Unpacking the Invisible Knapsack' and 'Some Notes for Facilitators.'" National SEED Project. 1989. https://tinyurl.com /y7u82cmg.

McLeod, Saul. "Mary Ainsworth: The Strange Situation." Simply Psychology. 2018. https://tinyurl.com/y9l4fpz3.

Medina, John. *Brain Rules for Baby: How to Raise a Smart and Happy Child from Zero to Five.* Seattle: Pear Press, 2010.

Miller, T. Christian, and Ken Armstrong. "An Unbelievable Story of Rape." ProPublica. September 16, 2019. https://tinyurl.com/q7on4mr.

Moffitt, Terrie E. "Childhood Exposure to Violence and Lifelong Health: Clinical Intervention Science and Stress-Biology Research Join Forces." *Development and Psychopathology* 25:4 pt. 2 (2013): 1619–34. doi:10.1017 /s0954579413000801.

Moreau, Julie. "LGBTQ Parents Face 'State-Sanctioned Discrimination,' American Bar Association Says." NBC News. February 6, 2019. https://tinyurl.com /ya76kqcg.

Morey, Glenn. "Adult Adoptee Voices Are Changing Adoption Narrative." *Psychology Today.* November 19, 2018. https://tinyurl.com/quxdjpt.

NAACP. "NAACP Policy Handbook: Resolutions Approved by the National Board of Directors 1976–2006." www.naacp.org.

National Association of Black Social Workers. "Transracial Adoption Statement, 1972." NABSW Position Statements. 1972. https://tinyurl.com/wy857oy.

Nelson, Christa. "What Is Healthy Attachment?" Attachment and Trauma Network. May 18, 2014. https://tinyurl.com/rqmpbn8.

Newcomb, Michael E., Michael C. Lasala, Alida Bouris, Brian Mustanski, Guillermo Prado, Sheree M. Schrager, and David M. Huebner. "The Influence of Families on LGBTQ Youth Health: A Call to Action for Innovation in Research and Intervention Development." *LGBT Health* 6:4 (2019), 139–45. doi:10.1089/lgbt.2018.0157.

Niequist, Shauna. *Bread & Wine: A Love Letter to Life around the Table, with Recipes.* Grand Rapids, MI: Zondervan, 2017.

NPR. "Six Words: 'Black Babies Cost Less to Adopt.'" NPR. June 27, 2013. https://tinyurl.com/t4fs4uw.

Owen, Liz. "Parents: Quick Tips for Supporting Your LGBTQ Kids—and Yourself—During the Coming-Out Process." PFLAG. June 21, 2017. https:// tinyurl.com/qldayy6.

Pecora, Peter J., Peter S. Jensen, Lisa Hunter Romanelli, Lovie J. Jackson, and Abel Ortiz. "Mental Health Services for Children Placed in Foster Care: An Overview of Current Challenges." *Child Welfare* 88:1 (2009), 5–26. https://tinyurl .com/ulhuko8.

Perez-Brumer, Amaya, Jack K. Day, Stephen T. Russell, and Mark L. Hatzenbuehler. "Prevalence and Correlates of Suicidal Ideation Among Transgender Youth in California: Findings From a Representative, Population-Based Sample of High School Students." *Journal of the American Academy of Child & Adolescent Psychiatry* 56:9 (2017), 739–46. doi:10.1016/j.jaac.2017.06.010.

Perry, Bruce Duncan, and Maia Szalavitz. *The Boy Who Was Raised as a Dog: And Other Stories from a Child Psychiatrist's Notebook: What Traumatized Children Can Teach Us about Loss, Love, and Healing.* New York: Basic Books, 2017.

Perry, Bruce D. "Stress, Trauma and Post-Traumatic Stress Disorders in Children." The Child Trauma Academy. 2007. https://tinyurl.com/rxh5tdr.

Peter, Tracey. "Exploring Taboos." *Journal of Interpersonal Violence* 24:7 (2008), 1111–28. doi:10.1177/0886260508322194.

Plotkin, Candace N. "Study Finds Foster Kids Suffer PTSD." *The Harvard Crimson.* April 11, 2005. https://tinyurl.com/s6jamyx.

Price, Alan, Penny A. Cook, Sarah Norgate, and Raja Mukherjee. "Prenatal Alcohol Exposure and Traumatic Childhood Experiences: A Systematic Review." *Neuroscience & Biobehavioral Reviews* 80 (2017), 89–98. doi:10.1016/j.neubiorev .2017.05.018.

Purvis, Karyn B., David R. Cross, and Wendy Lyons Sunshine. *The Connected Child: Bring Hope and Healing to Your Adoptive Family*. New York: McGraw-Hill, 2007.

Rosnati, Rosa, and Laura Ferrari. "Parental Cultural Socialization and Perception of Discrimination as Antecedents for Transracial Adoptees' Ethnic Identity." *Procedia—Social and Behavioral Sciences* 140 (2014), 103–108. doi:10.1016 /j.sbspro.2014.04.393.

Rourke, Mary T., Wendy L. Hobbie, Lisa Schwartz, and Anne E. Kazak. "Post-Traumatic Stress Disorder (PTSD) in Young Adult Survivors of Childhood Cancer." *Pediatric Blood & Cancer* 49:2 (2007), 177–82. doi:10.1002 /pbc.20942.

Rutman, Deborah. "Article Commentary: Becoming FASD Informed: Strengthening Practice and Programs Working with Women with FASD." *Substance Abuse: Research and Treatment* 10: suppl. 1 (2016). doi:10.4137/sart.s34543.

Ryan, Caitlin, Russell B. Toomey, Rafael M. Diaz, and Stephen T. Russell. "Parent-Initiated Sexual Orientation Change Efforts with LGBT Adolescents: Implications for Young Adult Mental Health and Adjustment." *Journal of Homosexuality*. 2018. doi:10.1080/00918369.2018.1538407.

Sekhon, Nirej. "Blue on Black: An Empirical Assessment of Police Shootings." *SSRN Electronic Journal* 2016. doi:10.2139/ssrn.2700724.

Selby, Laura. "Caring for Transgender Children: A Physician's Advice." The DO. February 3, 2017. https://tinyurl.com/snrh2qj.

Senecky, Yehuda, Hanoch Agassi, Dov Inbar, Netta Horesh, Gary Diamond, Yoav S. Bergman, and Alan Apter. "Post-Adoption Depression among Adoptive Mothers." *Journal of Affective Disorders* 115:1–2 (2009), 62–68. doi:10.1016 /j.jad.2008.09.002.

Shrestha, Praveen. "Maslow Hierarchy of Needs." *Psychestudy.* June 16, 2019. https://tinyurl.com/ycddecb8.

Siegel, Daniel J., and Tina Payne Bryson. *No-Drama Discipline: The Whole-Brain Way to Calm the Chaos and Nurture Your Child's Developing Mind.* New York: Bantam, 2014.

Spangler, G., and K. E. Grossmann. "Biobehavioral Organization in Securely and Insecurely Attached Infants." *Child Development* 64:5 (1993), 1439. doi:10.2307/1131544.

Spinazzola, Joseph, Bessel van der Kolk, and Julian D. Ford. "When Nowhere Is Safe: Interpersonal Trauma and Attachment Adversity as Antecedents of Post-Traumatic Stress Disorder and Developmental Trauma Disorder." *Journal of Traumatic Stress* 31:5 (2018), 631–42. doi:10.1002/jts.22320.

Stagg, Steven D., and Jaime Vincent. "Autistic Traits in Individuals Self-Defining as Transgender or Nonbinary." *European Psychiatry* 61 (2019), 17–22. doi:10.1016/j.eurpsy.2019.06.003.

Stavropoulos, Katherine. "Autism and PTSD: Similarities and Differences." *Psychology Today.* October 1, 2018. https://tinyurl.com/v8guuqy.

Tucker, Angela. *The Adopted Life.* www.theadoptedlife.com.

Turnage, Barbara, and Justin Bucchio. "Be Ready to Support LGBTQ Youth." Adoptive Families Association of BC. August 20, 2018. https://tinyurl.com/utahese.

Twohey, Megan. "The Child Exchange: Inside America's Underground Market for Adopted Children." Reuters Investigates. September 9, 2013. https://tinyurl.com/y8plaasr.

Valby, Karen. "The Realities of Raising a Kid of a Different Race." *Time.* n.d. https://tinyurl.com/yyah5uzk.

Van Dam, Nicholas T., K. Rando, M. N. Potenza, K. Tuit, and R. Sinha. "Childhood Maltreatment, Altered Limbic Neurobiology, and Substance Use Relapse Severity via Trauma-Specific Reductions in Limbic Gray Matter Volume." *JAMA Psychiatry* 71:8 (2014). doi:10.1001/jamapsychiatry.2014.680.

van der Kolk, Bessel. *The Body Keeps the Score: Brain, Mind, and Body in the Healing of Trauma.* New York: Penguin, 2015.

Van Der Miesen, Anna I. R., Hannah Hurley, and Annelou L. C. De Vries. "Gender Dysphoria and Autism Spectrum Disorder: A Narrative Review." *International Review of Psychiatry* 28:1 (February 2016), 70–80. doi:10.3109/09540261.2015.1111199.

Verrier, Nancy Ma. "The Primal Wound: A Preliminary Investigation into the Effects of Separation from the Birth Mother on Adopted Children." *Pre- and Peri-Natal Psychology Journal* 2:2 (1987), 75–87. https://tinyurl.com/yxy7b2hf.

Verrier, Nancy Newton. *The Primal Wound: Understanding the Adopted Child.* London: BAAF, 2009.

Wallin, David J. *Attachment in Psychotherapy.* New York: Guilford Press, 2007.

Warner, Elizabeth, Jane Koomar, Bryan Lary, and Alexandra Cook. "Can the Body Change the Score? Application of Sensory Modulation Principles in the Treatment of Traumatized Adolescents in Residential Settings." *Journal of Family Violence* 28:7 (October 2013), 729–38. doi:10.1007/s10896-013-9535-8.

Waterman, Barbara. "Mourning the Loss Builds the Bond: Primal Communication between Foster, Adoptive, or Stepmother and Child." *Journal of Loss and Trauma* 6:4 (2001), 277–300. doi:10.1080/108114401317087806.

Weir, Kirsten. "The Exercise Effect." *Monitor on Psychology* 42:11 (December 2011). https://tinyurl.com/yyrpkofy.

Winston, Robert, and Rebecca Chicot. "The Importance of Early Bonding on the Long-Term Mental Health and Resilience of Children." *London Journal of Primary Care* 8:1 (February 24, 2016), 12–14. doi:10.1080/17571472.2015.1133012.

Woronoff, Rob, Rudy Estrada, and Susan Sommer. "Out of the Margins." Lambda Legal. Child Welfare League, July 31, 2014. https://tinyurl.com/slfun3m.

Zill, Nicholas. "The Changing Face of Adoption in the United States." Institute for Family Studies. August 8, 2017. https://tinyurl.com/t7kzkj5.

Zill, Nicholas. "The Paradox of Adoption." Institute for Family Studies. October 7, 2015. https://tinyurl.com/rk3hwmt.

Index

About the Author

BARBARA CUMMINS TANTRUM, MA, LMHC, is trained and experienced in trauma-informed therapy. This includes working with children, adoptive and foster families, adult survivors of trauma and abuse, and marital couples. She is a cofounder of Northwest Trauma Counseling, a Washington State–based private practice specializing in trauma related to adoption and foster care, and author of their PATCH Protocol, a trauma-informed model therapy approach focused specifically on addressing trauma-related issues. A graduate of the Seattle School of Theology and Psychology with a master's degree in Counseling Psychology, she conducts training sessions regularly for groups, including social workers, teachers, adoptive and foster parents, and other support groups. In her personal life, Tantrum is herself a foster and adoptive mother and sister. This is her first book.

About North Atlantic Books

North Atlantic Books (NAB) is an independent, nonprofit publisher committed to a bold exploration of the relationships between mind, body, spirit, and nature. Founded in 1974, NAB aims to nurture a holistic view of the arts, sciences, humanities, and healing. To make a donation or to learn more about our books, authors, events, and newsletter, please visit www.northatlanticbooks.com.

North Atlantic Books is the publishing arm of the Society for the Study of Native Arts and Sciences, a 501(c)(3) nonprofit educational organization that promotes cross-cultural perspectives linking scientific, social, and artistic fields. To learn how you can support us, please visit our website.